INGO SWANN

ACCESSING

YOUR INNATE

ABILITY TO SEE

INTO THE

FUTURE

A FIRESIDE BOOK   PUBLISHED BY SIMON & SCHUSTER

NEW YORK LONDON TORONTO SYDNEY TOKYO SINGAPORE

YOUR

NOSTRADAMUS

FACTOR

FIRESIDE
SIMON & SCHUSTER BUILDING
ROCKEFELLER CENTER
1230 AVENUE OF THE AMERICAS
NEW YORK, NEW YORK 10020

DESIGNED BY SONGHEE KIM
MANUFACTURED IN THE UNITED STATES OF AMERICA

1   3   5   7   9   10   8   6   4   2

LIBRARY OF CONGRESS CATALOGING-IN-PUBLICATION DATA
SWANN, INGO, 1933–
YOUR NOSTRADAMUS FACTOR : ACCESSING YOUR INNATE ABILITY TO SEE
INTO THE FUTURE / INGO SWANN.
P.   CM.
INCLUDES BIBLIOGRAPHICAL REFERENCES AND INDEX.
1. PROPHECIES (OCCULTISM)—HISTORY.   2. FORECASTING—
MISCELLANEA.   3. NOSTRADAMUS, 1503-1566.   4. NEW AGE
MOVEMENT.   I. TITLE.
BF1791.S92   1993
133.3—DC20   93-18876
                                                             CIP

ISBN: 0-671-75058-5

THIS BOOK IS DEDICATED TO

MARTIN EBON
AND
MARTY EDELSTON

FELLOW VOYAGERS AND SOURCES OF INSPIRATION

ACKNOWLEDGMENTS

Hundreds have contributed to the increase of my understanding and thus to this book. Of these, in memory are my maternal grandmother, Anna Paul McCraney, who foresaw, especially in emergencies; and Dr. May Schwender, Leo Katz, Buell Mullen, Dr. Jan Ehernwald, Jo Chamberlain, Dr. William Wolf, Dr. Shafica Karagulla, and Harold Sherman, all of whom also foresaw and who *forced* my mind to try to grow upward and psychically open.

I am indebted beyond repayment to Marty Edelston, who made possible the one-year experimental future-seeing project reviewed herein; to Martin Ebon for two decades of profound emotional and moral support; to Marilyn Ferguson, who expands most everything she touches; and Dr. Gerald Epstein, who guided me in confirming that image-building is tantamount to psychic perceiving. I thank Dr. Eldon Taylor for his telephone conversations on how the subliminal mind functions; Rolf Osterberg for discussions concerning the world economy; and Mrs. Robin Chandler Duke of the New York branch of the Population Crisis Committee, who provided me with the committee's excellent population statistics.

I am profoundly grateful to my literary agent, Sandra Martin, whose enthusiasm for this project brought it into existence; to my sister Murleen Ryder; to Sam Matthews, Barbara Gess, and Sheila Curry for their welcomed editorial overseeing; and to Thomas Joyce, who executed the illustrations. I am also indirectly indebted to those authors listed in the bibliography.

Everyone *can see something of the future*—provided *that they adapt their intellects to do so.*

C O N T E N T S

CONTENTS

PART TWO

THE OUTER PHENOMENA OF THE FUTURE-SEEING MOSAIC

MAKING THE ASHES

CONTENTS

PART THREE

THE ULTIMATE PIECE OF THE FUTURE-SEEING MOSAIC

INTRODUCTION

My interest in how the future can be seen began as a child. I was witness to my own spontaneous future-seeing episodes and those of many others. I began an organized literature research on the subject in 1962. My entry into full-time parapsychological and psychoenergetics research in 1972 opened a wider basis for future-seeing experimentation. By 1985 I had developed a set of theories regarding future-seeing, and I finally had the opportunity to test them during a year-long experimental project in 1990 (which is reviewed in chapter 14).

The sciences and philosophies of the Modern Age did not accept psychic forms of future-seeing. But many postmodern advances have been made in physics, biology, anthropology, psychology, bioenergetics, information theory, and energy-information transfer. So the scientific limits that characterized the Modern Age (roughly between 1847 and 1968) have been expanded.

Postmodern terms and phrases such as "virtual time," "virtual reality," "interdimensionality," "linear-time transcendence," "cross-time continua," and "interrelated cross-dimensional events" have come into usage. If not yet exactly understood, these terms and phrases are increasingly seen as meaningful to the strange human phenomenologies via which the future has been seen and forecast.

The sum of my understanding and workable seership discoveries reflected in this book must be augmented by others yet to come. But I am certain that every human possesses the future-seeing capabilities discussed in this book and that those who elect to make the effort to do so will be able to locate them.

Your abilities to foresee aspects of the future are determined by *inner* mind-dynamic processes and by *outer* circumstances, events, and realities that influence you and everyone else. It is sometimes very difficult to separate the inner from the outer "pieces," because they are interrelated and fit together like a mosaic. Part one comprises what I have discovered regarding the inner mind-dynamic processes, whereas part two relates those processes to outer circumstances.

That the future *is foreseen* is beyond question. As has been recorded since early antiquity through today, it is spontaneously foreseen in dreams, waking visions, and by achieved seers. Historical and contemporary resources to this effect are enormous, though marginalized, and the more reliable and accessible sources are given in the bibliography. In part one I describe four general kinds of future-seeing. Three of these are commonly and widely experienced spontaneously, and many readers will recognize them. The fourth kind refers to achieved future-seers who have brought various degrees of conscious control to their art.

Whether the future *can deliberately be foreseen*, though, is a problem that eludes resolution in a philosophical and scientific sense because the "mechanics" of foreseeing and the real nature of time and time-transcendence are either not understood or misinterpreted. Many of these misunderstandings have led to debates regarding the evidence that the future *is* foreseen versus the philosophical and scientific problems attendant to whether it *can* be foreseen. This is the first book to take a position midway between the two poles of these debates.

The age-old question of whether the future is predetermined and already fixed or whether we are freely determined to create it cannot be resolved within the scope of this book. This question has been volcanically debated and has fiercely divided religious, social, scientific, and philosophical venues.

I will not enter into this debate, because evidence supports both sides of the question. Cycles researchers have shown that an amazing number of phenomena approximately repeat themselves periodically, and in this sense they are "predetermined." Self-limiting mind-sets exhibit certain kinds of predetermining factors. But the future can be changed by those who foresee what will happen if they don't change it. And, indeed, the basic reason for studying future-seeing *is* to enhance our abilities to transform the future into a better one.

This book, then, seeks to escape the chimeralike arguments. It focuses instead on discarding or reinterpreting old, misunderstood factors and introducing new ones appropriate to gaining a better and more functional understanding of future-seeing.

ESSENTIAL DEFINITIONS

Five terms strategic to the discussions will be used continuously throughout:

Intellect. 1) That part of our mind-dynamic systems active only when we are awake and via which we accumulate the knowledge-experiential basis for our particular self-limiting forms of reason and logic; and 2) that computerlike part of our mind-dynamic processes housing the basis for our choices, decisions, and actions resulting from them.

The Nostradamus Factor. 1) In the individual, a specialized mind-dynamic presence "beneath" intellect, which foresees the future and spontaneously (though only occasionally) alerts the individual through dreams, waking visions, and autonomic urges; and 2) in given groups, the shared intuition of forthcoming future events or conditions.

Future-Seeing. 1) As a process, the sum of all combined available methods that result in correct perception of what is about to happen; and 2) as a "mind," the sum of all the processes that result in correct perception or foreknowledge of what is about to happen.

Image-Building. As used in this book, *the physical action* of sketching, drawing, graphing, or diagramming both simple and complex elements of future-seeing into a pictorial synthesis, the precise goal of which is to activate dormant or latent *"seeing-synthesizing"* components of your mind-dynamic processes.

Psychic. As used in this book, those mind-dynamic processes that incorporate perceptions that exceed or extend beyond the ranges of our physical senses.

The "pieces" of the future-seeing mosaic are many. But two of them can been seen as having preliminary importance: first, erecting an increasingly precise vocabulary that refers to specific future-seeing phenomena; and second, increasing image-building skills. Precise vocabulary expands those functions attributed to the left hemisphere of the brain; image-building enhances those attributed to the right hemisphere.

Any conscious control of your future-seeing capabilities you might acquire *cannot* be achieved unless both criteria above are also achieved.

Linguistic limits are an immediatge drawback if we wish to enlarge our intellectual understanding of future-seeing phenomena. Some traditional words are not adequate, and Western languages do not include words for hitherto unidentified future-seeing phenomena. As you will see, the "pieces" of future-seeing cannot be jumbled together; they must be fitted together with precise understanding. And this begins with precise word definitions via which our intellects process information.

I do not like to erect neologisms, though. To avoid doing so, I have elected to link well-known terms together, combining their dictionary definitions. Unless otherwise noted, I have depended on the older *Webster's Seventh New Collegiate Dictionary*.

Regarding image-building, it must be adamantly stated that our mind-dynamic systems utilize *mind-images* to present psychically acquired information to intellect, and that intellect itself utilizes mind-images to crystallize understanding. It is through images that we think more effectively. In fact, many researchers have wondered if words are even necessary to thinking—as discussed, for example, by Rudolf Flesch, the renowned authority on writing-improvement, in his important book *How to Write, Speak, and Think More Effectively*, first published in 1946 and still in print.

If the future is to be fore-*seen*, it is to be seen through mind-dynamic *images*—and so increasing image-building skills is an unavoidable prerequisite for psychic-improvement perceiving in general and for aspiring future-seers in particular. Our Western cultures are appallingly inadequate in the arts of image-building skills, even though the enormous appeal of comic and picture books, illustrated texts, movies, and television is taken for granted. But we look at or watch (in-flow) these only, while we are hardly encouraged to externalize (out-flow) images of our own making.

Many have found, though, that they can "work things out" on paper by sketching, doodling, or diagramming things that they have difficulty understanding in verbal contexts alone. The reason for this is understandable. In his book entitled *A Second Way of Knowing* (1991), the perceptual researcher Edmund Blair Bolles shows that perceptual meaning is achieved via a number of laws, among which is the "law of proximity."

We group things that are near or related to each other into a whole figure (mind-image). We then perceive the whole figure, but we often mind-miss or do not mind-perceive its parts. But when we undertake to sketch or diagram the whole figure we are obliged to "spot" all the functional parts that make it up. Unless we spot, by sketching or diagramming, all the functional parts of something, we may understand something only generally but not precisely. And unless we understand mind-dynamic processes precisely, we cannot achieve precise conscious control over them.

I have included a small selection of illustrations not principally to illustrate the verbal text but as examples of how easy a difficult concept can be reduced to a simple illustration that will enhance your image-building capacities. Merely copying out these few illustrations will activate deeper image-building understanding—but your own efforts to draw out additional ones will do so even more.

Chapter 12, for example, contains a number of "laws" of future-seeing, each of which can and should be diagrammed by the serious would-be future-seer. If you diagram only one or two of them, for example, you will soon notice that your mind-dynamic processes function more easily regarding those than the ones you have not diagrammed. You may, of course, read this entire book at the verbal level and achieve some intellectual understanding of the text. But if it is NostraFac activation you are after, then increasing your general image-building skills is "where it's at."

Future-seeing has commonly and popularly been called "prophecy." This term will not be used in this book. The reason is specific: from early antiquity until approximately the middle Renaissance, a prophet was considered to be someone who conveyed or pronounced the words of God or the impulses and revelations of the Holy Spirit. In this sense, the prophet was a religious, theological, or spiritual amanuensis *only*. Whether spurious or not, this type of revelation can still be claimed to exist, and it consists of a topic that would need separate treatment.

By the end of the book, you will see that the distinctions between *future-seeing* and *futurology* can become entwined. The reason is that the future-seer can utilize the established methods of futurology to enhance his or her image-building—seeing into the future. *Futurology* is defined as projecting probable futures based on identifying and measuring existing trends and conditions and extrapolating forward in time from them. Futurology is definitely part of the sum of all *combined available methods* that result in more correct perceptions of what is about to happen.

Future-seeing is divided from futurology by two mutual misunderstandings. It is popularly believed that psychics can automatically see the future without recourse to mundane forms of help. This sometimes appears to be the case, but it is not true generally. Futurologists popularly believe they can extrapolate the future without recourse to psychic insights. This likewise appears to be the case sometimes, but it not true generally.

Futurology as a science *does not* incorporate psychic inputs. Its methods are not therefore capable of foreseeing the completely *unexpected* and *unanticipated*, which can radically alter the status and meaning of ongoing conditions and trends. The basic element of future-seeing that can "spot" what will disrupt the ongoing belongs to the Nostradamus Factor, as will be described here in detail. The best critical examination of futurology so far will be found in Max Dublin's 1991 book *Futurehype: The Tyranny of Prophecy.*

Although the word *psychic* is used in this book of necessity, it is problematic in that no good definitions exist for it. It covers a wide range of mind-phenomena for which no causes or sources can be found via the material sciences, especially if the phenomena apparently do not correspond to the known laws of matter, energy, space, and time. This was the grounds in modern science for rejecting psychic phenomena entirely. However, as it is turning out in the advancing sciences, matter and energy and space and time *also* do not correspond to those known laws at certain levels of their activity—as was discussed in Gary Zukav's *The Dancing Wu Li Masters: An Overview of the New Physics* (1979), among other recent notable books.

Part two discusses outer pieces of the future-seeing mosaic that influence or impact on our inner future-seeing processes. Most of these outer phenomena cannot be discussed unless treks into actual predicting are undertaken to demonstrate how, why, and to what degree outer phenomena impact on inner mind-dynamic processes. I have selected predictions that roughly refer to what I believe will occur up to the year 2010, and perhaps a bit beyond. Since the twentieth century will end and the twenty-first will begin during this period, I will refer to this epoch as the "millennial transition."

It must be borne in mind that the predictions are given only in an experimental sense to illustrate certain future-seeing aspects that I could not otherwise describe. *In no instance do I claim that I am able to see the future.* I am an aspiring or ostensible future-seer, and I am still learning how the future can be seen rightly.

Some of the predictions may prove to be wrong (some I even hope will be). These prediction failures would only reflect on my personal future-seeing capacities and in no way jeopardize the possibilities for others seeking to implement the future-seeing mosaic the text represents. No one will ever see the future correctly all the time, but this is no reason for many not to try to foresee it correctly some of the time.

With regard to the prediction-sets given, I have avoided two areas of ongoing activity because they are centered on volatile debates.

These are the abortion issue and the Jewish-Muslim impasse. Attempting to predict the outcomes of these two issues would upset many and distort the purposes of this book; and in any event, other predictions can serve the illustrative purposes intended.

Finally, although a great deal of new information is offered herein, much of it extends from existing information whose sources are found in the bibliography. In my opinion, future-seeing theoretically has been possible for some time not only because we possess natural Nostradamus Factors but because others have dealt with and understood some of its issues. The whole of these issues, new and known, have been brought together for the first time in this book.

Ingo Swann
New York, September 1992

P A R T ONE

THE INNER PHENOMENA OF THE

FUTURE-SEEING MOSAIC

"Something" in us foresees the future.

Virtual time exists.
Our inner mind-held concepts can prevent us
from entering it.

1

JUMPING THE TIME BARRIER

Like many others, I've had good reasons during my life to assume that the future can be seen. But if I had any doubt it would have vanished as a result of an astonishing forty-five seconds when I found myself in Detmold, then in West Germany, in the spring of 1988.

Detmold is near the beautiful Teutoburger Forest and a famous pre-Christian shrine, *Horn-Externstein*, which is a pile of towering rocks riddled with sonorous caves. Until the time of Charlemagne it is said that Nordic kings came to Horn-Externstein to consult seers about the future.

I was invited to Detmold by Herr Manfred Himmel in April 1988 to give a series of lectures about psi research. This was Herr Himmel's fifth "esoteric" conference, and it was well attended by several hundred people. Herr Himmel was ardent about psychic matters, and the talks of his other speakers were interesting to me. Some of these speakers were also practicing psychics who were busy giving individual "readings" and making predictions about the future.

I was billed as the famous American superpsychic who had "astonished scientists" since my first formal laboratory experiments in

1970. But I have never given individual "readings," and I *never* made predictions about the future.

Many of Herr Himmel's conference attendees were visibly disappointed that I did not give the expected readings and did not foresee the future. Although I had studied "prophecy" and predicting for many years and had even experienced some novel insights about it, I was well aware that most predictions turn out to be wrong. I felt I had a scientific reputation to protect, which would be damaged if I accumulated a list of erroneous predictions. Moreover, I didn't view myself as a future-seer in any professional sense, and I thought that predicting should be left to those who were or at least tried to be.

I gave several lectures and workshops at the conference, as well as the keynote address. I had worked hard at preparing this address, entitling it "Revising Psychic Research Methods and Expectations in the New Age," and even gave the opening statements in German before continuing in English with the aid of a translator.

This was, I thought, an important lecture. And, indeed, the audience listened attentively. When the talk was over, I asked for questions. The hall was silent—until an elderly woman sitting in the second row stood up and meekly asked: "Herr Schwann, won't you give us as least *one* prediction?"

Caught very unexpectedly and in clear view between the proverbial rock and the hard place, I began grasping for a diplomatic way to get out of making a prediction.

I was quite angry to be put in this position. But as my anger rose, there was a "noise" or rushing sound around me, and I had a sense of getting "larger." Then there was a clarity of some unfamiliar kind, which somehow was liquid—and in this liquidness what seemed like a thousand pictures flashed through my consciousness. I had the distinct, lightninglike impression that most people in the audience *already knew the future* at some "place" deep within them. And I knew that their conscious minds were disconnected from this deep place.

And I knew what they knew, so to speak, and one aspect of this hidden knowledge boiled up into my intellectual consciousness. Without deciding to do so, I said: "Okay! You want a prediction?

Here's a prediction. The Berlin Wall will come down in eighteen to twenty-four months." I spat this out intensely and fast, holding on to the podium with both hands.

The translator standing by my side looked at me with wide eyes. My own narrowed. "Translate it—translate it NOW!"

She did. When it appeared that the audience had not heard it correctly, she translated it again, this time somewhat nervously. The initial silence of the audience was complete. Then they began to rise to their feet, one by one. Someone began to clap, and in the next moment the audience lost its composure and became unglued. Several burst into tears and began to hug each other. And some rushed to the podium and began to hug *me*.

"Wait a moment," I tried to yell into the melee. "It's *only* a prediction."

And when it was over, I was absolutely astonished that I had spoken the words in the first place. "Lord," I thought, "my colleagues back in the States are going to think I've lost it. And the skeptics will have a field day." In April 1988 the Soviet Union and the Berlin Wall seemed destined to ride intact into the twenty-first century.

Once back in New York, I was glad enough to forget that I had made this rash prediction. And it was doubly rash because I had *given it a time-window*—eighteen to twenty-four months as of April 1988. *Anyone* could have predicted that the Wall would come down at some indeterminate future time—and it probably would. But I had said *when*.

Nineteen months later, the Berlin Wall came down almost overnight, a historic event that caught everyone (including the CIA, MI-5, the Mosad, and even the KGB) by complete surprise, if the media are to be believed. And I had one of the most rewarding experiences of my life—lying in bed eating potato chips, watching my prediction come true on real-time television right before my eyes. Somehow, something in me had spontaneously foreseen a bit of the future, and that part had ultimately manifested itself in the physical universe.

How does what begins as a mind-image in someone's inner sensing systems ultimately become or manifest itself as fact in the physical universe? How is it that our inner sensing systems can transcend the "absolute" linear time of our physical universe? And *why* is it that this awesome and important faculty, reported since the dawn of human activity on earth, has the low esteem it does today?

What is involved here are mysterious processes that we do not know about or, if we do, understand very well. Could everyone foresee better if they understood those processes? And why didn't I realize that I could future-see—even though I had studied predictions and seers for over thirty years (as part of my overall interest in psychic matters)?

I am not, of course, the first, nor will I be the last, to foresee some completely unanticipated bit of the future. Aside from the great number of successful predictions recorded since ancient times, stunning examples of future-seeeing are always taking place. The psychic Jeanne Dixon predicted that President Kennedy would be assassinated in Dallas. A year ahead of time, the psychic Alan Vaughan (who also predicted Kennedy's assassination) forecast that in June of 1972 Pennsylvania would experience enormous floods causing mass evacuations—which duly occurred.

One of the worst plane crashes in U.S. history, which occurred on May 26, 1979, in which 272 people died, was foreseen to the day by at least five future-seers, including one who died in the crash because he ignored his forewarning. During a live radio talk-show, a psychic living in the state of Washington forecast the date and approximate time of the eruption of Mount St. Helens. At least two psychics taking part in TV interviews predicted the explosion of the Challenger space shuttle in January 1986. Future-seeing is not confined to famous psychics, though, as we shall see. Momentous forthcoming events "leak" into the consciousnesses of "average" people, and sometimes hundreds foresee bits and pieces of them.

The only feasible explanation is that we possess future-seeing powers that remain consciously undeveloped in most of us but that can manifest themselves spontaneously even in those who do not suspect they have such powers.

As I watched the first breaches in the Berlin Wall open up I found myself saddled with the problem that automatically followed from this successful prediction. Could I foresee other things?

By the end of 1990, I had discovered that the answer to this question was yes—with certain qualifications and reservations. And this answer is partly the justification for this book.

But there is another justification. I am firmly convinced that what scientists call the "hundredth monkey syndrome" has a great deal of truth to it. Some time ago, researchers discovered that a number of monkeys on an island began learning how to wash their food in streams or the sea. Soon, all the monkeys on the island could do the same. But on another island nearby, all the monkeys started to wash their food the same way *without* seeing the monkeys on the first island do so.

In short, so the theory goes, if a hundred monkeys learn something, all monkeys will soon acquire this knowing even in the absence of any sensory contacts with the learned monkeys. An unknown form of "learning transmission" is thought to exist, which would explain all this. Such learning transmission is presumably *psychic*, since it is of some nonsensory quality. Critics say this is all bunk, but the facts remain. With a wide expanse of ocean separating them, monkeys learned something in a way that no standard or prevailing explanation can account for.

It is rather well known that humans possess psychic states that influence those around them. And there is also a phenomenon of people separated by vast distances "having the same idea at the same time." By extension and implication, then, if more people understood the processes by which future-seeing is achieved, more people might become future-seers—or at least become so more easily.

This assumption helps to account for one phenomenon I experienced in April 1988 when the entire audience in Germany accepted my Berlin Wall prediction without reservation and with a collective enthusiasm that is not easily explainable. Skeptics might opine that the response arose from collective wishful thinking. But the Wall did come down. I experienced a flash in which I "saw" that the whole audience already knew of this event at some deeper level other than their waking consciousness. When I verbalized this shared deep-knowing, the apparent truth of it welled up in the entire audience. If the audience contained any doubters, none of them presented themselves.

I believe what all the evidence suggests: that all of us foresee at some level deeper within us, and it is this assumption that constitutes the first argument in favor of future-seeing. And as more and more people gain understanding about future-seeing, there will be increased future-seeing potential for all. This possibility is the second and more important reason that I wrote this book.

My research substantiates the conclusion that during the twentieth century, future-seeing (in its variety of forms) has been at its historical all-time low as an acceptable social phenomenology. And, a few individual future-seers notwithstanding, it has been the twentieth century that collectively has made the most mistakes in even approximating what will happen in the future. In this sense, the hundredth monkey syndrome appears operative in negative as well as positive respects. If a lot of us forget or ignore one of our powers, eventually the rest of us, by "dis-learning transmission," may do so also.

Although it was the Berlin Wall sequence that convinced me that I should get down to future-seeing business and organize all the information I had acquired about it, what can be called my academic interest in predictions and seers began much earlier.

As a child, I probably had more than my share of previsions of the future, either dreaming, visualizing, or intuiting things that I thought were going to happen—and that often did. But since the prevailing wisdom of the day held that the future could not really be seen because it did not yet exist, most people told me that other, more logical reasons existed for my experiences. I suppose I accepted this "logical" reasoning. As I grew up, this kind of foreseeing subsided—as it probably does with many young people who are reverse-trained to ignore or suppress contacts with their own anticipatory capabilities.

However, in the early part of 1962, when I was twenty-nine, I had a sudden flare-up of future-seeing *dreams*. I did not at first recognize these for what they were, thinking they were merely symbolic of what was going on in my subconscious (which was the theory of the day). But shortly afterward I began encountering situations that were near-exact replicas of what I had seen in the dreams.

One of the dreams that immediately came true involved seeing myself arriving one morning at the crowded intersection of Forty-Second Street and First Avenue in New York, where the United Nations buildings are located and where I was working at the time. In the dream I saw a man with tattooed arms, in an orange shirt, being chased by cops. My view of this scene in the dream was from a point near the fleeing man's face, where I could see his unshaven cheek, smell him, and hear his breath, his heartbeat, and sense his fear. He turned and fired a gun at the cops, and they shot him on the corner. *In the dream I knew that the sound of bullets would be heard and that they would wake me up.* The sound of bullets flying actually woke me up out of the dream. My own heart was beating fiercely, I was sweating, and I "knew" his fear.

Two days later as I arrived at that corner on my way to work, bullets suddenly began flying. I backed up against a wall. A man with tattoos and an orange shirt was running down First Avenue toward the intersection. He had turned and fired at the cops who were chasing him. The cops were yelling at people to get out of the way. They shot the man in the orange shirt. He fell on the sidewalk into a pool of his own blood. He was not dead, and soon he was whisked away in an ambulance. The only difference between the event and the dream was that I was not near his face but crunched against the wall. Otherwise everything else *was exactly the same.*

I did not know this man and had never even seen him before. I had no idea why I had seen either him or the shooting event in the dream. But I was immeasurably impressed—even though most of my colleagues at the UN said that all this was probably just a coincidence. I thought that this "logical" explanation was more than a bit lame—especially when not a few of those colleagues later began telling me that *they had seen the future in dreams, too!*

The shooting dream left me grappling for an explanation—*any* explanation that would make sense. Why should I have dreamed of someone I had never seen before and never saw again—a man and an event that had nothing at all to do with me? I made one decision quite early—which I later realized was almost correct. The fulfilled dream of the tattooed, orange-shirted man clearly had nothing to do with what was going on in my subconscious—*unless* that subconscious was involved with seeing into the future.

I made some decisions as a result of this dream and its fulfillment, which more-or-less line up as follows:

1. this experience, with all its exact details, whatever else it may have been, had nothing to do with coincidence;
2. something "in" me could see into the future and present its sightings in dreams;
3. I began remembering earlier times that I had seen the future in one way or another;
4. I decided, at first as a serious hobby, to take up in-depth research with regard to seeing into the future; and
5. I realized (after some time had passed) that when I heard the real shots in the street and witnessed the dream fulfillment, I "woke up" to the *reality* of future-seeing—which *caused* me to undertake long-term, serious investigation into the matter.

In this roundabout way, my subconscious (if that is what it was) *did* wake me up to the realms of future-seeing—and this, as I have since taken it, was the purpose of the prevision.

The implications of this prevision are awesome. For one thing, we possess a factor that can see the future. For another, I interpreted that something in me also wanted me to become aware of that factor—and "used" the dream to make it so. In retrospect, the whole of this at first apparently simple, nonsensical dream, its fulfillment, and its aftermath was actually quite complex, especially because I *did* strive to find out about how we can future-see—an effort that has now resulted in being able to compile this book approximately thirty years after the fact.

THE METHOD OF THIS BOOK

The cumulative results of my research clearly indicate that seeing into the future is a multilevel mosaic of different mind-dynamic phenomena that fit together to produce time-transcending warnings, alerts, or predictions. A review of the multilevel mosaic therefore has determined the method of this book.

There is a class of phenomena called *epiphenomena*, meaning *secondary* phenomena. Epiphenomena arise from primary phenomena. Epiphenomena are distinguished by the fact that they remain mysterious and unexplainable no matter how much we study them alone. The reason is that they are *end-products* of *other phenomena that come together in processlike forms*. The how and why of the end-product can be understood only if its primary-causal phenomena are located and understood first.

All reports of future-seeing, whether ancient or modern, are fascinating to the interested reader. But in all cases they are reports of epiphenomena. If we focus exclusively on them we will never locate, understand, or learn to work with the primary phenomena that produced them. Thus, I will use selected reports of future-seeing epiphenomena only to familiarize the reader with specific types of foreseeing I have identified.

Otherwise, the substantive bulk of the book's first part, and some of the second part, will be devoted to ascertaining and describing "technical" aspects of the primary phenomena of the mosaic. These technical aspects, as they relate to future-seeing, have not been discussed anywhere until now, and so this book is the first of its kind to assemble them into their mosaiclike form.

The primary-phenomena aspects are found in our mind-dynamic systems. You will be able to recognize them in yourself. And your recognition and control of those systems will become refined to the degree that you activate your psychic image-building capacities by sketching out concepts as discussed in the introduction and explore the introspection exercises I suggest. I have used image-building sketches and introspection exercises to expand my own capacities.

There is no quick, easy route to achieving high-quality foreseeing. Only a patient increase in your overall understanding will contribute to that. Our mind-dynamic processes, though wonderful, are also very complex systems. The suggested sketching exercises will help you break up old patterns of thinking and begin to erect new ones that are propitious to seeing into the future.

When the primary aspects are assembled in your own intellect-awareness, you will realize that all together they represent a new and unfamiliar realm of mind-dynamic activity that is tantamount to an undiscovered future-seeing reality.

As it happens, this future-seeing reality is consistent with new advances in scientific understanding regarding human biopsychic functioning, bioelectromagnetism, quantum and virtual time, and new understandings of vitalistic consciousness. These, then, must be discussed, since they are part and parcel of the future-seeing mosaic.

2

CONSTRUCTING AN INTELLECT-BRIDGE TO OUR INDWELLING NOSTRADAMUS FACTOR

A good anecdote reporting successful future-seeing is to me what viewing a rare stamp is to a stamp collector, or what watching a perfect touchdown is to avid football fans. And I have collected thousands of them.

Anecdotal reports of spontaneous future-seeing experiences can convince us that future-seeing is possible and inspire us to want to learn "*how* to do it." But if we do not realize that anecdotes are only secondary epiphenomena we will not think of looking for the primary phenomena that produced them. And this mistake will cause us to ignore the fact that something in us is *already seeing into the future* even though our conscious intellects have not yet learned how to recognize what it is or even know that "it" exists.

Two access points to future-seeing are (1) familiarizing ourselves with the processes that precede the final event reported in anecdotes;

and (2) identifying and linking up with that "something" in us that naturally sees into the future and gives rise to the epiphenomena of spontaneous future-seeing experiences.

We can find these two access points only if we look far afield. First of all, there is the matter of how little we really know about what we are and what our powers are. And then there is the matter of how little of our powers we utilize.

During the two decades in which I have been scientifically active in "paranormal" or parapsychological research, I have repeatedly been impressed with a single fact: Anyone who develops extensive contact with our parapsychological or "psi" nature soon begins to realize how little we understand about ourselves. We are clearly a species with extraordinary and marvelous capabilities. As is often said, our real realities are more astonishing than any astounding fiction that can be devised by imaginative writers.

Yet it is also clear that a great many of us conceive of ourselves in ways that neither flatter nor awaken our extraordinary and marvelous capabilities. Rather, it might be said, we exist within the small realms of our waking intellects (which themselves are epiphenomena) and let the rest of ourselves go unawakened. Brain-mind specialists began to realize over eighty years ago that the average person utilizes less than 5 percent of his or her brain-mind potential and that even the greatest geniuses rarely employ more than 15 percent.

These words may be intellectually meaningful to you. But if you first draw out a large circle that stands for *all* of your unawakened potential and then place in it a very small circle that stands for the 5 to 15 percent of your awakened potential, you will instantly achieve a change in perception that words alone cannot stimulate.

If you now take a pencil and black out the bigger portion of the circle, you can begin to get a variety of ideas. For example, your entire mind-dynamic potentials are like the Broadway theater district in New York City—except that most of the theaters are dark or closed down. One of these darkened theaters represents your indwelling Nostradamus Factor—and there is no contact-bridge between it and the lit-up theater that is your waking intellect.

Here are several great mysteries. Why do we posssess brain-mind potential far in excess of what we normally use? And what happens to that which we do not use? Do they atrophy, as might be supposed? It is unthinkable that we were provided with *greater* brain-mind potential and not intended to use it.

The fault, then, must lie within ourselves, within the many self-limiting ways we *intellectually* conceive of ourselves, within our beliefs, convictions, and worldviews—all of which are products of our epiphenomenal intellects. Indeed, it is very easy for us to consider ourselves less than we are and quite difficult to conceive of ourselves as more than we appear to be. And we tend toward dysfunctionality when we diminish or deny our sense of our greater capabilities and toward increased functionality when we enhance our sense of them.

My interest in researching future-seeing antedates my scientific parapsychological work by twenty years. And it is the future-seeing research that reveals more than any other how little we understand of ourselves. When I began that research (in 1962), I was under the general impression that foreseeing could only be accomplished by special people who mysteriously possessed specific talents for doing so. I certainly did not number myself among such extraordinarily gifted individuals, even though I'd had certain spontaneous future-seeing experiences as a child.

But as the years rolled on and I became more knowledgeable about the true dimensions of future-seeing *of all kinds*, several important new understandings began to dawn on me. One of these was that as a group, "ordinary" people are more likely to have correct future-seeing episodes than are "achieved" seers. For example, many achieved future-seers blossomed into acclaim at the beginning of this century. But only one of them foresaw the sinking of the Titanic in 1912—whereas two hundred–plus ordinary people foresaw the disaster, some of whom saw this event quite clearly. There is no way, of course, to tabulate the exact percentage of nongifted future-seeing throughout history; but it is of such a magnitude that we may as well consider it universal.

The only real differences between gifted and nongifted future-seeing is that it occurs less frequently among the nongifted and that the gifted have done something the nongifted have not: developed some kind of intellect-control over it. It is the *intellectual interest* in developing the control that seems to stimulate increasingly gifted future-seeing.

It is true, though, that a certain number of people are born with high-stage future-seeing gifts that are apparently "natural" to them. But these people may actually number, say, less than one in ten million. A somewhat larger percentage, speculatively one in three million, *train themselves* to enhance their future-seeing potential in some way. In my estimation, *most* acclaimed future-seers have trained themselves into their calling or profession. But these are still very few when considered against the great numbers of people who spontaneously experience occasional future-seeing episodes that are both meaningful and *accurate*.

THE NOSTRADAMUS FACTOR

Early in my future-seeing research, then, an awesome fact began to dawn on me: our *species* must possess some kind of Nostradamus-like factor composed of natural processes that can and do transcend time and connect up to certain future events that are meaningfully relevant to the progress of our lives. And I also realized that this Nostradamus Factor resides among those brain-mind powers we normally do not develop and use.

At least four different kinds of these natural processes can be identified:

> NostraFac experiences of the first kind—spontaneous fore-
> warnings occurring in dreams during the sleep state;
> NostraFac experiences of the second kind—spontaneous alerts
> occurring during the waking state;
> NostraFac experiences of the third kind—forewarnings and
> alerts communally experienced by numbers of people in
> either the waking or sleep state; and
> NostraFac experiences of the fourth kind—consciously con-
> trolled future-seeing achieved by seers.

I'll collectively refer to these natural processes as *our* Nostradamus Factor in honor of the great future-seeing sage Michael de Nostradamus (1503–66). Nostradamus made hundreds of predictions five hundred years ago, many of which have periodically come true since. His name is practically synonymous with seeing into the future.

Perhaps Nostradamus *was* especially gifted to begin with. But he was as human as we all are, and his specialness (if that is what it was) began with his inner and natural future-seeing processes, to which he must have added some form of adaptive, intellectual understanding. And from what few biographical details of Nostradamus remain, it is clear that he studied future-seeing matters very deeply. It was from those studies that he was able to enhance his innate future-seeing processes, bringing them under some conscious control.

Only a natural, indwelling factor could account for universal, spontaneous future-seeing experiences—experiences that sometimes occur even among individuals who do not believe it is possible to see the future.

This latter comment is very strategic. If someone who believes that it is *not* possible to see the future *does* spontaneously experience an episode of correct future-seeing, then that experience is taking place in spite of his or her conditioned intellectual beliefs. This is tantamount to establishing something most people do realize: that we possess powers outside the peripheries of our conscious, intellectual beliefs and concepts; we transcend the limits of our physical senses. And these powers *operate on an agenda of their own*—which gives rise to their "spontaneous" nature.

When I made this realization in about 1965 (and it has never ceased to be staggering), I began to understand that the correct target for future-seeing research was not so much the study of gifted individuals or their anecdotes as it was the pursuit of this indwelling factor inherent in everyone. And I have no hesitation at all in stating that everyone who reads this book will be able to remember one *of their own* future-seeing experiences—and if not, they will experience one soon after reading it.

It is the universal *communality* (not individual specialness) of spontaneous, time-transcending experiences that constitutes the basic case for future-seeing. And it is this communality that, although it is known by a few researchers, has not been described in sufficient detail and whose processes certainly have never been isolated and presented so that people can learn from them.

Your own Nostradamus Factor exists somewhere in the bigger darkened part of the circle you sketched out. You might indicate your NostraFac as a small circle somewhere in that darkened part. Your NostraFac occasionally spontaneously sends hints and clues of the future to your waking intellect—normally called gut feelings or intuition. Thus, erecting a more vital bridge between it and your intellect must be possible. Sketch in a line between your NostraFac and the 5- to 15-percent circle that constitutes your waking intellect. As discussed in the introduction, this simple sketching process constitutes image-building, and images strike more deeply into your consciousness than words alone do.

It is almost certain that the only difference between nondeveloped and developed future-seers is that the latter have constructed some kind of *intellectual bridge* between their Nostradamus Factors and their conscious, intellectual processes. This bridge might occur naturally with some. But historical evidence indicates that most achieved future-seers have had to *work* at becoming proficient— and work with as much devotion to succeed in their goal as is necessary in any other discipline, craft, or art. Most assuredly, it is by self-learning that we can recognize future-seeing processes inherent in our brain-mind potential.

Once this intellectual bridge is established, the seer consciously emerges and can peer from the doorstep-of-the-Now into changes coming in the future (and predict them if he or she has the courage to do so).

The realms of our Nostradamus Factor, though, are strange. As seen from our familiar and concrete Now, the familiar laws of linear time and the physical universe are topsy-turvy in what amounts to nontime "geography." But as daunting as this might seem at first, I can state with conviction that once your intellect *and* your image-building mind grasps the whole of it, deep processes beneath the intellect will begin to respond. We are far more than the sum of our epiphenomenal intellectual conscious processes, and deeper learning goes on sometimes even in spite of them.

The *processes* of our deep-level future-seeing powers remain obscured and unlocated not only because they are deep-mind functions but because they are intellectually obscured by myths, misinterpretations of evidence, inappropriate intellectual assumptions, and sometimes outright denial of future-seeing phenomena. Most of us assume that what we think is correct simply because we cannot believe that we could think incorrectly about anything. Thus it is difficult for us to consider that we might be misinterpreting evidence or possess inappropriate intellectual assumptions. We feel we are correct in denying the things we do, and myths and misunderstandings are merely what *others* possess.

So we defend our "correctness," ofttimes to the death. But by considering the possibility that we might be incorrect, or at least not fully informed, about some things, we are already beginning to dissolve our intellectual blocks to future-seeing.

The intellects of individuals that are ill-disposed to future-seeing possibilities rather naturally will not have developed an intellectual bridge to their *own* Nostradamus Factors. Thus, when they do experience a spontaneous future-seeing episode, chances are that it will cause them a great deal of intellectual confusion—confusion that may manifest itself as denial, disbelief, or some other kind of psychological stress.

If our intellect contains antifuture-seeing constructs, then we probably will *not* be able to construct that intellectual bridge. The problem of accessing our natural future-seeing capabilities then boils down to an intellectual problem—one that is peculiar to each individual. The royal road to achieved future-seeing is not learning how to do it but realizing *what is keeping us intellectually alienated* from our own indwelling powers.

I got onto this tactic some time ago from a very unlikely source when I chanced across a statement published in an edict (Bull) by Pope Benedict XIV (1675–1758), recognized by historians as a patron of learning: "The recipients of prophecy may be angels, devils, men, women, children, heathen or gentiles; nor is it necessary that

a man should be gifted with any particular disposition to receive
the light of prophecy—*provided his intellect and senses be adapted for
making manifest the things revealed to him*" [emphasis mine].

Adapted? After I made sure this was not a mistranslation of, for
example, "learn," a very subtle nuance dawned on me. *Adapt* means
"to make fit for a specific new use or situation, often by modifying."
We normally do not think of adapting our intellects to anything.
Rather we use them to *acquire* knowledge.

We then adapt what we encounter so that it fits with the knowledge we have learned—and, of course, we often reject what doesn't
fit.

Modern psychologists have known for some time that it is very
difficult to get someone to *readapt* to anything. Once our mental-
intellect "circuits" have become established they are usually set for
life. But over two hundred years ago, Benedict XIV was suggesting
that if one's intellect can "be adapted" to future-seeing processes,
he or she may see the future.

Thus, adaption or readaptation plays some role in relinking each
person's bridge-building intellect to his or her future-seeing capabilities. But can our intellects be readapted so as to become more
experientially sensitive to our innate future-seeing processes? The
answer is yes. If we change our intellectual thought-patterning,
different adaptation "affects" occur—a phenomonology that is the
basis for all psychodynamic therapies, creativity, and self-improve-
ment techniques.

This is easier said than done, as we all know. But it is worth the
try, especially if our future-seeing powers might be enhanced by
doing so. The one thing that permits readaptation is *information*.
And in this sense, information about ourselves, about what we *are*
is a good place to begin our future-seeing readapting.

So, what *are* we? One of our more interesting aspects is that we
picture and identify what we are by setting up "explanations" to
explain to ourselves what we are. Consider this last sentence very
carefully, for it reflects one of the most important conundrums we
can encounter. We explain *to ourselves* what we are. Or at least we
try to. In terms of explaining what we are, we are in the odd position
of *being what we are BEFORE we try to explain what we are.*

First comes the human—which, in the primary instance, is what it is. Somewhere along the way, the human *then* needs to set up an explanation of what it is in order to "know" itself. The human then puts together, and adapts to, what information it can perceive about itself and its relationship to other things, and from that information conjectures a concept regarding what it is. The human then explains itself to itself via the concept it has itself conjectured.

But all such conjecturing is *secondary*, or an epiphenomenon, since it is a product of and not the *primary cause* of the human. In this way, we can architecturalize any explanation of ourselves that we want. But that all such explanations are epiphenomena quickly comes into view when we discover anything *new* about ourselves and our primary facts. At that time, we have *to alter our secondary explanations* of what we are in order to incorporate the new primary facts. In doing so we alter our conjectured images of what we are and in effect "know" ourselves differently.

For example, Western theology taught that we were created by God and were in essence a soul in a body. But when the theory that we were only physical-matter mechanisms became scientifically popular during modern times, many accordingly changed their concepts of what we are. It was assumed that souls might occasionally foresee the future, but physical-matter mechanisms could not transcend time and space. It is now being realized that we are principally bioelectromagnetic entities, and our ideas of what we are will change accordingly—as we will see in part two.

The scope of this testy problem has dismayed many throughout history and has led some to assume that we will never know ourselves completely since our knowledge of ourselves will always be limited to what we *think-believe* we have learned about ourselves.

But our essential primary facts remain extant beneath whatever we secondarily think-believe about ourselves. Clearly, what we think-believe we are *has NOT created us*. Our primary facts doubtless have remained unchanged for many thousands of years. Only our secondary explanations of what we think-believe we are have changed, sometimes radically so.

This discussion is particularly relevant to future-seeing because one of the primary facts is that we *can* see into the future. Seeing into the future is documented in some of our earliest documents, including the Bible. The ancient Greeks and Romans recorded noted examples of future-seeing that occurred in their times, as did the Chinese and all other cultures up to our contemporary times. But it is equally true that this primary fact can be occluded by secondary think-believe phenomena that *we produce ourselves*. When our secondary think-believe phenomena cannot accommodate some aspect of our primary phenomena, then those phenomena lie beyond our think-believe cognitive reach. If, for example, our secondary think-believe phenomena are themselves encased in misleading myths about future-seeing, such myths will act as barriers to future-seeing.

So, there are two impediments to putting the future-seeing mosaic together and building the desired bridge to our Nostradamus Factors:

1. limited or erroneous concepts of what we are; and
2. myths about future-seeing that limit our perceptions.

Needless to say, a myth is an epiphenomenon too, a *production* of ourselves.

3

NOSTRAFAC EXPERIENCES OF THE FIRST KIND: SPONTANEOUS FOREWARNING INTRUSIONS DURING THE SLEEP STATE

Our existence is characterized by four commonplace but astonishing facts. The first is that we have dreams while asleep. The second is that many dreams have had enormous impacts on how human history has unfolded. Third, we have achieved very little understanding of why or how we dream, even though our species has been dreaming from time immemorial. And fourth, *some of our dreams show us the future*—or bits and pieces of it—and so are important to our welfare and life directions. It is this last fact that is the topic of this chapter.

Throughout history many future-seeing and other kinds of dreams have redirected human-caused routes into the future. The most concise book so far regarding the culture-shaping impacts of dreams on human affairs, *The Understanding of Dreams, or the Machinations of the Night,* by the dream historian Raymond de Becker, was published in 1968. De Becker shows that in all civilizations ancient and modern, dreams have played many roles—therapeutic, philosophical, psychological, divinatory. Important theories and inventions that have changed history, and thus the shape of the future, have emerged from dreams (for example, the steam engine, airplanes, economic theories, and new art forms).

De Becker also shows that dreams are not merely the expression of rechurning and repressed activity but often are a rough plan for action, for good decision-making and the means of approaching those decisions. And it is this particular aspect of dreams that is of utmost importance to future-seeing and to gaining understanding of the Why of our Nostradamus Factor.

Spontaneous Dreamtime Foreseeing Alerts

A more precise description of what is happening during sleep is that our dreams take place when *our waking intellects are suspended and not operative.* We have little willful, volitional, rational, or logical control over why, how, or to what end our dreams take place. They occur because of some automatic function in us. This function is an autonomous thinking function in its own right, working independently of our waking intellects. We are completely justified in assuming that it is a mind in its own right.

Thus, the dreaming-mind differs considerably from our intellect-mind. For one thing, our waking intellect-mind has a very difficult time perceiving what *really will happen* in the future. For another, the dreaming future-seeing mind produces future-seeing information that often challenges the logic, reason, and beliefs of our waking minds. When the dreaming mind does this, we are placed in a particularly confusing situation. The dreaming mind produces future-seeing information that our waking minds can argue with, doubt, or disbelieve altogether. Two minds, then, do entirely different and separate things.

The easily verifiable evidence that our dreaming mind spontaneously foresees the future, often in spite of our intellect's failure to do so, is the best and most crucial evidence we have that we possess the natural future-seeing capability I have dubbed our Nostradamus Factor. I refer to the dreaming mind's future-seeing alerts and forewarnings as "NostraFac experiences of the first kind" principally because humans universally share them and they are the most frequently reported of all foreseeing experiences.

In the mid-1970s, I met a young neurological student preparing for his doctorate at a New York university. He was hired as a consultant on a psi project with which I was involved. He told everyone that he did not believe in psi or any of that "occult garbage." Yet he possessed certain qualifications for brain-wave analysis that were important to the project. He was married and had a young son.

About a week after the project got under way, he approached me somewhat sheepishly, saying that he had had a dream several nights in a row that he was riding with his son in a car. The car came to a crossroad where it was hit by a truck that came out of nowhere. His son was killed. He went on about the probable psychological symbolism inherent in the dream. Did he somehow wish his son dead, or such?

I am not a dream analyst, but I have always been convinced that our dreams must have a purpose, even though our intellects might not immediately figure out what that purpose is. Instead of discussing the dream as a symbolic interlude, I asked him where the crossroad was. He didn't know, except that it was somewhere in a strange, moonlike landscape, which seemed surreal to him. Beyond establishing the character of the landscape, neither of us knew what to think about the dream. A few days later he told me that the dream had not occurred again.

Some five years later I got a telephone call from him late at night. He was very excited. In the intervening years, he had divorced his wife and had taken his son on a tour of the Arizona deserts. While driving on a certain road in the arid, hot landscape, he began to notice that the surrounding topography resembled a moonscape. He recognized it as the landscape in his dream.

He was so shocked that he stopped the car on the side of the road just in time to miss being at a hidden crossroad when a sixteen-wheeler roared through. If he had not stopped, the car would have been crushed, and his son quite likely killed. He was very grateful to me for having directed his attention to what the landscape looked like. He would have paid no attention otherwise, figuring it was just eerie dream stuff. "Jesus Christ!" he yelled over the phone. "I *saw* the future in a dream five years ago! This was no *coincidence!*"

The *warning* nature of this NostraFac experience is obvious. The intent of the NostraFac in the dream was to impress into the man's intellect the nature of the locale in which the accident would take place, to *alert him* to the danger of that locale. The goal of his Nostradamus Factor, via the dream, was to save his son's life and probably his own, too. He, at least, had no doubt about this, and neither do I.

But we have to remember that this man was a disbeliever in future-seeing so far as his intellectual realities were concerned. His antifuture-seeing intellect, however, did not act as a deterrent to his deeper, indwelling NostraFac, which apparently "decided" to *push* the warning repetitively through his mind-set resistance until it lodged somewhere in the vicinity of his waking intellect.

After this close call, the former disbeliever in "psychic stuff" became very amenable to the idea that in addition to what we call our consciousness (meaning our waking intellectual consciousness), we possess *another* kind of consciousness, which *can* penetrate the future and alert us to momentous situations at a time yet to come.

Few of us, I think, would deny the fortunate, life-saving nature of this event. But many people are likewise dream-alerted to future events and *do not take advantage* of their alerts because of intellectual resistance. And I regret to say that I have been one of them on occasion.

In the early 1960s, I dreamed three nights in a row that I should buy Madison Square Garden stock. I was then financially naive and knew very little about the stock market. I couldn't imagine that Madison Square Garden issued stock publicly, thinking that it must be a fully owned business of some kind. But in looking at the stock lists in the newspaper I found its stock selling for thirty-three cents a share.

I had no idea why I had these repetitive dreams regarding a topic I knew nothing about and had no interest in at all, but I consulted a woman who played in stocks. Her broker said that the stock had not moved in years and probably never would. In any event, I was working at the United Nations at the time for a slave's wage, and though I could have borrowed $1,000 from the UN credit union, I did not, mainly because I was too lazy.

Barely six weeks later, the Madison Square Garden Corporation announced its ultrasecret plan to build a new Garden in New York, and within four days the stock was selling first for nineteen dollars a share and finally for thirty-five dollars—a great jump from thirty-three cents! My $1,000 investment would have netted me more than $35,000.

I was absolutely shattered—and for three reasons: first, that *something in me* had surely seen the future in a dream; second, by the correctness of the dream alert; and third, by my own disbelief and stupidity. But like most people who suddenly experience a spontaneous NostraFac alert, it caught me completely unaware and very unprepared to act upon it.

My own NostraFac apparatus has not since given me another stock tip, even though I have tried every process to encourage it to do so. This has led me to the conclusion that our NostraFacs are very stubborn and are not easily pushed around by our mere intellectual desires—another testament to their autonomy. They seem to stick to some mysterious agenda of their own and push up information, when they do, for reasons of their own. But this amusing alert and my failure to act upon it did have a by-product, one that could only be seen in retrospect years later. As can easily be imagined, I began to take a more focused interest in psychic matters and our innate predictive capabilities.

In the mid-1970s, after my newfound career as a subject in parapsychological experiments had begun to attract attention in such media outlets as *Time* and *Newsweek*, I began to be invited to speak at conferences and to give seminars about psychic potential and development. At one of these, put on by Spiritual Frontiers Fellowship at Carleton College, I gave a talk about future-seeing dream-alerts. After the talk was completed, a woman came up to the lectern, stared at me blankly for a few moments, and then burst into tears. Another nut-case, I thought. Not knowing what else to do, I took her for coffee, during which she told me her sad tale of intellectual resistance to *her* NostraFac apparatus.

During her mother's yearly checkup, the family doctor pointed out a minor condition that was not dangerous but that should be rectified by a brief operation lest it develop into something untoward. The mother immediately decided to undergo the surgery two weeks later, the doctor promising that she would be in and out of the operating room quickly.

About a week before the surgery, the daughter had a dream in which a "being in radiant light" appeared and advised her to seek a second opinion about her mother's impending surgery. "I did not do this for two reasons," she explained. "It would have created an uncomfortable situation with the family doctor, who had been our doctor for years. And because I had been taught that dreams were merely psychological manifestations through which we worked out our suppressed desires and fears. I was worried about my mother, and I thought that was all the dream implied."

Her mother underwent the surgery and was indeed in and out of the operating room in a short time—but she died in the recovery room from a reaction to the anesthesia. An autopsy revealed that the woman had not had the minor condition to begin with. As might be imagined, the daughter was devastated, because a second opinion might have revealed that the mother did not have the condition.

Even twelve years after the event, the daughter felt that she had failed. "How could I have told anyone," she asked, "that a dream had alerted me to the possibility that the original diagnosis was incorrect? I didn't at first see that this dream was a predictive one, but a certain futureness was implicit in it. If I had obeyed it, my mother's and my own future would have turned out differently."

Our social norms expect us to discount dream contents save those that might apply to our own personal psychological problems. And, admittedly, a large percentage of our dream materials do seem to be involved with these problems. But imbedded in this woman's dream was a "content" that had nothing to do with her own psychological situation. "I am most angry with *myself*," the woman told me. "But this dream-alert made me realize how much I was a product of our ignorant [her word] culture, how much I modeled myself after it. We are taught to be ignorant in these matters and ridiculed if we do not live up to the status of this ignorance." The woman went on: "We have many different kinds of dreams. Why doesn't someone get to work and find out how we can identify the different kinds and help us identify those dreams that forewarn us of something that will happen in the future?"

One researcher who *has* focused on future-warning dreams is Atlanta clinical psychologist Dr. David Ryback. In his 1988 book *Dreams That Come True*, he establishes that from his sample of dream subjects, it is apparent that one out of twelve people experience future-seeing dreams that come true. I personally think that the statistic must be much higher if a broader spectrum of people is considered. I have not been able to find anyone who will say he or she has *never* seen something of the future in dreams. If some exist who have not, they are among an unfortunate minority.

So far as I can tell, future-alerting dreams can easily be distinguished from other dreams by any or all of four clues:

1. they are usually more vivid than other kinds of dreams;
2. they are often repetitive, meaning that the same dream occurs more than once;
3. they are usually remembered into the waking state and leave us with the feeling we ought to be doing or anticipating something with regard to them; and

4. if we are to respond to the meaning of the dream, *doing so will require some unusual action on our intellectual part.*

It is this fourth clue that is the most problematical. After all, the autonomous future-seeing mind is trying to alert us to a forthcoming event that our intellect-mind rationally and logically does not expect and thus cannot identify. The warning demands that we actively respond to what we cannot yet perceive and, if we are to respond, requires us to take actions *others will probably criticize.*

I've talked with many who don't have this problem and have benefited from their NostraFac warnings and alerts. But by and large, most Westerners have been taught that the future does not exist, and so it cannot be foreseen. Although for thousands of years before our modern epoch people very carefully tapped dreams for what they offered, the rationalist trend against doing so has, bluntly, made us afraid to try. Fear of social criticism is a very strong deterrent to many of our activities and our powers as well.

We *can* take advantage of some dream alerts in secret—in the closet, so to speak. But often the alerts *require us to take unusual actions* in the broad light of day and in full sight of others.

In the first example in the preceding, the driver of the car had to be careful of a hidden crossroad whose location was identified by the "moonscape" encountered in the dream and later in physical reality. He stopped the car (the unusual action) more out of surprise than because of any intellectual decision to do so. If, as he later said, he had told someone that he should stop the car because of a dream, he would have been considered foolish.

If I had acted upon my stock dream, I would have purchased some shares that the broker said were "dead" (first unusual action). I would have had to borrow the money to do so (second unusual action). Since the UN credit union did not loan money to invest in stock purchases, I would have needed to invent another "need" to justify the loan (third unusual action).

In the third example, the woman would have had to convince her mother to disregard the family doctor's opinion (unusual action), probably insulting him in the process. She decided not to undertake this unusual effort, and her mother died.

You have to be very determined in order to take an unusual action, even in logical and rational circumstances. Taking unusual actions in anticipation of something that has not yet happened leaves you open to guffaws and derision. Social fears encase us. But, as we shall see ahead, sometimes there are heavy prices to be paid when we allow those socially inspired fears to defeat our NostraFac alerts—and sometimes significant rewards when we rise above those fears.

THE FUTURE-SEEING PRODUCING-RECEIVING PROBLEM

In his book entitled *Four-Dimensional Vistas* (1916), Claude Bragdon (1866–1935?) discusses the fact that something in us (our Nostradamus Factor) transcends time and space in dreams and participates in a fourth-dimensional vista where the future is apparent to it.

He uses the analogy of sound-producing and sound-receiving mechanisms to describe the specific difficulty we encounter regarding dream forewarnings. When we cannot hear or interpret a sound clearly, this is not because there is a defect in the sound-producing source. Rather, the deficiency is with limitations of the sound-receiving mechanisms—in this case our auditory apparatus. Our future-seeing mind produces foreseeings, and so far as I can tell they are not defective in doing so. But our foreseeing-receiving apparatus is our intellect, where our powers of understanding, action, volition, judgment, and decision-making reside.

In other words, our future-seeing deficiences do not arise from our indwelling Nostradamus Factor, which produces foreseeing, but from within our intellects, which may be defective receivers of what is being foreseen. If our waking intellects do not possess adequate understanding or criteria regarding our natural future-seeing powers, then any "sound" produced by them will be defectively received by those intellects.

The anecdotes given in this chapter illustrate this producing-receiving problem, which is the primary underlying theme of this entire book. The extent of this problem in each individual will determine how he or she will be able to piece the future-seeing mosaic together and how viable the mind-dynamic bridge to his or her own indwelling Nostradamus Factor can become.

Many have learned that they should write out their dreams, but Dr. Gerald Epstein, a noted waking-dream therapist in New York, holds that *sketching or drawing* them may be more important. In his book *Waking Dream Therapy* (1981) he notes that pictorial reports complement the written because they show the positions of elements, figures, settings, colors, and so on, which may be missing from the written reports. He also notes that the quality of the draftsmanship is unimportant (so don't feel inadequate if you can't draw).

I have undergone many waking-dream sessions with Dr. Epstein and discussed the special importance of drawing with him. For one thing, if a quick sketch of a dream is made before it fades away, a mere glance at the sketch will cause the dream to flood back into conscious memory in all its details, even years later. Written reports usually do not serve as well. If anything can indicate the dramatic mind-dynamic functional difference between words and image-building, the knowledge that even the briefest sketch can bring about complete recollection of dream episodes, and that words cannot, certainly is meaningful.

If you experience a dream sequence that apparently refers to something in the future, make a quick sketch of it *before* you transliterate the dream images into words. Doing so "locks in" the dream better than words will, and you will be better able to recognize the forthcoming event as it begins to happen. Dr. Epstein agreed with me that the future-seeing mind deals with images, not words, and that one of the ways to enhance contact with it is to make a practice of image-building.

In this sense, then, you might want to work out an image-building sketch of the contents of this chapter—which will show all the elements of the future-dream mechanisms and how they try to push a bit of forewarning into waking intellectual consciousness.

The sketch or diagram may be elaborate or simple. Creating it may take some time and thought, and you may want to add new elements to the drawing as you discover them. Very few have ever thought this was necessary, but one of the yields of doing it is that the intellect-bridge to your Nostradamus Factor will become stronger and more functional. And this will add meaning to all the other mosaic elements of your future-seeing enterprise.

4

NOSTRAFAC EXPERIENCES OF THE SECOND KIND: SPONTANEOUS FOREWARNING INTRUSIONS DURING THE WAKING STATE

Our dreamtime might be fertile territory in which NostraFac forewarnings can emerge, but we can also spontaneously experience them when we are awake. I call these NostraFac experiences of the second kind. They are also widely reported, but they have two characteristics that distinguish them from other future-seeing experiences.

First, a perceptible sense of urgency is usually associated with them. And second, the experience compellingly *tries* to overwhelm the individual's intellect-held reason and logic. In fact, when they occur, NostraFac experiences of the second kind *surprise* people.

After I had finished my undergraduate education in 1955, I joined the Army and eventually found myself stationed in Korea. I was assigned to work on the General Staff, then headed by General I. D. White, who was commander of all military forces in the Pacific area.

After the cessation of active hostilities, North and South Korea were divided by a demilitarized zone that ran approximately along the thirty-eighth parallel. On either side of this zone soldiers dug in and sporadically exchanged shots that sometimes resulted in casualties. At Kaesong in the zone, a few prefab-type buildings had been erected in which officials of the United States, South Korea,

and other nationalities met monthly with their North Korean counterparts to discuss hot issues and resolve problems.

I was required to go along on some of these trips to Kaesong,
mainly to help organize some aspects of protocol, but sometimes to
take notes. During these meetings, protocol demanded that each
person occupy an assigned seat and not move from it for the duration
of the talks. Each side was worried about the possibilities of assassination, and any untoward move by anyone was more than just
frowned upon. The situation was very tense, and everyone had to
be very alert to prevent any mishap, breach of protocol, or debacle.
Outside the buildings, soldiers of both sides were ordered to not fire
random shots in either direction across the demilitarized zone.

I had been in my assigned chair at the end of the second row of
"observers" for about five minutes after the meeting-confrontation
had begun. Only the principals at the table were permitted to speak,
and then only in accord with items on the agenda, and according
to their rank. I was very surprised, therefore, when I heard someone
behind me say: "Get up, get up now." This was not just a whisper.
I heard it as a high-volume command.

I stood up, and in doing so realized that there was no one behind
me at all. The eyes of everyone in the room turned toward me. All
conversation stopped, and hands reached for guns.

At that moment there was, in quick succession, a pop, and a
thung. A bullet ripped through the prefab wall and hit the back of
the chair where I had been sitting, striking right where my heart
would have been if I had remained seated.

The North Koreans stood up and silently walked out. Most of
the rest of us retired to the club-bar at Kaesong, tossed a few down,
and then took some photos of the hole in the wall. These were
later confiscated by investigative authorities, and the whole incident
was hushed up. I was, of course, asked why I had stood up. I decided
to be very honest: "A voice told me to do so, and I am goddamned
glad I did." There was no official reprimand, since no one wanted
to pursue *this* aspect of the case.

Years later, in New York, when the Walkman craze had just
begun, I bought one because I realized I could listen, at high volume,
to the thunderous music of Richard Wagner while I walked through

the streets of New York. One morning I donned the headset, upped the volume, and set out for the grocery store. At the corner, I looked both ways and, since no cars were coming, moved to step off the curb. At that moment, a voice said, over the volume of the music: "Stop!" I stopped, leg in midair, and moved back about three inches from the curb to recover my balance, wondering how a *word* had gotten into the tape.

At that moment, from *behind* me a car whizzed past, hitting the curb, and the air flow from it knocked me down. That speeding car was followed by a police car, lights ablaze. I had heard none of this over the loud volume of music and obviously would have been crushed had I been even three inches off the curb. Later, when I had recovered, I rewound the tape and listened to see if the word *Stop!* was there. It was not.

The two examples above are among the six instances in my experience when my NostraFac foresaw something decidedly threatening about to happen, took over my autonomic systems, and saved my life—leaving my rational-logical intellect in increasing appreciation. But such happenings have taken place throughout history— even though they sometimes do not involve matters of life and death.

One of the most charming experiences in my life took place while I was working at the United Nations during the 1960s. One morning, a co-worker came in with a large assortment of candles, which she inexplicably began setting up in containers. She could be a bit addled at times, and when asked what the candles were for, she answered: "I don't know, really. I stopped in Woolworth's on the way to work, and something made me buy them. I have no idea why I am getting them ready."

So, those candles sat there all through the day and into the long evening hours we were working while the General Assembly was in session. Suddenly, the lights faded in one of the most extensive blackouts in history. We used those candles to wend our way through the totally dark corridors to get out of the building. Two hours later, there was not a candle to be bought in the whole of Manhattan.

It is also quite usual to find that NostraFac alerts of the second kind remove us from our rational-volitional precincts, or attenuate any possible interference that might emanate from those quarters. We jump when the voice says "jump," and if we perchance do not, then we find ourselves under the ten-ton rock that has just fallen.

As a group, mothers are probably more sensitive than others to NostraFacs of the second kind, especially where their children are concerned. The wide incidence of telepathic bonding between mothers and their children has, I think, been convincingly established beyond any reasonable doubt. But telepathic bonding alone cannot explain how a mother can, for example, suddenly leap out of her house, dash down the driveway into the garage next door, and retrieve her child from some danger about to befall it. Reports of this nature are legion. And I had the opportunity to be present at one such occurrence.

I was visiting some married friends for dinner. As the mother was serving some snacks, she suddenly let the tray crash to the floor. She bounded up the stairs in near-hysteria, with all of us following her in amazement. Her child was safely asleep in its crib, but the mother broke into sobs and would not allow herself to be removed. Her husband tried to quiet and restrain her.

She grew even more hysterical, broke away, and snatched the sleeping child from his crib. At that moment, a large limb of a tree outside broke away and came crashing through the window, smashing the crib into the floor. The mother then fainted but with the baby protectively tucked in her arms.

When she was revived, she claimed she could remember hardly any of the scene, save that she heard something say she should go instantly and get her baby. "All I could see was something terrible coming from the window. I don't even remember coming up the stairs," she said. The father then compounded the mystery. "Well," he said, "I had a dream in which we decided to remodel this room, the nursery, and we decided to cut down the tree outside. I should've done that right away, shouldn't I?" We all thereupon went outside and purposefully cut down the tree, an old oak obviously past its prime.

The mother's part of this is an example of her Nostradamus Factor attending to what presumably is its normal business, albeit in the emergency mode characteristic of spontaneous NostraFacs of the second kind. The father's part we already recognize as a NostraFac of the first kind—a leisurely forewarning.

Regarding NostraFacs of the second kind, it is not unusual for voices, images, visions, and prosurvival urges to occur together. One example I like very much goes as follows: a few years ago, I was invited to speak to a small gathering of people interested in future-seeing, and I brought up the issues of voices *and* images. At that, everyone in the group began telling of their experiences. One woman told of how she was planning to fly overseas to Africa. She made her reservations to do so and set out to pick up the tickets.

In the taxi, she heard a voice say: "Do not buy that ticket. Something awful is going to happen. Look, now, and see!" Then followed a vision of a plane colliding with another on a runway, a tremendous ball of smoke and fire erupting. The scene then shifted to long rows of body bags.

The woman went ahead and bought the ticket anyway, thinking all this was the product of her fertile imagination. Three days before the trip, she was tending her plants on the edge of her porch. Again she heard a voice: "Sorry to do this." She was surprised and then felt "someone" push her. She stepped back, right off the porch, twisting her ankle painfully. She could not make the trip. The plane on which she had been scheduled to fly collided with another on a landing field, and both burned—but her body was not among those in the long rows of body bags depicted in newspapers.

Sometimes a NostraFac alert of the second kind fails to get the message through. I once talked with a man who had a significant scar on his neck. He told me that the scar was the result of not following his gut feeling. He had turned into a street in New York but had experienced "a faint impression that he should not go that way." Since he had walked that street many times, he saw no real reason not to continue. Midway down the block a gas main exploded, and the force of the explosion pushed him through a storefront window. His jugular vein was slashed. He lived, but he openly states that he "sure as hell will pay more attention next time."

In another example reported to me in 1989, a man and a woman who had just gotten married were hiking in the mountains above Aspen, Colorado. At a certain point along a cliff edge, the man paused and then said that he had a gut feeling that they should go another way. The wife scolded him, pointing out that the path they were on was the recommended one. He proceeded. One small rock in the path gave way and he plunged to his death. The widow blamed herself for her insensitivity to his anticipatory gut feeling.

MIND-DYNAMIC DIFFERENCES BETWEEN NOSTRAFAC FOREWARNINGS OF THE FIRST AND SECOND KINDS

Most forewarnings experienced during sleep tend to be passive in that they usually do not demand that we wake up and immediately undertake some unusual action. Rather, we can wake up and consider their meaning at our intellectual leisure. Most spontaneous forewarnings that happen when we are awake tend to demand relatively quick responses. An active urgency of some kind is usually connected to them, so much so that split-second timing can be involved.

One way of understanding this is to consider that passive forewarnings *suggest*, but active forewarnings *urge*—*urge* meaning to force or compel into an indicated direction when no apparent reason or logic can account for why. This kind of NostraFac happening can be very dramatic. Any event that involves the suspension or countermanding of our rational-logical intellects and causes us to respond often against our will clearly can be called a *happening*. And it is during such a happening that we can see our indwelling Nostradamus Factor in its most independent state, powerful enough to take over temporarily and command all our other mind functions, including our autonomic nervous system.

As an example, not long ago in New York a woman peacefully having coffee and cakes in a cafeteria suddenly felt the urge to run into the street. For a few moments she repressed the urge, thinking it silly. But in the next moment she found herself dashing, against her conscious will, through the door without paying the bill. The cafeteria had been remodeled in years past, and just as the woman found herself inexplicably standing in the street the dropped ceiling came loose and collapsed, killing some of the other customers.

The woman had no idea at all why she had dashed. More precisely, her rational-logical intellect had no idea, and her dash to safety had taken place as if that intellect simply did not exist. Her Nostradamus Factor took over her autonomic nervous system and, without any intellect participation at all, caused her body to get itself to a place of safety. Thousands of similar reports exist, and by asking your friends and acquaintances you can probably track down one or more of them. Doing so will help convince your intellect that such experiences actually occur.

In fact, at this point it would benefit you to put the book down and undertake the following self-educational steps:

1. intellectually assume that such happenings do take place;
2. reflect on why they do;
3. try to describe where the urge comes from; and
4. try to describe how the urge "knows" that such an apparently extreme action is necessary.

A PRIMARY ERROR ABOUT OUR FUTURE-SEEING POWERS

We have made a great error in attributing *thinking* to only our conscious waking intellects because these are what constitute our abilities to discern differences, to compare meanings, and to make decisions. We use these abilities *to survive*. NostraFac experiences of the second kind reveal that another mind-dynamic function in us is also interested in our survival and can warn us of dangers our intellects cannot perceive. The nonintellect interpretation that a given danger exists clearly cannot take place unless our Nostradamus Factor, in its own right, can also discern differences, compare meanings, and make decisions.

In this sense the term *survival* begins to take on importance and must somehow prominently figure into why we possess a future-seeing mind. In its popular usage "survival" is usually defined as continuing to live. But when a dictionary is consulted we find that it refers to continuing to live *afterward* (i.e., after a time, event, condition, or situation). Survival, then, is not a continuous or automatic state in and of itself but rather is completely linked to continuing *after* something has transpired or been encountered.

If the concept of survival-as-continuing-after is applied to our composite mind-dynamic systems, the whole of these systems must adopt right-choice parameters in order to achieve the continuing. Our whole mind-dynamic system, then, must possess unequivocal foreseeing capabilities in order to decide upon what choice to make. Indeed, if we suppose that our evolutionary mind-dynamic systems survive by merely guessing at random choices, they would then in effect be in the same situation as a gambler in a casino.

Our waking intellects might find themselves in the gambler-casino situation at times, but it is unthinkable that our other, more pro-found decision-making systems could survive beyond one second if they were. From the quantum level upward our energyinformation systems make *trillions* of foreseeing decisions minute by minute— and if the results of those decisions do not predictively and correctly get the life-unit to the *after*, then symptoms of nonsurvival imme-diately become apparent.

With all this in mind, it now becomes impossible to separate *survival* from *foreseeing*—which come neatly together in the term *anticipatory* (or anticipate). "Anticipate" means to foresee and deal with in advance; to act before so as to check or counter; to act prior to an event to take into account or forestall a later action; or to visualize a future event or time. We may intellectually vilify visu-alizations of a future time or event. But in actuality, all our other energyinformation processing systems are actively participating in their own anticipatory mechanisms—for if they were not we would soon be a pulsating, random heap of molecules and energies with little more hope of getting to the after than a casino gambler has of hitting the big one.

Right choice and right action play significant roles not only in the conduct of our lives but with regard to how we can begin to understand the purpose and nature of our future-seeing capabilities. Our intellects can be misarranged so as to discount or discredit the information being produced by our NostraFacs. But in this sense the defect resides in our intellects, which receive the information.

There are many reasons why individual intellects become defective with regard to receiving future-seeing information being produced by our future-seeing powers. But there are communally shared defects also. We will examine three of these shared defects before going on to NostraFac experiences of the third and fourth kinds—after which the latter will make more sense.

5

"REALITY" BLOCKS TO FUTURE-SEEING

Most people intuitively feel and will admit that they have, at some deep mind-dynamic level, an undeveloped power to see into the future. If, though, you ask the same people why they have not developed this power, most of them will say they don't know.

This kind of survey, which I have undertaken myself, reveals the existence of widespread information gaps that act to keep the future-seeing powers of the majority undeveloped. These gaps become important when we ask why they exist and *how they are kept in existence*.

The only possible explanation that accounts for information gaps is that we intellectually select certain realities and reject others—after which we accept information that fits with the realities we have selected and reject information that fits with the realities we have rejected. Accepted information, if it is wrong information, accounts for part of an information gap, while rejected information, if it is correct information, accounts for the rest of it. In this sense, then, the absence of information represents only information defects in ourselves.

Now, it must frankly be stated that most people *do not* like to entertain ideas that they may have reality information gaps, and even more of them will fully resent any suggestion that the information that constitutes their realities is defective in any way. These are volcanic issues, and information gaps are maintained because most of us learn to navigate very diplomatically around the defective information gaps of others, and others maneuver diplomatically around ours.

This overall situation constitutes the sole reason that people do not know why they have not been able to develop their foreseeing powers. This situation prevents the future-seeing mosaic from being put together in a mind-dynamically effective way and of course prevents the intellect from constructing the bridge between it and the indwelling future-seeing mind.

Having established the existence of our Nostradamus Factor as an autonomous, thinking mind in its own right, we are thus faced with two developmental goals: first, discovering how to adapt our intellect-mind so that it can learn to work with the indwelling Nostradamus Factor; and second, discovering why our intellect-mind has failed to do so in the first place.

Since our future-seeing powers *have not developed* even though they obviously exist, our intellects must have accumulated mind-dynamic *blocks* that have prevented their development. *If we undertake identifying these blocks and deconstruct them*, the natural information-transfer routes between our NostraFac and intellect-mind will automatically revitalize. We can then become sensitive to those process routes (or pulses) and learn anew how to work with them. Otherwise, the continuing existence of mind-dynamic blocks obviously would *interfere with and distort* future-seeing capabilities *and* future-seeing information-transfer pulses.

Everyone's mind-dynamic blocks to future-seeing are, of course, subjective ones, and so they can be deconstructed only by introspective efforts—going meditatively into one's own mind-dynamic systems, locating and retrieving them, and more consciously realigning the correct-versus-incorrect information out of which they have been constructed. The exact nature of these blocks varies widely from individual to individual—which accounts for why standardized introspective formulas or step-by-step routines do not work across the board.

But people largely share at least four major subjective obstacles to future-seeing:

1. incorrect myths and superstitions that confuse or mislead our expectations about our real and vital future-seeing powers;
2. our adaptations to social resistances to future-seeing, which decrease individual future-seeing reality;
3. the failure to realize that future-seeing is the virtual basis of right decision-making and right action; and
4. what-we-believe-we-are misconceptions.

All these, or any combination of them, account for why we can believe that the future cannot be seen.

MYTHS AND SUPERSTITIONS ABOUT FUTURE-SEEING

Both myths and superstitions differ widely, depending on the people involved. But all myths and superstitions are identical in at least one respect: they are what *others* have. We do not have them ourselves.

Myths and superstitions are people's ways of "explaining" phenomena they do not understand, by encapsulating those phenomena within a kind of reasoning and logic that they assume are correct. But an assumption is always involved. Myths and superstitions, then, are *kinds* of explanations, or secondary (epiphenomenal) intellectual contrivances.

History is full of examples of future-seeing events whose predictive details are astonishing and mind-boggling—and so some kind of mythic "explanation" must be established for them. The phenomena must be accepted-explained or rejected-explained. Rejective-myths exist as do acceptive-myths. In either case, superstitial behavior soon manifests itself as "explaining it" or "explaining it away."

In the distant past it was believed that only gods and goddesses could foresee the future. They foresaw on behalf of those who asked them to do so. Some have believed that when the future was foreseen, it was an act of God intervening in human affairs via one of His prophets (this being the classical definition of "prophecy"). These two mythic beliefs gave rise to the "explanation" that only some Power external and superior to the human could foresee. When a human *did* foresee (such as an oracle or sibyl), the human was temporarily "inhabited" by one of these supernatural forces.

In less distant times, future-seeing became surrounded by two particular (and contradictory) mythic superstitions: first, that only a "gifted" individual can see into and predict the future (the lay acceptance-myth); and second, that the future does not exist in any way, and so it cannot be foreseen (the Modern-Age scientific rejection-myth).

These myths and superstitions are challenged if we consider that each of us possesses innate future-seeing processes of the first and second kind and also experiences intuition, gut feelings, and premonitions. But if your realities are mind-dynamically anchored in them, these myths and superstitions can intellectually block you from connecting to your Nostradamus Factor and its process-phenomena.

When I first realized the scope of this problem—that obstacles to working with my own future-seeing powers existed in *my own* mind-dynamic systems—I decided to try to identify these obstacles. I began by making a list of all the acceptive and rejectve ideas I had ever encountered and trying to figure out how they assisted or blocked my intellect from my future-seeing mind.

For example, I remembered having heard as a child that only special people could see into the future, Why, then, did I also have future-seeing experiences? And why did others who were not "special" in any obvious way have them? I had also been taught in my Psychology 101 course in college that future-seeing was "abnormal." But then, in creating my list, I was obliged to wonder if future-seeing dream alerts or prosurvival urges experienced in the waking state *were* abnormal.

I first viewed this list as a kind of introspective mind game I played with myself. But slowly and surely my reality basis began to alter more on behalf of my own future-seeing powers. And the more this occurred the more aware I became that, with patience, an intellect-bridge could actually be constructed between my waking intellect and my own Nostradamus Factor.

SOCIAL RESISTANCE TO FUTURE-SEEING REDUCES INDIVIDUAL FUTURE-SEEING AWARENESS

Most of us can imagine what social resistance to future-seeing might be. But two good examples of it can be appreciated. Many alleged "witches" were burned or drowned during the infamous Salem witch trials because there was evidence that they may have been seeing the future. Doing so was considered to be the work of the devil, and his future-seeing minions were executed accordingly. These executions served notice on society that future-seeing elements should be communally and individually resisted.

During the nineteenth and twentieth centuries, many influential scientists opted to proclaim that time could not be transcended, and any who claimed otherwise could not be considered scientific. And neither could they be admitted to the scientific mainstream or its societies, professions, or fraternities. Scientific mind-sets largely shaped the mass consciousness of the twentieth century and that of aspiring young scientists who accordingly adapted to this particular antifuture-seeing dictum. Academe and the media followed suit, and through them antifuture-seeing sentiments leaked down through the social systems of the century. Anyone who had scientific goals, hopes, or pretensions socially resisted future-seeing potentials.

Social resistance to future-seeing has a great deal to do with NostraFac dysfunction not only in society but within individuals as well. Most people know they possess powers that they have not developed. But when we do not develop one of our powers, we usually think it is we who have not worked hard enough to do so; we perceive that the fault is ours at the individual level. Social environments demand that only those beliefs, abilities, attitudes, and levels of performance be developed that will *adapt-fit* us into what is socially acceptable.

Complying requires that we deadapt from our indwelling powers that will not fit well into the social environment. We become a suitable, nonindividualized replica of our society this way and do so in large measure without even realizing it. We become part of the myths and superstitions and duplicate in ourselves their information gaps.

Many have asked me how they can *learn* to develop their future-seeing powers or improve their psychic powers in general. They ask as *individuals*, assuming that they can enhance themselves by individual efforts. This assumption seems so logical that it is difficult to introduce the idea that *the disdevelopment of innate human powers comes primarily from social factors outside us.* And unless the outside existence of social restrictions to our powers can be identified, the aspiring future-seer cannot intellectually learn how to separate his or her developmental consciousness from them.

The situation, then, becomes clear. We possess indwelling Nostradamus Factors, and most of us intuitively feel we do. But we have also been exposed to social disbelief and intolerance of seeing into the future. We observe socially inspired conflicts about our future-seeing powers and *carry such observations in memory.* These can mind-dynamically distort or block future-seeing impulses originating in our NostraFac mind.

There is a predictable outcome to all this. A good case in point is the example given earlier of the woman who lost her mother because she had adapted her intellect to antifuture-seeing beliefs of her society and thus *was not able* to take advantage of the information contained in her dream.

I am a great believer in objectifying my thoughts by noting them down on paper or making sketches of them. The idea that I may have developed obstacles to future-seeing because of social influences irked me considerably. What were these influences? I made a list. As the list expanded, I began to recover bits and pieces of antifuture-seeing trivia I had experienced but had forgotten.

I made two introspective lists:

1. memories of when I had observed or experienced *outside* social conflicts about future-seeing—and judged the psy-

chodynamic, *contractive* impacts they had on my developmental awareness; and

2. memories of when I had experienced some future-seeing event myself, or of when I had heard or read of someone else doing so—and judged the psychodynamic, *expansive* impacts they had on my developmental awareness.

I worked at constructing these two lists sporadically over about six months' time, but eventually I was able to see that most of my future-seeing blocks and information gaps had come from outside me. In this introspective way, finally an early memory popped up of a particular event in my childhood that I had long forgotten: I remembered asking about how the future could be seen.

Since no one knew, eventually I was shunted to my Sunday school teacher, a woman who was the proverbial pillar of the community. She held up a Bible and thunderously and fearsomely exclaimed in front of the Sunday school class, and in the best Salem witch-hunt style, that seeing into the future was the work of the devil. "Do you *want* to become a minion of the devil?" she asked with visible emotion. Indeed I did not, and I was nearly frightened to death by the possibility—as well as being mortified in front of my Sunday school peers.

Here are all the makings of an antifuture-seeing reality-point. First, interest on my part, then thunderous emotion on her part, followed by fear on my own part, along with being made to feel wrong in front of the whole class for having an interest in the first place and then finally "forgetting" the whole affair. After this incident the reality-point, now a very sensitive one, subsided to some subconscious depth where it resided with its energy and information intact until I restored it to mature intellectual scrutiny. At that point, it deconstructed.

There are terrible prices to be paid because of social resistances to future-seeing powers. Not only do these resistances install obstacles to future-seeing in the mind-dynamic systems of individuals, but by doing so society suffers on the whole. To illustrate this, I will perform a future-seeing "autopsy" of the assassination of Abraham Lincoln, one that shows that he died needlessly.

Academic biographies of Lincoln almost completely avoid any mention of his interest in what we now call the paranormal. But his interests were extensive, and it is quite likely that at least some of his most important decisions came from such unlikely sources as discarnate beings. Very few official biographies mention what is well known in psychic research circles: like millions of others throughout history, Lincoln experienced dream-forewarnings of his own impending death.

One good account of this dream-forewarning appears in *Seeing into the Future* by Harvey Day, published in England in 1966, which is in accord with information found in several memoirs eventually published by members of his Cabinet and friends of the Lincoln family.

A few days before his death, Lincoln confided to his wife and to a friend, Ward Hamon, that he had had a dream in which he was wandering from room to room in the White House. From every room came the sound of sobbing. In the East Room he came upon a catafalque in which lay a corpse clothed in funeral vestments. Surrounding the soldiers on guard was a throng of weeping mourners. When he asked, in the dream, who lies dead in the White House, the guards answered, "The President! He was assassinated!"

The afternoon before he was shot, Lincoln's Cabinet entered a council room for a meeting and there found Lincoln already seated, his head buried in his hands. Again he had had a dream, he told them, of being in a boat, alone, helpless in a boundless ocean. "Gentlemen," he said, "before long you will have some important news. Perhaps tomorrow, perhaps in just a few hours, you will have important news."

The news of his death-dream had already circulated among his Cabinet, and some, to their credit, urged him to cancel his public schedule, specifically not to go to the theater that evening, and to stay in a secure place for a few days. But can a President run scared before a mere dream? To do so would have necessitated taking an unusual action, one imperative if the forewarning was to be acknowledged.

Quite likely Lincoln had to assess what might happen to his reputation (i.e., consider the social conflicts) if he ran scared before a dream and canceled his public schedule. In the end, he went to the theater—and barely five hours after he and his Cabinet had discussed the matter, he was dead.

But the Lincoln story has an added future-seeing aspect, one quite buried in history but that I am including in the NostraFac autopsy of his death. Lincoln was assassinated on April 14, 1865. Previously there had lived in Philadelphia an astrologer, one Dr. Luke Dennis Broughton, who, even though his house was stoned by those who thought he was doing the work of the devil, published a periodical entitled *Monthly Planet Reader and Astrological Journal.*

In the winter issue of this journal, published in September 1864, Broughton pointed out that Lincoln would be reelected, but shortly thereafter his planetary aspects would be bad, and he should be on guard against attempts to take his life and especially against "fire arms and infernal machines." In the spring 1865 issue of the journal, Broughton updated his prediction by emphasizing that "a noted general or person in high office dies about the 17th or 18th of April."

Since Lincoln was the nation's highest "general" and occupied its highest office, it was immediately assumed that it was Lincoln that the astrologer Broughton was referring to, and the Lincoln death-forecast raced up and down the East Coast accordingly. Although I have not been able to verify the fact, it is quite likely that Lincoln's secret service was in possession of this astrological forecast, since it was their duty to discover any information involving the President. But it is almost certain that Mary Todd Lincoln had received Broughton's journal, since she was deeply interested, almost to distraction, in such matters. So, *two* astrological warnings existed, but heeding them in any form would have necessitated unusual actions and added to social conflict.

If all these future-seeing elements could have been packaged together and acknowledged as *meaning something* and *pointing to an undisclosed future event,* clearly the assassination could have been avoided. But most people, including presidents, are not willing to fly in the face of what the surrounding social environment considers acceptable. The social conflicts about future-seeing prevailed. Result: a dead visionary and leader, perhaps one of the greatest the United States has had.

This future-seeing autopsy of the NostraFac experiences preceding Lincoln's assassination clearly illustrates that taking them into account would have been the *right action*. And in this way, we come in the next chapter to an aspect of future-seeing that has never been brought to light—one we should consider very carefully if we are to come anywhere near the *why* of future-seeing.

Several important conceptual points regarding attempts to revitalize future-seeing capabilities have been made in this chapter. *But it must be stated very clearly that image-building is extremely important with regard to them.* You'll get nowhere if you try to deal with these points only by intellectualizing the word-based concepts "inside your head." *Based on YOUR experience and points of view*, you'll need a more permanent image-building "map" or diagram that reflects incorrect myths and superstitions, adaptations to social resistances, and so forth, to which you have been exposed. Few can construct, visualize, and maintain this map in their heads.

My own image-building maps went through several generations each time I located some new mind-dynamic-block tidbit. I started by merely listing (on paper) social antifuture-seeing stuff I had encountered. But soon I was cutting them apart and rearranging them in various ways to see how they seemed to fit together.

The earliest mind-blocks occurred when I was defeated as a child after asking how the future was seen. Blocks acquired in childhood, then, were closest to the deep layer of consciousness containing my NostraFac, while antifuture-seeing teachings of "science" accumulated later. In between were myths and superstitions I heard or read about.

Your NostraFac must send its impulses (in image form) "up" into your waking intellect-consciousness, but the impulses have to negotiate all the acquired blocks. A box-and-flow diagram, easy to construct, serves the image-building purposes of all this very well. A typical one is offered on page 69, in which some of the common mind-block sources are identified by category.

My own diagram, though, contained—as yours should—specific instances and information appropriate to my antifuture-seeing ex-

YOUR FUTURE-SEEING PERCEPTIONS
modified by anchor points and reality threshold.
Some perceptions may be blocked.

YOUR REALITY THRESHOLD

SOCIALLY-CONSTRUCTED MYTHS
and superstitions about future-seeing that
you have "bought" into.

MIND-CONSTRUCTED ANCHOR POINTS
may be dynamic blocks to future-seeing.

Deep-level cognitive consciousness:
YOUR NOSTRADAMUS FACTOR

THE FUTURE

perience. Eventually, I achieved a bigger image-built picture of what was involved, one that surpassed the *limits* of my imagination and any visualizing built on it. Also, the blocks and the bigger image-built picture were invisible before I rendered it into a diagrammed form, and few of us can visualize what is invisible to us.

Getting all this out on paper in a self-organizing way served to discharge or deconstruct the blocks because *both* the left and right hemispheres of my brain could now perceive the bigger diagrammed *picture* involved. Your own map can be as simple or complex as you wish.

6

FUTURE-SEEING AS RIGHT ACTION

This short chapter points up what I hold to be the most fundamentally important aspect of future-seeing: the most likely reason *why* humans, as biopsychic life-units, have future-seeing powers in the first place.

If we consider one important fact of our lives, we can begin to see something that integrates our Nostradamus Factors with the moment-to-moment progress of those lives. Living our lives requires an ongoing and never-ceasing activity that is referred to (in *The Encyclopedia of Philosophy*), as "choosing, deciding, and doing." Many Eastern philosophies, though, refer more inclusively to choosing-deciding-doing as *right action*. Buddhism, for example, identifies right action with the cessation of or escape from suffering. The way to achieve this is by the Noble Eightfold Path, which leads to right views, right aspiration, right speech, right conduct, right livelihood, right effort, right mindfulness, and right contemplation.

The Noble Eightfold Path requires choosing, deciding, and doing, in which *each* of us is required to participate on a continuous basis. Buddhism's Noble Path, though, is mounted on far more ancient knowledge. From time immemorial, in all countries and among all races, the problem of right versus wrong action has achieved considerable importance. In very ancient texts, right versus wrong action is referred to as the right-handed path of "light" and the left-handed path of "darkness." The right-handed path leads to *destiny* (freedom from suffering and to achievement and positive fulfillment); while the left-handed path leads to *fate* (increase in suffering, negative fulfillment, failure, and doom).

In using the phrase "right action," I am not referring to moral concepts, which at best can be only *relatively* right or wrong depending on circumstances. Rather, I am referring to actions that set into motion chains of subsequent events that in the future culminate in positive or negative ways. An action or choice that leads to some kind of future-negative outcome can hardly be seen as having been a right action or choice.

In our Western context, choice is thought of as doing x rather than y, either choice leading to some kind of z. It is often argued that choice itself is a kind of doing that mitigates and decides between x or y. Choice is practically synonymous with freedom, for we feel not-free when we find we are prevented from choosing between x and y. And when we must obey or experience z whether we choose to or not, we know we are not free and that the course of our lives is determined by z rather than by *our* choosing.

What is little understood about all this is that *any* choosing, deciding, or doing automatically implies a future result of some kind. In other words, *some kind of foresight* is implicit within any choice we make. Most of us will not set in motion an action *if we can foresee* that it will result in an increase of suffering and possibly in failure and doom.

In this sense, then, if our powers of foreseeing are attenuated, not active, or clogged by conflicts, impediments, and deterrents, the chances of attaining positive results of any choosing we decide upon are no better than fifty-fifty and sometimes worse. In this context our future-seeing powers are a vital and absolutely necessary part of the choosing-deciding-doing processes that proceed continuously within us—and that none of us can avoid.

Interestingly, no mention of foresight or future-seeing is made in all the philosophical texts I have read with regard to the problems of choosing-deciding-doing. In other words, the problems of choosing have not been intellectually linked to the problems of future-seeing. Even discussions of Buddhism's Eightfold Path skirt around this particular linkage.

We have to return to ancient days to find that a link between choosing and future-seeing once existed. Then, people consulted seers and oracles to discover what would happen if they chose x or y, and also to discover if any particular z would interfere with either choice. The ancients knew that a direct link existed between action and future-seeing. Only this can explain why they culturally erected and preserved *social* institutions for foreseeing.

To the ancients, the only practical way to determine the difference *ahead of time* was to foresee the future—or have someone else try to do so on their behalf. The ancients were clearly aware of NostraFac experiences of the first and second kinds. They knew the future was "revealed" to them in both dreams and waking visions. If they did not understand the "message," they consulted interpreters, sages, or soothsayers who ferreted out the message. Hence, most ancient texts contain *teachings* that link right action with future-seeing that were meant to convey the meaning of the link.

The tale in the Bible, for example, of Pharaoh's dream of seven fat and seven lean cows is not just a biblical story recorded through the centuries as trivial gossip. Pharaoh had this dream more than once and suspected it was a future-seeing warning of some kind.

Unable to determine the message himself, he called in the Jewish seer and sage, Joseph, to interpret its meaning. Joseph advised that Egypt would experience seven good years of plenty followed by seven years of famine. The warning was that Pharaoh should conserve and store food during the seven good years so that Egypt would survive the seven-year famine to come. Pharaoh *chose* to do so, and his action proved to be the right one. This *teaching* links foreseeing to action decided upon in the present.

Although our society has intellectually detached future-seeing from our choice-making, we are still saddled with the same problems that involved the ancients. Wrong actions decided upon in the present will result in disasters up the timeline, whereas right actions will result in successes. But we have an additional problem that results from detaching our future-seeing poowers from our choosing powers: we cannot tell if our choosing will result in negative or positive outcomes *until it can be seen that they do when the future arrives*.

Here we come across one of the most noted deficits of reason and logic. We believe that reason and logic are primary things in themselves. But, indeed, they *are not primary phenomena*. They are mind-dynamic epiphenomena. It is well known that the mind-dynamic processes underlying reason and logic can compute and analyze based only on experience. We build mind-dynamic reality-points based on what we have experienced. Realities and phenomena that fall outside that experience cannot be integrated into the computations and analysis that produce reason and logic any more than a computer can operate beyond the limits of its installed software programs.

Thus our reason and logic are limited and dysfunctional when it comes to computing and analyzing possibilities that are not expected to occur within the contexts of experience. In short, reason and logic cannot expect what they cannot expect.

The dilemma of the mind-dynamic realities underlying reason and logic, then, is that they cannot *recognize* the unexpected since they possess no experiential basis for doing so—that is, *unless those mind-dynamic realities have integrated with indwelling future-seeing powers*.

To help illustrate future-seeing choices of right action, there is the amazing case early in this century of a celebrated evangelist named Moody. Moody was a Spiritualist who had attracted a large following in London and, it would appear, a few enemies along the way. As a Spiritualist believing in the continuity of life after death, and that the future could be foreseen from the spiritual point of view, Moody had probably resolved any culturally implanted conflicts to future-seeing pulses.

He reported a strange event that took place one night as he was walking down one of London's streets. At a certain point he "felt" a powerful impulse to cross over to the other side of the street. He looked around, but could see no reason for this impulse. But he crossed to the other side anyway, puzzled by his own irrational behavior.

The reason for this impulse would never have been known were it not for another strange occurrence that took place several years later. His following had grown by then, and a new convert to his Revivalist-cum-Spiritualist brand of philosophy came to him one day to "confess." The follower told Moody how he had once hated Spiritualism and especially Moody. This hatred had boiled in him to the extent that he had decided to murder the Spiritualist.

To this end, one night several years earlier he had followed Moody in the shadows of a darkened street, and just as he was about to lunge forward and plunge a knife into Moody's back, Moody suddenly dashed to the other side of the street. Since the would-be murderer could not follow him without revealing himself he desisted. Moody's urge was a prosurvival, right-choice one, spontaneously experienced without his knowing, at the time, why it occurred.

Making the connection between future-seeing and right action serves as the basis of one of the most important realizations any aspiring future-seer can experience. I would like to give the testament that brought the realization to me not only because it is a fabulous future-seeing anecdote, but because like Pharaoh's dream it involved making a *conscious* choice between right and wrong action.

In October of 1973, I came across an anecdote given by Harvey Day in his book *Seeing into the Future* (1966), a book rich in the astonishing details of future-seeing, which also reports on forewarnings worldwide. This particular anecdote had a deep impact on me, mainly because whereas I could accept hunches or gut feelings about things about to happen, I could not really entertain the idea then that the future could be seen very far in advance. I had the somewhat ambiguous idea that the farther away the future was in time, the more "fuzzy" and undecided it must be. I conceived that near-time was probably linked to the outcome of events of the present, but that far-time ahead was composed only of "potentials."

The tale of Adrian Christian, after I had gone to some lengths to ascertain its legitimacy, brought an end to my particular misconception while at the same time giving birth to the realization that future-seeing and right action are directly connected. In 1833, on the Isle of Man, situated in the Irish Sea between Ireland and England, a young boy named Adrian Christian dreamed that he had become a captain of a ship and that his family on another ship was in danger. He rescued them. He recounted his dream to his family, especially his brother, Thomas, and they related it to family friends. The facts of this dream were exchanged in family letters that remain today, and so the fact that the original dream took place is verified.

In 1880, forty-seven years later, Adrian Christian had indeed become a ship's captain—of the vessel *British India*, which was bound from Sydney, Australia, to Rangoon. A few days after the sailing, Christian dreamed of a ship in distress whose name *Family* appeared in flaming letters at the end of the dream. Remembering his dream of decades earlier, Captain Christian *decided* to double his vessel's lookout, a decision that caused grumbling among his crew. But when he had the same dream on the next night, he gained the impression that the distressed vessel was due north of his present route.

Christian was in that strange position in which the reception of NostraFac information places anyone: what to do? An unusual action was required—in this case, diverting his own vessel to the north from its present course to the west, which would make the *British India* late in arriving in Rangoon. Naturally, his other officers protested the change of course because he had *only* dreamed of a ship in distress to the north. But over these protests, Adrian Christian *did* alter his own vessel's course—which proved to be a *right action*, and in spades.

Two days' sailing passed, the ship's other officers grumbling all the while. But toward the end of the second day they sighted a smoking, sinking hulk on the horizon. The name of the doomed vessel was *The Family*. From it were rescued 269 very relieved people—among whom, to Christian's great surprise, was his own brother, Thomas!

The realization of the close relationship between right action and future-seeing brings into focus many unresolvable questions about future-seeing and why we possess its powers. Consider this: it is almost unthinkable that our biopsychic organisms could evolve if they were perpetually balanced fifty-fifty between right and wrong choices. The human evolutionary processes *themselves* must be naturally tipped in the intuitive direction of right actions. The only possible way they could be tipped this way is if evolutionary processes contain anticipatory processes that increase survival.

Evolution cannot possibly be only a hit-or-miss matter. Nor, for that matter, can creation. Evolution and creation must "know" which "choice" is the right one, in exactly the same way that our spontaneous future-seeing episodes do—which means at the human level that first, those whose future-seeing powers have become attenuated because of artificially installed mind-dynamic blocks are probably aimed toward a negative future; and second, those whose future-seeing powers are *not* attentuated will probably survive the best into the future. The latter is a fact that hardly needs arguing.

Making the connection between right action and future-seeing, though, caused me to undertake something on my own behalf that, so far as I could tell, had never been done before. I was determined to introspect my mind-dynamic systems yet again, but this time with different goals in mind. I set about making two lists of experiences:

> The first would contain those predictive instances that I could attribute only to my own logic and reason. This list was to be subdivided into two categories:
>
> 1. those logical and rational expectations that proved to be true; and
> 2. those that proved to have been wrong.
>
> The second list would contain instances of future-pulses that had run against my logic and reason. This list would also be subdivided into two categories:
>
> 1. those pulses that I obeyed and therefore benefited from; and
> 2. those that I did not obey and from which I therefore suffered some kind of negative consequence.

At first this seemed like a confusing and fruitless game I had decided to play with myself because my memory did not cooperate at first. But after a certain point, I felt as if something in me had "gotten the idea." Although itemizing these lists took several months during which memory coughed up bits and pieces at odd moments, I am certain that persisting in this self-imposed introspective task served to demobilize some mind-dynamic obstacles about future-seeing. My intellect finally identified the *value* of future-seeing.

I could eventually see for myself that my logical and rational "right" actions usually had misled me (especially in that I apparently had forfeited no less than three marvelous job opportunities and one entire career path I had decided against by reason and logic). And I could easily see, too, that my spontaneous future-seeing episodes, when I responded to them in a right-action kind of way, had been one of the graces of my life.

Anyone who aspires to revitalizing his or her own future-seeing links would be *required* to undertake some self-imposed introspection exercises like this. Our intellect can discriminate among information we organize for it, and it is via such exercises that we can make clear those conceptual errors that act as obstacles to our own future-seeing powers. Our intellects are glad enough to erase errors once it is seen that it is advisable for them to do so.

I fully believe that what command over my own future-seeing powers I have managed to achieve began with these listing activities (as a form of introspective meditation). The intellect-bridge could finally be "walked" over.

In chapter 9, I will again pick up the theme of future-seeing as right action as part of the discussion about what we are. But to prepare the ground for that chapter, it is necessary to discuss the two remaining kinds of future-seeing, since their elements lead naturally into the discussion of what we are.

Since most people have experienced some intuitional forewarnings, dreams, or waking visions, it is easy enough to make lists of these and revivify them in your mind-dynamic systems. What did the forewarnings consist of? Did you take advantage of them or not, and why? What were the social situations involved? It is also easy enough to erect another image-building box-and-flow diagram showing when the forewarnings took place and how they affected your life.

You can contrast this diagram with the one of blocks that was suggested in the preceding chapter. If you construct these two diagrams, you will for the first time be able to compare in image-building form the extent of the negative and positive NostraFac elements regarding yourself. If you feel your mind-dynamic systems beginning to "readjust" as a result, don't be surprised.

7

NOSTRAFAC EXPERIENCES OF THE THIRD KIND: COMMUNAL OR GROUP FUTURE-SEEING

Social resistance to our Nostradamus Factor results in reducing the collective visibility of active future-seeing in the society as a whole. The resistance not only defies the primary evolutionary principle and purpose of indwelling future-seeing powers but also "permits" humans blindly to pursue wrong actions and choices that *will result* in future-negative situations that increase individual and collective suffering.

But these two future-negative factors also work to blind us to something else that, if ignored, can lead to absolute failure and destruction. It is this: all traditions regarding seeing into the future rest on two simple premises: first, that *the future always foreshadows itself*; and second, that this foreshadowing "leaks" into human awareness not only via individual but also through communal NostraFac experiences.

A very old axiom is founded on these two premises: that "many shall know the future." If the future *does* foreshadow itself, and if we all possess an indwelling Nostradamus Factor, then it must follow that the foreshadowings *must* leak into the consciousnesses of the many. In other words, *group* or *communal* foreseeing of future events should take place if the two premises and the axiom above are true.

It is the purpose of this chapter to show that communal foreseeing experiences do take place. I have dubbed these communal foreseeings as NostraFac experiences of the third kind.

COMMUNAL FORESEEING

As a child, I encountered one of these group future-seeing functions (although I did not realize what it was until about forty years later). I was born in Telluride, Colorado, in 1933. Set in a high, narrow valley, the town is near timberline, and it is surrounded on all sides with towering peaks, majestic, thousand-foot cliffs, and deep, perilous canyons. The raw beauty of that then—largely unspoiled enviroment was "beyond compare," as it was perpetually described.

But dangers lurked in this beauty. Cliffs occasionally broke and slid, unwary people became lost in endless forests or fell down canyons. Rock slides occurred all the time. Sudden cloudbursts created avalanches of water, mud, boulders, and broken timber. Lightning struck trees, rocks, cliffs, buildings, and people alike. Winter snow, beautiful to look at and ski upon, tended to mass up and sweep unmercifully down slopes. Telluride was a mining town, and in the mines tunnels collapsed, and every once in a while one of the huge tailing ponds (where mine by-products were stored) broke.

The body count that resulted from these dangers was quite high at times—especially, but not exclusively, among tourists who managed to find their way into the beauty but mistakenly assumed they could behave as if they were on the streets of Topeka, Kansas. As we experienced mountaineers knew, there was a psychic art to living safely in the rugged mountains.

This art did not really have a name. But it was the mix of common mountaineering sense, the knowledge that dangers could be encountered unexpectedly, and a phrase that was repeated to me time and again: "You gotta know what's gonna happen before it do, or you're a goner." There was no arbitrary division between intuition and the learned logic of common-sense mountaineering. Rather, these blended into a consciously maintained state of anticipatory awareness, or the marriage of *intuitus-intellectus*, which will be discussed later. Neither intuition nor logic took precedence over the other. When this unnamed art was not in some kind of functioning mode, many fell victim to the miscalculations of their reason and logic or to the vicissitudes of nature.

Telluridians did not actually talk of themselves as if they were psychic, and the Modernist idea that psychic stuff was irrational was socially accepted at one level. Nonetheless, on another level most paid attention to their gut feelings, dreams, and forewarnings—not only individually but as groups.

Many times I witnessed group-foreseeing events similar to the following: a certain day dawned. Various telephones started ringing and people would say something like "there's an avalanche gonna come down today." The central telephone exchange then still required an operator to connect telephone lines. She usually listened in on the conversations, and then forwarded the information to her friends, who forwarded it to theirs, until word circulated throughout the town.

Later in the morning, certain people began standing on Main Street surveying the slopes and cliffs nearby. Groups would form—and eventually they would all point in the same direction, even though there was no indication that an avalanche would take place where they were facing. " 'Bout three-thirty thizafternoon, I'd expect," someone would say. "That's up by the mine," someone else would thoughtfully note. "Better call up there and have 'em get ready for it."

The call, perhaps several of them, would be made. Experienced mine officials would peruse the cliffs above the mine with their own intuitus-intellectus. The mine would let off its shift early. About three, some brought chairs and beer into the street to "watch for the avalanche." The avalanche would occur at close to the predicted time, taking out a building or two, a tailings pond perhaps, and, as usual, some electric power lines. The damage was cleaned up. Business resumed as usual, as if nothing untoward had taken place. The next communal networking alert would come when it did.

I recall another group foreseeing event: our school was a large brick building, standing quite near the mouth of a deep, narrow canyon in whose depths was a beautiful waterfall a thousand feet high and whose water source was a large basin between several peaks that rose behind it. The entire school (grades one through twelve) had only about fifty students, so the absence of a few students was definitely noticed.

One day several students did not come in. When the teachers called their homes to find out why, they were told by several mothers that there was going to be a cloudburst that day, and that all the kids should be sent home. The teachers went to the school principal with the forewarning of this motherly collective foreseeing. The bell rang shortly, and everyone *was* sent home—to the great joy of the students.

It was a brilliant, sunny day with hardly a cloud in the sky. About noon, though, the whole town began to notice that a huge dark cloud had formed in the peaks above the canyon behind the school. Not a drop of rain fell anywhere in town, but we knew what those dark, cloudburst elements portended. Shortly, a wall of water, rocks, and mud some twenty feet high roared out of the canyon's mouth. In seconds, it had crashed through the basement windows of the school, where the first- and second-graders would have been.

As I grew up and moved to other locations, I forgot about being witness to the demonstrated communal future-alert systems of my childhood. But my memories were triggered many years later when I came across what may be the first example of a *group-foreseeing* *"autopsy"* in modern times. It confirms that wide forewarning leakages did take place prior to the sad disaster that occurred in 1966 in another small mining village—Aberfan, in Wales, about twenty miles north of Cardiff.

The village of Aberfan sits at the bottom of a narrow valley, with its coal mines in the mountains above it. Since the engineers working on behalf of the mining enterprise needed someplace to put the coal and mining wastes, they fanned enormous amounts of it out along the mountain sides in what are called "coal-tips."

One such coal-tip steadily grew to massive size directly above the Aberfan schoolhouse. On October 21, 1966, the coal-tip, weakened and slicked by rain, gave way and slid down on the schoolhouse and surrounding homes and buildings at 9:15 A.M.—just moments after the town's children had arrived at school to begin their day's work. Body count: 16 adults and 128 children.

The forewarning autopsy of this event shows that it *need not have occurred*. First of all, reason and logic alone could have prevented it. Aside from asking why an unpredictable coal-tip should have been allowed to form above the schoolhouse, many in the village had speculated that a slide was imminent. And indeed the coal-tip had already exhibited the beginnings of its downward movement. Nothing was done, and so the much-overvalued powers of reason and logic failed completely in averting one of the greatest national disasters Wales has ever experienced.

But the legendary communal powers of foresight did not fail—at least insofar as they can been seen in retrospect by reading the forewarning autopsy conducted by one J. C. Barker, M.D., a psychiatrist at Shelton Hosptial, Shrewsbury, who rushed to the scene and offered to help assuage the psychological traumas engendered by the deaths. At the scene, Barker quickly became apprised of the fact that many in the town had had premonitions of the disaster. At least three of the dead children had described NostraFac dream-alerts of their impending deaths in black mud. This inspired Barker to launch newspaper appeals requesting that anyone who had "suffered" an Aberfan premonition contact him.

Within two weeks he had received over two hundred letters, *seventy-six* of which were considered verifiable because their authors could prove they had told others of their forewarnings. Forewarnings of this disaster had begun to leak into the "now" via conduits that we can recognize as NostraFac alerts of the first and second kinds. The leaking began *ten months* before the disaster took place, but as its time drew nearer, the alerts increased in number, amplitude, and *accuracy*.

Three weeks before the event, a woman in Ryde, not far from Aberfan, had a "technicolor vision" of a coming tragedy in which a little girl dressed in a Welsh costume called out the name of "Aberredfan," an archaic name for Aberfan. Eighteen hours ahead of the disaster, one Mr. J. T. of Stacksteads, Lance, had a dream in which he saw a desolate row of destroyed houses and heard the name "Aberfan." Six hours before the tragedy, a Mr. E. H. of Newcastle-on-Tyne experienced a vivid "fantasy" in which the name of Aberfan was linked to some terrible event. Many others "saw" children in Welsh national costumes being killed by a massive avalanche of black mud and then buried in those costumes in a large communal grave (as the children were).

The implications point to the fact that we possess communal forewarning systems that spontaneously leak parts or full descriptions of approaching events piecemeal into the *consciousnesses of many*— in other words, NostraFac experiences of the third (communal) kind.

Here, then, is a resource *indwelling within ourselves* that, if properly understood and implemented, could *change* the directions of future events.

The dramatic sinking of the luxury liner *Titanic* on April 14–15, 1912, on its maiden voyage is a well-known event. The *Titanic* was considered *the* seagoing marvel of the Industrial Age, advances in technology having made it "unsinkable." It struck an iceberg at sea and sank anyway, claiming a little over fifteen hundred lives.

The sinking was unique in another way, which you may not be aware of. An enormous number of communal foreseeing leakages presaged the sinking. Various researchers estimate that far more than fifteen hundred people experienced either imprecise or very precise forewarnings.

The strangest of these forewarnings came from Morgan Robertson, whose 1898 novel *The Wreck of the Titan* proved to be an exact preview of the actual event, down to minute details of the *Titanic*'s sinking. Other subtle leakage-type phenomena manifested themselves as the time of the *Titanic*'s sailing drew nearer. The sailing was a very significant *social* event at the time, and trendsetters who could do so made plans to be on board. Yet the rate of canceled reservations was very high. Three sailors jumped ship while the *Titanic* was still negotiating the English Channel after its initial departure. In later interviews, they said they did so because of "feelings" that the *Titanic* was going to sink.

After the sinking, it became rather broadly known that the sinking had been spontaneously foreseen, or actually predicted, by many.

The cautious parapsychologist Ian Stevenson later made an attempt to draw together the sum of these previsions and was able to establish that at least twelve of them contituted "significant" evidence that the sinking had been foreseen. But the number of foreseeings is actually much greater than those selected by Dr. Stevenson for parapsychological research. Of the various kinds of forewarnings experienced, the total number probably adds up to more than two thousand. (Stevenson's report, and a reprint of Robertson's novel, can be found in The Doomed Unsinkable Ship, edited by William H. Tantum [Riverside, Conn.: 7 C's Press, 1974]).

Research regarding group forewarnings shows, first, that they occur to people regardless of their social status; and second, that the more important the foreshadowed event, the more widespread the communal leakages are. If this is the case, then the assassination of President John F. Kennedy should have been preceded by a great number of communal forewarnings, since his murder was one of the most socially significant events of this century.

The fact that the assassination was preceded by numerous previsions is well known. But the writer Herbert B. Greenhouse is the only one who has performed an adequate forewarning autopsy. In his 1971 book Premonitions: A Leap into the Future he estimates that at least fifty thousand persons had premonitions that President Kennedy would be shot.

I don't know where Greenhouse obtained this estimate, but I do know from my own research that communal forewarnings about Kennedy's assassination were very numerous—and my own forewarning can be included among them. One morning early in that fateful November, while relaxing in the tub, I heard a shot that I thought came from the street. I then "saw" Kennedy slumped over in a car. "My god!" I heard someone say. "He's been killed." When I went into work that day at the United Nations, I mentioned to a friend that I thought Kennedy was going to be assassinated. He looked at me in surprise. "I had a dream," he said, "in which I saw Kennedy lying in a coffin."

Even if Greenhouse is in error with his estimate of fifty thousand forewarnings, the advance leakage of Kennedy's approaching assassination was still one of the most widely circulated in contemporary history. Forewarning alerts were received throughtout the world, and even noted psychics "got" the picture in awesome detail. Of these, Jeanne Dixon's is probably the most remembered.

In addition, though, the late Arthur Ford's prediction of the assassination was taped in Washington, D.C., in the presence of many politicians, including Senator McClellan of Arkansas. At the time of the 1960 Presidential campaign, Adrienne Coulter, a Flushing, New York, psychic, heard a voice say: "Nix on Nixon. Kennedy will become President and will be assassinated." A New Jersey psychic, Mary Tallmadge, "saw" Kennedy facing a coffin, the national flag at half-mast. A voice told Jeanne Gardner, a West Virginia housewife, that Kennedy would soon be killed, and in August 1963, she "heard" the name Oswald but did not know what it meant. In 1962, during a hallucinogenic drug experience, a New Jersey psychologist had a vision of the President's death.

As the event drew nearer, the frequency of premonitions increased, some depositing the word "Dallas"—the very city to which Jeanne Dixon tried vainly to warn the President not to go. Even the noted parapsychologist Stanley Krippner had *his* vision of the assassination two years in advance. At least twenty-four young children reported that they "knew" in advance that the President would be murdered.

The psychic drums leaking and beating out the intelligence of the future Kennedy assassination began thumping at the time of his election and, as in the case of the Aberfan disaster, increased in their frequency up to the very day of the sad event.

A thousand individuals can experience foreseing episodes that refer to a thousand different personal events. But these can be explained away and have no social meaning because they do not link into the communal forms of shared consciousness that bind societies together. Shared consciousness is more important and powerful than individual consciousness.

But a thousand individual future-seeing experiences that refer to the *same future event*, and have no immediate relevance to the individuals themselves, cannot be explained away so easily. There is only one explain-it-away contrivance that can be brought to bear:

mass hallucination. This contrivance falls rather flat when the event communally foreseen by the many comes to pass.

With this kind of evidence in mind, it appears that the ancient axiom that "events foreshadow themselves" *is* true. When it can be shown that communal foreseeing leakages do occur, the question of whether time can be transcended is no longer a question but an obvious certainty.

Three kinds of NostraFac experiences have now been described. The future-seeing mosaic fits together better and the strength of your intellect-bridge to your Nostradamus Factor is increased if your intellect becomes more certain that these experiences occur. You may increase this certainty by going beyond the examples given in this book.

Seeing into the future is always a good topic for social conversation, and you might begin asking if others have ever foreseen something. If you adopt a poise that conveys that you are really interested, most people will confess they have—or that they have heard of someone else who has. You can begin categorizing their responses, and somewhere along the line you will encounter those who have communally foreseen important events—NostraFac experiences of the third kind.

8

NOSTRAFAC EXPERIENCES OF THE FOURTH KIND: CONSCIOUSLY CONTROLLED FUTURE-SEEING

Successful future-seers are people who have integrated their innate future-seeing capabilities with their intellect-processes—

a feat that falls into the category of *ability*, meaning an acquired skill. This integration results in what I designate NostraFac experiences of the fourth kind, to differentiate them from the other three kinds, which are spontaneous.

Many different degrees of this integration are possible, of course. But the essential characteristic of these seers is that they have decided to develop it. The integration takes place when our three major mind-dynamic systems are in a state of alignment: our deep structures, our subconscious strata, and our intellects. (This complex alignment will be discussed in detail in chapter 10.)

Most of the achieved future-seers I have studied do not maintain this alignment 100 percent of the time and thus have variously produced inaccurate predictions and forecasts. But the more outstanding among them have published their predictions in advance of the events to which they refer. These predictions are so rich in precise details of the forthcoming event that it is impossible to believe the predictions consisted just of vague, lucky guesses. It is clear that they did transcend time. Many of them gave exact dates at which their predictions would be fulfilled, this being a very important "detail" as we shall see presently.

Achieved future-seers have had several things in common. Most, but not all, were spontaneous future-seers as children and for whatever reason grew up maintaining a serious interest in the matter. They adhered to their interest in future-seeing despite social resisance to it. They were outsiders, and none sought scientific, academic, peer, or social approval in order to pursue and maintain their interest. A high level of courage is implicit here—and perhaps a high degree of stubbornness, too.

None left adequate autobiographies, possibly because there was no social encouragement for them to do so. And the few biographies that others have attempted to write tend to be shallow, overemphasizing the "gee whiz" aspect of successful predictions or social awkwardness that was sometimes colorful and dramatic enough. Finally, none of the achieved foreseers left any commentary on how others might develop future-seeing abilities. Because of this autobiographical and biographical deficit, it is not easy to arrive at deep insights regarding their psychology or to reconstruct their holistic overview or viewpoints of the cosmos, of life, or of human nature.

Most notable future-seers were students of the occult, and the most successful ones were astrologers—as was Michael de Nostradamus. Astrology, the historical queen of the predictive arts, was used to buttress their innate future-seeing capacities. Others utilized devices (such as crystal balls, cards, beads, sticks, stones, mirrors, or pendulums). Successful future-seers who relied only on psychic perceptions have been rare. As a group, these tend not to see the future very well if the low success rates of their published predictions is reviewed.

Prediction and *forecast* are words generally used interchangeably, but there is an important difference between them. *Predict*, literally "fore-*say*," means "to declare in advance." Anyone can declare something in advance, that thus-and-so is going to happen, or may happen, or might happen, or is likely to happen. But exactly *when* it might happen is altogether another matter. It could happen tomorrow, or a thousand years from now. Including a *date* in a prediction makes it a forecast. The importance of this distinction is that general or vague predictions are not very useful in practical ways. But precise forecasts are.

For example, one of the most famous *predictions* in history is attributed to one Ursula Shipton, commonly known as Mother Shipton, who, it is thought, was born in 1488 during the reign of Henry VII, near Knaresborough, Yorkshire. A collection of Mother Shipton's predictions was published in 1641, and a copy of this collection is preserved in the British Museum. That 1641 collection contains the forecast given below, approximately 412 years before our modern technological age began:

> Carriages without horses shall go,
> Around the earth thoughts shall fly
> In the twinkling of an eye;
> Through the hills man shall ride,
> And no horse be at his side.
> Underwater men shall walk,
> Shall ride, shall sleep, shall talk.

In the air men shall be seen,
Iron in water shall float,
As easily as a wooden boat.
Gold shall be found and shown
In a land that's not now known.
Fire and water shall wonders do,
England shall at last admit a foe.
The world to an end shall come
In eighteen hundred and eighty-one.

Some elements of this forecast have been interpreted in different ways, but as Henry James Forman pointed out in his book *The Story of Prophecy* (1940), there is no "mean assortment" of foreseen technological advances. We easily recognize our *own* modern times in which the automobile, telegraph and radio, submarines, aircraft, steamships, railways, and tunnels were developed. Vast amounts of gold *were* found, after 1641, in the New World, the amount of which changed the economic structure of the then-known world. The 1776 American Revolution, in a land "that's not now known," did cause England to acknowledge the existence of a "foe," which that great nation did not conquer. And we recognize 1881 as the approximate date that separates the nontechnological world from its technological successor, the time at which the nontechnological world ended.

Time-relevant data are not always given in terms of the calendar dates we normally use and might be given, as is sometimes the case in Nostradamus's forecasts, in terms of specific *planetary arrangements* whose timing can be deduced by referring to an ephemeris of planetary movements and places. Some dates can be implied only indirectly, such as when such-and-so can be seen to happen then, too, will this or that happen.

As critics of future-seeing have pointed out, predictions may be useless unless they contain date-time data, just as it would be impractical to begin planning for something that may happen a thousand years from now. There are great differences between seer-predictors and seer-forecasters.

SOME ACHIEVED FUTURE-SEERS

Out of the great many available, I have selected the following examples to highlight the date-window accuracy that achieved future-seers have accomplished, a factor that immediately lifts their predictions and forecasts out of the realms of chance or coincidence.

In 1927, a book entitled *New and Enlarged Edition of Cheiro's World Predictions: The Fate of Nations* came out in New Delhi. Cheiro (pronounced like Cairo) was actually Count Louis Hamon (1886–1936), an ebullient, pear-shaped fellow, born in Ireland, an astrologer-palmist-numerologist whose international fame was worldwide at the turn of the century. And for good reason: his seer-forecasting abilities were completely staggering.

In the 1927 book, Cheiro produced a forecast that was extraordinary for his time: as of 1980, "the Jews, or as they will again be called, Israelites, will have made enormous strides in wealth, world position and power" and will have restored themselves into the homeland of Palestine. Cheiro prefaces this astonishing forecast by outlining the complex numerological-cum-astrological equations that allowed him to arrive at this dated and timed forecast.

In the same book, Cheiro made another forecast, which was considered laughable in 1927. After giving complex astrological reasons for this particular forecast, regarding the then–prince of Wales, later briefly known as Edward VIII, he indicated that the prince "will in the end fall a victim of a devastating love affair" and "give up everything, even the chance of being crowned, rather than lose the object of his affection."

This forecast was considered lunacy in 1927, for no British monarch had ever abdicated the throne because of a love affair. Indeed, in 1927 the prince of Wales was enjoying extraordinary popularity, and the whole of England was eagerly awaiting his accession. The existence of the infamous Wallis Warfield Simpson, the eventual object of the prince's affection, was completely unknown to anyone in 1927, and the prince met her only briefly in 1930. Even after the "affair of the century" became well known, no one dreamed that Edward would give up the chance of being crowned for this twice-divorced American woman. But he did, in 1936, just after his father died.

The time-window is implicit in the prediction. "The chance of being crowned" implicitly figures that the abdication would take place between Edward's inheritance of the throne and his coronation, the official ceremony in which he would have been invested as king of England and all its realms. Strictly speaking, having done so before his inheritance would merely have removed him from the line of succession, not from a confirmed chance at the crown.

These two forecasts are important because they were published in advance of their occurring. Additionally, what they forecast was so unlikely that the usual explanations regarding lucky guesses, chance, or coincidence do not suffice.

After the turn of the century, another eminent future-seer was at work in equally astonishing ways—Walter Gorn Old (1864–1929), born in Harndsworth, Birmingham, England, who himself adopted the pseudonym of "Sepharial," one of the many who used that name. Whereas Cheiro was a social type of fellow who circulated in the highest strata of society, Sepharial was a rather grey eminence acting behind the scenes. He published a great many of his predictions and forecasts in advance, mainly through a series of pamphlets called *The Green Book for Prophecies*, then sold on newsstands in England. Many of these are preserved in the New York Public Library.

A large set of his forecasts was printed in book form in 1913 under the title *An Astrological Survey of the Great War, Being an Examination of the Indications Attending the Outbreak and the Presumptive Effects of the Conflict*. Now, the Great War (later known as World War I), which began during the summer of 1914, *did not begin to be called the "Great War"* until the spring of 1915, when it was realized that the war was neither temporary or small. Chalk one up for Sepharial's nomenclature.

Sepharial's forecasting accuracy was positively awesome. He had first predicted a "great war of nations" in his 1896 *Manual of Astrology* as "coming soon." In his 1913 *Survey* he gave the date for its commencement as "about July 25, 1914." Just prior to this date, he predicted that there would be war talk through Europe, and that the "Balkan concert would now be disturbed and affairs tend to a crisis in Austria" beginning on June 28, 1914.

On June 23, 1914, the archduke Franz Ferdinand of Austria and his wife, Sophie, were assassinated by a Serbian assassin in Sarajevo, the capital of the Balkan nation of Bosnia. The Austrian government demanded on July 24 that Serbia be suspended as a state and be absorbed into the Austrian empire. Serbia immediately refused to be suspended and prepared to defend against the takeover. Serbia's refusal of suspension is historically accepted as the commencement of the "great war," which commenced on July 25, 1914—exactly on the day Sepharial had predicted in 1913.

Walter Gorn Old did not like the Germans of the time, referring to their Hohenzollern dynastic leaders as "the great beasts." In his series of *Green Books* and other publications, he gave the step-by-step events, often accompanied by date-windows, leading to their total doom. He forecasted that by 1931 their line would be completely "rooted out" and shortly predicted that after this rooting-out yet another German "great beast" would arise who would cause "a second great devastation for which the Great War would seem like only a dress rehearsal."

In 1931, the remaining claimant to the Hohenzollern throne of Germany was rooted out of Germany and in permanent exile in Holland. And in 1933 Adolf Hitler began the meteoric rise that culminated in World War II, the second great devastation for which the first indeed had been only a "dress rehearsal."

In his 1913 forecasts and predictions, Old also turned his future-seeing competence toward assessing the future of Russia. Of all the monarchies that might fall (though none of them were expected to fall), the House of Romanov was certainly the least likely contender. Yet, *in 1913*, Old boldly forecasted that it was unlikely that the tsar, Nicholas II, would survive the Great War and that by the time Nicholas reached forty-nine years of age there would be "a great revolution" that would "see the end of the dynastic succession" in Russia. He also predicted that Russia would not emerge from the Great War or from its revolution "with any measure of success."

The Russian Revolution occurred in 1917 when Tsar Nicholas II was forty-nine years of age. He was executed in July 1918 (along with his family). He thus did not survive the Great War, which ended five months later in November 1918. The fact that Russia did not emerge from its revolution with any measure of success is one of the clearest phenomena of the world order as I am writing this book in 1991–92.

Neither Hamon nor Old was completely correct in all his predictions and forecasts. But considering their published predictions and forecasts, they made relatively few future-seeing blunders. I would like to give more examples of NostraFacs of the fourth kind, but doing so would make this book overly long. I refer you to the bibliography.

If you were to take a survey of people regarding whether they had experienced some kind of reasonably accurate forewarning (intuition, premonition, dream, vision, etc.,) 80 percent or prehaps all of them would say they have. You can satisfy yourself in this regard by asking all those you know (you will find that doing so makes for good conversation). It is a simple fact that humans experience various kinds of future-seeing episodes.

So, the human species MUST *possess mind-dynamic processes that can and do transcend time.*

If these processes can be identified—even partially, if not yet in their entirety—then it is reasonable and entirely logical to assume that our intellects will become increasingly adapted to "working" with them. The next four chapters discuss these inner processes as I have been able to identify them.

You should be prepared to note three phenomena associated with these processes:

1. They will appear difficult to comprehend at first. But they belong to that strange category of mind-phenomena that, if difficult at first, become simple *after* they are understood. These processes after all are part of ourselves, part of our minds, and they are unfamiliar and apparently complex only because we have not intellectually organized our understanding of them.

2. Printed words can describe these process-phenomena in secondary ways; but the actual primary phenomena the printed words can only approximate are nonverbal or, so to speak, preverbal. Thus, they are best understood by attempting to build images of them on paper in the form of diagrams or sketches. I will provide as suggestive models a limited number of diagrams regarding certain strategic concepts that you might utilize by first copying them yourself and then adding to or changing them as your image-building understanding increases. But all the concepts discussed can be illustrated. If and when your illustrations become complete enough you will find you are mind-resonating with them.

3. The mind-dynamic systems of each person are put together in ways that often are highly individualistic. Yet our mind-dynamic processes through which the future is perceived must be relatively similiar. For example, our eyes and ears all have near-identical structures that function in similar ways even though what each of us sees or hears, and the particular ways in which we do so, can be highly individualized. I will refer to the *similarity* of our future-seeing processes as "structure," which can become "architecturalized" according to how our intellects are "designed" by our experiential and educational backgrounds. Our future-seeing processes are best identified by locating (and diagramming) their structure. The lists I encourage you to make refer to how your intellect has become architecturalized for or against future-seeing.

9

FUTURE-SEEING AND OUR MULTIPLE
MIND-DYNAMIC SYSTEMS

Our intellect-perceptions determine our interests, beliefs, choices of action, and goals. All these, though, are governed by the *limits* of our intellect-processes, which are controlling the perceptions in the first place.

But we don't actually see it this way. Instead, we speak from *within* our intellect-limits by saying, "I think" thus-and-so, or "I believe" thus-and-so, or "my realities" or "my logic and reason" hold this or that. We seldom consider that our thoughts, beliefs, realities, or logic and reason are *limiting*—largely because they seem big (and correct) enough to us and because it is somewhat ego-destructive to consider that they consist of limits.

Our intellect-awareness is built out of what we have experienced and learned or, frankly, "bought into." As children, our intellects are eager for experience and information. But at a certain point, the experience and information begin to attain some kind of architecturalized form. We begin to accept what fits into this architecture and reject what does not. In this sense, then, intellects can function as closed circuits, or closed loops, which accept or reject information packages that fit or do not fit with the information previously packaged into the self-contained closed circuit.

On average, our Nostradamus Factor is *not* incorporated into our architecturalized intellects, and so we have not developed any intellectual pathways to deal with even its spontaneous manifestations. But spontaneous forewarnings come from somewhere in our minds; and so we have to postulate the existence of deeper, less limited processes existing in what we call "other forms of consciousness," which many assume to be "greater" than our limited conscious intellects.

This situation is particularly pertinent to the goal of building an intellect-bridge to your future-seeing powers, especially if the realization has set in that you possess not one but many forms of consciousness.

If we illustrate these as a spectrum, we have greater, limitless forms of consciousness at one end of it and our intellects (which may be closed circuits) at the other. Between the two ends exist multiple intermediate forms of consciousness. Information originating in less limiting forms of consciousness must pass or be processed through these intermediate forms in order to arrive, if it can, into waking intellectual awareness. The whole of this equates to what can be called our *consciousness spectrum*.

It is mandatory for the serious future-seer to try to diagram and visualize this spectrum. But this is difficult to do because the intellect can visualize only *within the limits* of what it already contains—and it has great difficulty in perceiving what is outside of those limits. If, for example, you try to visualize your other forms of consciousness (try doing so now), all you will probably "see" is something equivalent to being inside a round ball in which some nondescript images are floating aimlessly.

The reason for this is that your intellect has not been provided with a literal picture of the consciousness spectrum—an absence that you can immediately correct by sketching out one for it. The figure on page 97 is provided as a hypothetical (and probably quite idealized) model for this spectrum. You can begin by *copying it*. If you copy it (rather than just look at it), you will *have to use your image-building, right-hemisphere functions*. These functions will involve your autonomic nervous system (in ways that are not understood in science), but the effect will be a restructuring of your intellect.

This model, however, is *my* model, and copying it gives your intellect only an idea of what is required. Try to diagram your own versions of it. If you watch it do so, your intellect will now reorganize itself and begin to provide a model that is more appropriate to you—so long as you image-build (by actually sketching or diagramming)

CONSCIOUSNESS SPECTRUM

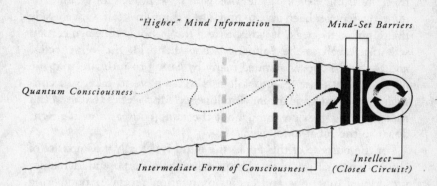

what is being visualized. In fact, as you read on, your model will *change* to accommodate the increasingly precise information to follow. You will also find that the images you sketch out are now more permanently present in your visualizing intellect and that what you visualize is patterning itself differently.

MORE THAN ONE MIND?

We consider and explain the whole of this spectrum as *the* mind (in the singular) and assume that *the* intellect (again in the singular) is its strategic command center. But a problem with this explanation emerges when we realize that spontaneous episodes of future-seeing originate not from the intellect but from other minds when the individual is asleep or in some altered awake state.

The term *mind* as used today may be less than a thousand years old (our recorded history began about six thousand years ago), and the concept of a *mind* is much more recent. Our ancient ancestors had no word for mind, and they did not believe that thinking went on in the brain. They thought that *awareness* went on in different parts of the body, and even outside of it—much in the way the new sciences are discovering.

The word *mind*, as we know it today, is derived from root words meaning "to think," "to intend," and "to remember," but especially those meaning *memory*. Scientists who have probed for or into the mind have never been able to find it as a thing-in-itself. Once inside the mind, so to speak, it vanishes as a thing. Some time ago certain scientists, such as the eminent Wilder Penfield, Sir John Eccles, and Sir Karl Popper, alarmed many by daring to intimate that the mind did not exist. Neurobiologists today have to take into consideration the new quantum "intelligence" discoveries that establish that thinking goes on throughout the mind/body as a whole right down to the subatomic level.

For the purpose of this book, the mind is actually a composite of "mind-dynamic" processes. The processes have purposeful, dynamic, prosurvival functions and energyinformation receptors numbering in the trillions. Millions of these processes and their receptors do what they do in microfractions of seconds. Your future-seeing powers are embedded in this fantastic and astonishing composite of mind-dynamic processes.

Simply put, your mind does not see the future, but your mind-dynamic processes at some functioning level ALREADY *do*—and this shift of intellect-understanding is very significant. You cannot learn to do something that is already going on in your mind-dynamic systems. You can only learn to recognize it and then prepare your intellect to work with it.

A great deal is known about how our mind-dynamic processes work. But what is strange about all this is that very few of us are taught much about how they function. Having even the least idea of all this can change your intellect pathways considerably.

For example, consider the mind-dynamic processes that result in what we call vision. We fully believe that when we see a cup, a dog, or a lover, we are "seeing" what is out there. Well, yes; but mainly no. What we are actually seeing when we are looking at something out there are pictures of it that our remarkable mind-dynamic *sensors* have constructed in our *inner* visualizing mind. Our physical eyes possess a vast array of sensors (called rods and cones) that scan-sense what we "see" in bits and pieces. It is the bits and pieces that are forwarded to our minds, which reconstruct them into inner images. Neurophysiologists have definitively established that what we see when we are looking at something outside of us is a mind-reconstructed-image of it *in* our minds. The inner mind-dynamic processes by which inner images, with unimaginable speed, are arrived at, so to speak, are truly staggering, as is shown below.

1. Our eye sensors literally break apart the energy and information they are registering into bits and pieces, forwarding them along neural pathways from the eyes to the brain, where an enormous collaboration of other neural activities recompose them into pictures, after which

2. other neural frameworks "look" at the "photo" and "decide" which

3. *other* neurons to send it along to for *interpretation*, after which

4. the interpretation is thence once again forwarded to neurons whose business it is to *decode* its "meaning," after which

5. the meaning is forwarded to other neurons that "decide" whether the "package" should be routed along to

6. conscious intellectual awareness neurons,

7. to subliminal, subconscious memory storage,

8. perhaps to the "thinking" immune cell neurons circulating watchfully in the body, or

9. to emotional electrochemical molecules in order to

10. trigger further electrochemical molecules that "produce" sensations of fear, happiness, contentment, or desire, etc., or, as it may happen, trigger

11. future-seeing neurons that "compute-anticipate" what is going to happen, which

12. may then forward the *prediction* to our cognitive-awareness neurons—at which time

13. if the prediction-infoenergy does not get derouted by already-installed reality-points that are disadapted to future-seeing, *we will "suffer"* a foresight.

Our mind-dynamic processes of intellect-understanding are exact parallel processes in that our "understanding" is the sum of our "think" (as a noun, not the verb). Our "think" is, itself, the end-product of an astonishing subarray of electro-chemical-magnetic molecular routings and reroutings that convey our understanding-stimuli (the best term, but insufficient) through about a trillion neural switches and decoders *before* whatever is involved results in what we fondly call our understanding, which is the sum of our thinking processes.

A sizeable portion of our understanding-stimuli is routed to subliminal memory storage *if our waking, conscious intellects have not been prepared (or programmed) to receive them.* If, for example, your intellectual reality-anchors have become coded to believe that future-seeing is available only to the gifted or is impossible because the future does not exist, then when your future-seeing receptors are twanged by a "bit" of future-relevant energyinformation, Lord only knows where it will end up in your systems. But chances are it will not emerge in your waking intellectual consciousness—except, perhaps, via a dream or sudden gut feeling.

In other words, if your reality-anchors believe that the future can be seen and that you possess future-seeing receptors, then you automatically facilitate your indwelling future-seeing processes.

You can become intellect-aware of *processes* by realizing that nothing is frozen into the permanent present. All processes are future-oriented and are changing *into the future.* And they all will have outcomes, whether these be negative or positive.

How aware are you of the processes going on within you? If you can find and intellect-identify with a given process, your innate future-seeing powers will go to work and in some way inform you about the future outcomes. For example, romantic or sexual attraction between two people is actually a series of processes going on between them. If you can introspectively identify not with either or both of the two people but with the processes taking place *between* them, I can assure you that you will foresee the outcome of the processes. Intuition, one of our great foresensing capabilities, results not from seeing what is out there, but from sensing the ongoing processes between things. You may be surprised at how fast the foreseeing of the outcome takes place (remember, our mind-dynamic processes work with microsecond speed). And you may be even more surprised to discover that, as it is often said, "something in you knew it all along, anyway."

I have already recommended several introspective lists you might make. Use these lists now to find items of myths, beliefs, and obstacles to future-seeing. Select one or more that seem "magnetic" or interesting, and try to perceive the processes that made that item what it is. Once you can spot the processes surrounding the item, you will be able to foresee or at least intuit their outcomes.

OUR MULTIPLE MINDS

If we do not have *a* mind that contains/produces our thought processes and that is centered in the brain, which in turn is in the body, then what then *do* we have? Spontaneous future-seeing episodes have an autonomous nature that becomes clearly defined when the warning or alerts in the episodes contrast very highly with our waking intellect's functioning. As we have seen, our waking intellect can disagree or doubt the information contained in the spontaneous alert or warning and decide to disregard it.

Any mind-function that is autonomous and whose function-ing contrasts highly with other mind-functions can really be said to be a separate mind in its own right. The autonomous future-seeing mind is different from the intellect-mind that can disagree with the information being provided by the former. In this sense, then, we have at least *two* minds that work in variable ways with each other. The idea of two minds brings up the issue of *multiple minds*.

It is clear that our intellects (which function only when we are awake) constitute only a small fraction of our multiple minds—a fact that is now thoroughly accepted in science and psychology. In their attempts to preserve the concept that we have *one* mind, though, modern scientists divided the mind into "levels." But postmodern scientists have begun to realize that "our" mind is composed of interacting networks of multiple minds, some of which cannot be said to be "ours" simply because our waking intellects have little or no control over them.

The confirmed concept of multiple minds gives rise to the concept of multiple *intelligences,* which has succinctly been set forth in Howard Gardner's lively book *Frames of Mind: The Theory of Multiple Intelligences* (1983). As Gardner points out, there is persuasive evidence for the existence of several "relatively autonomous intelligences." But research since 1983 has begun to establish that some of these minds *are* completely autonomous and possess "thinking" neural-energy-information-transfers and processes exquisitely of their own.

The problem regarding our intellect rises out of the modern *rationalist* definition of it—which we now need examine to find out how it blocks access to our future-seeing mind.

About three hundred years ago, when the philosophy of rationalism began to emerge, its exponents began changing the definition of intellect by eliminating its historic and traditional contexts and substituting meanings relevant only to rationalistic principles. *Rationalism* was (and still is) defined as the theory that reason is in itself a source of knowledge superior to and independent of the sense perceptions. In reflecting this theory, modern dictionaries came to define *intellect* only as the capacity for rational thought and knowledge, defining this capacity as the power of knowing as distinguished from the power to feel and to will since those powers are intimately associated with sensed perceptions.

In establishing, theoretically, that *reason,* as distinguished from the *senses,* was not only the prime source of knowledge but the pure function of intellect, hard-line rationalists were able to draw boundaries between *sensed* energyinformation packages and *ideas brought to conscious by, but not derived from, sense experience.*

The theory that the intellect and the senses are separate arose, in large part, from the ideas of the French philosopher Rene Descartes (1596–1650), who formulated a doctrine of "innate ideas" not derived from sensory experience. Descartes, and, more important, his subsequent followers, held that the body is part of "mechanical nature," but that the mind, which interacts with the mechanical nature, is a "pure thinking substance" unique to itself. Not all philosophers agreed. The equally influential philosopher John Locke (1632–1704) insisted that "there is nothing in the intellect which was not first in the senses." But Locke's statement was amended by the rationalist German philosopher Wilhelm Leibnitz (1646–1716), who added "except the intellect itself," in order to establish what was later called a "consistent rationalism."

All this adds up to something very difficult to comprehend if *all* our life processes are taken into account. But this line of reasoning permitted rationalists to *separate* intellect from information sensed from other sources (from our NostraFacs, for example) and ultimately to place the detached intellect as the prime source of knowledge above sensed forms of knowledge.

Understanding the misleading influence of this separation is crucial to aspiring future-seers when it is realized that

1. spontaneous episodes of future-seeing do not originate from within the intellect but from some sensing states or from mindlike, autonomous mechanisms clearly independent of them; and
2. future-seeing derived from nonrational sources is considered irrational in the rationalistic perspective.

The negative mind-dynamic effects of the rationalistic misleading influence begin to fall away when (as the American philosopher William James [1842–1910] and other consciousness researchers have pointed out) it is realized that our normal, waking, rational intellects are a specialized kind of awareness, and that all around them are other forms of consciousness, entirely different.

INTUITUS-INTELLECTUS

The rationalist definition is of relatively recent vintage, yet the term *intellect* is very old. In researching the problem of adapting our intellects to our future-seeing powers, I decided to undertake an archeological autopsy to find out how it was defined *before* it was colonized by and converted into its exclusive rationalistic definition.

In tracing the history of *intellect* backward from the present, it was surprising to find that the once-authoritative 1892 *Encyclopaedia Britannica* did not have an entry for "intellect."

That encyclopedia, however, does provide commentary on "intellection" and "intellectual feelings"—neither of which is used today. Together, apparently thought of as synonyms, these are defined as "not only the feelings connected with certainty, doubt, perplexity, comprehensions, and so forth, but also . . . with what are called the higher, *par excellence* feelings which are regarded as entirely determined by *the form of the flow of ideas* [emphasis mine], but not by the ideas themselves."

This definition is a very good one with regard to how we actually experience our intellects. We do not experience them as logic or reason per se but as flows of ideas (the processing of energyinformation packages) that result in deductions—deductions themselves being *stabilized* energyinformation packages.

Put another way, *intellectus* is composed of the flowing processes of ideas relating (or misrelating) to each other. In this sense, intellect becomes that specialized function of waking awareness in which ideas and knowledge flow with, in, and around each other, ultimately forming perceived relationships. Discernment of flowlike relationships (or *processes*) is the principal *experienced* output of intellect.

Even though rationalistic definitions hold that intellect is the power of knowing as distinguished from the power to feel and to will, it is difficult to see how the power to feel can be left out of the discernment-of-relationship processes.

We can *feel-sense* many relationships that do not fit in with our established rational and logical deductions. And if the intellect is not supposed to feel or to will, then what *is* it supposed to do? If we consider, as has been scientifically established time and again, that our first threshold of perception of *any kind* is feeling, then we are to wonder how our intellects can function effectively in its absence. The answer is that we cannot. Indeed, we literally feel our intellects working, and the popular phrase "I am feeling my way" through this or that information or experience reflects a direct, felt perception of our intellect processes.

The principal definition of *feeling* is to touch in order to achieve not just tactile sensations but also conscious perception. Since no relationship is "visible" to us unless we can feel-judge its existence in qualitative ways, then the perception of relationships fundamentally rests upon our power to feel.

We come very quickly into contact here with the definition of at least one future-seeing word that is completely pertinent to this book—*intuition*. This is defined as a *sensed* knowing or gut feeling of meaningful relationships that is, as most dictionaries define, *independent of intellect*. But when the apparent *processes* of intuition and intellect are considered, we find it difficult to determine which is which, since *both* consist of feelings or flows of sensed relationships.

The only real difference between the two is that what we consider intuition often flies in the face of what we consider to be rational or logical. But if it is considered that what we acknowledge as rational or logical is more likely determined by installed mind-set reality-points, then neither reason nor logic is a primary product of either active intuition or intellect *processes*. They are both epiphenomenal products of how flowing energyinformation packages are judged against positively or negatively loaded reality-points.

It is quite possible, then, that the prerationalist definitions of intuition and intellect were the same. The *Oxford English Dictionary* points up that the Latin *intuitus* meant "*to look at* and contemplate *felt* relationships," while the Latin *intellectus* meant "*to perceive* and discern felt relationships." The products of *intuitus* and *intellectus*, in a felt–looked-at–perceived kind of way, are identical: a discernment, a meaning, a feeling, a signification, any or all of which equate to *an* understanding.

At the very least, then, so far as their similar mind-dynamic processes go, intellect and intuition symbolically are often thought of as brother-sister minds. But both produce *ideation* (from the Greek *idein*, "to see"), which, technically speaking, is a cognitive seizing by and within the mind-dynamic systems of energyinformation packages being sensed-experienced by those systems and thus perceived or looked at.

A double mistake in the rationalist's misdefinition of *intellect* is now evident. In the first instance, they were ignorant of the now-known fact that the whole biopsychic (body-mind) system is *one* system and that it registers and interprets energyinformation at many different biopsychic levels because that information is literally felt-perceived at those levels. Second, they had not evolved anything resembling information theory. This deals with the *efficient* transfer of energyinformation packages between integrated and integrating systems—of which our waking awareness is only one of all those we possess.

This double mistake has done dreadful damage to how we have conceived the potential powers of our intellects, since it conceptually detaches them from participating in the information exchanges going on, via perceived feeling, throughout our whole mind-dynamic systems.

Once it becomes conceptually permissible to relink knowledge with our power of feeling, then intellect stands a conceptual chance of reintegrating itself with the whole mind-dynamic system of which it is a part. And, as we will now see, reintegration requires the deconstruction of inadequate reality-anchors and the construction of new ones.

This chapter is particularly rich in concepts to image-build. If any of the concepts introduced here were difficult for you to understand, simply go back and diagram or sketch them until you achieve a functioning, image-built picture of them. The *diagrammed* relationships between feeling and intellect, and between intuition and intellect, are particularly important.

10

THE RELATIONSHIP OF MIND-DYNAMIC
ANCHOR-POINTS TO FUTURE-SEEING

When the conscious intellect conceives that it is merely one member of a community of minds with different functions, it begins to construct cognitive bridges to those other functions. It does so by changing its reality anchor-points.

Reality anchor-points are the mind-dynamic points of view your intellect uses to establish your mind-set reality thresholds. These points of view and thresholds can vary considerably from person to person. We may be one species biologically, but when it comes to reality thresholds, we can, as it is often said, "come from other planets."

We judge future-seeing information or impulses by filtering them through our installed reality-anchors.

Each aspiring future-seer must work in tandem with his or her own reality-anchors. If we consider that these anchors can help, influence, distort, or block future-seeing information, it becomes understandable that the make-break point between successful and unsuccessful future-seeing depends on our reality-anchors. The exact reason is that we use our reality-anchors to process any and all information we encounter in any form—and it is our reality-anchors that architecturalize the information into what we call "our realities."

In other words, we do not process reality directly. We process information *about* it and, through the processing, end up with indirect assessments that are shaped by the nature of the information, which, in turn, has "gone through" our reality-anchors. The aspiring future-seer, dealing with information from the future, must acquire a fairly broad understanding of what reality-anchors are; and this understanding begins with conceptualizing the nature of information itself.

INFORMATION

Information theory deals with the *efficiency* of information transfer between information-processing units or systems. We conceive of our waking intellect-mind as one such a system and our NostraFac mind as another. Our NostraFac mind exists "deeper" than our surface intellect-mind, and the former is closer to larger realities since, by the evidence, it can transcend time. When our waking intellects cannot foresee the future as our indwelling Nostradamus Factors can, then the efficiency of information-transfer between the two systems is disadapted and dysfunctional.

To inform means to give form, character, and essence to. When a spontaneous future-seeing experience emerges into intellect-consciousness in the form of a dream, vision, gut feeling, or direct urge, a deep information-transfer process is giving us the *constructed* form, character, and essence of some future facts. These constructed forms are the exact equivalent of our conscious thoughts. *Thinking* is taking place in levels much deeper than our waking intellects. The future-seer has to adapt his or her intellect to that thinking.

Once such an adaptation has taken place, it serves as a new conceptual *anchor-point* in our whole mind-dynamic system. The conceptual anchor-point is then stored in the vast memory networks, most of which reside in the subconscious. Our mind-dynamic systems then use these stored anchor-points to "help" interpret whatever experience is encountered by the individual. Since the interpretation is anchored in memory strata, the waking intellect may or may not be aware of the anchor-points without making an effort to recover them. For example, the memory of my Sunday school teacher connecting future-seeing to the work of the devil had receded deep into my memory banks. But I eventually retrieved it by introspection.

Once they have become installed in experiential memory, antifuture-seeing anchor-points act as "noise" if and when the individual experiences some kind of future-seeing signal or impulse. This noise is experienced as confusion during the conscious waking state when the intellect is operative. The confusion arises because the energyinformation of the future-seeing impulse literally *cannot be fitted into* the energyinformation of the installed antifuture-seeing anchor-points. NostraFac information is then usually rejected or filtered out as being wrong, illogical, or irrational.

Our installed anchor-points are surrounded by an array of defensive mechanisms that actually flare up into activity when a bit of misfitting energyinformation is experienced. This can be observed especially in the case of "closed-circuit" intellects. Psychologists have long recognized the awesome destructive power of negatively "charged" anchor-points. Locating these and discharging their reality-making energyinformation frees the mind-dynamic systems from their influences. This is the sole basis for all reconstructive mind-dynamic therapies, including psychoanalysis, self-help, and meditation.

Usually just consciously locating the memory-stored anchor-points (sometimes seen as past events) serves to discharge their installed energyinformation patterns, and this kind of activity *edits* the sum effects of all installed anchor-points. The mind-dynamic system is then free to "work" without them.

Thousands of conceptual future-seeing barriers may exist, of course (some of which have been discussed earlier), and any mix of them will act as anchor-point blocks to the processing of future-seeing information. Resolving the problems and barriers to future-seeing requires

1. restructuring our intellects so that they can appreciate information about future-seeing processes that is correct; and
2. discharging incorrect energyinformation from our installed anchor-points so that they no longer automatically react defensively against correct estimations of future-seeing processes and impulses.

ANCHOR-POINTS ARE THE FOUNDATIONS OF OUR VALUES, VIEWPOINTS, JUDGMENTS, AND WORLDVIEWS

The absolute importance to future-seeing of our installed anchor-points becomes apparent when we realize that they serve us as mind-dynamic foundations for how we perceive and react to what we perceive in the way we have perceived it. And the implications of this become clear if we consider, first, that *real reality does exist* independently and outside of our reality anchors, but second, that our perceptions of real reality are modified by the various ways we perceive it via our complex reality-anchors, which give us our networks of values, beliefs, viewpoints, judgments, and worldviews.

It is the sum of an individual's reality-anchors that produces his or her mind-set orientations, which, in turn, group people into closed-circuit mind-set collectives. We all realize that we have values, viewpoints, beliefs, and so forth, but we do not always realize why we have those that we do. Our beliefs, viewpoints, and worldviews (which mitigate our perceptions of all things, including the future) are extensions of values to which we have become either positively or negatively adapted.

We seek out, identify with, and support what we *perceive* to be positive values. We avoid, do not identify with, and do not support what we *perceive* to be negative values. Our mind-dynamic juxtaposition between our positive-negative value perceptions governs not only our views of reality but how we unfold and develop within that reality. Existing *within* a perceived reality may be considerably different from existing within real reality. Our perceived realities may or may not correspond with real reality. This is a situation that can be very crucial to our lives and to the aspiring future-seer—so crucial, indeed, that it determines whether the aspiring future-seer will be able to take advantage even of his or her *own* spontaneous future-seeing episodes.

Understanding the nature and function of reality-anchors, then, is of extreme importance to the aspiring future-seer.

VALUE NORM ANCHOR-POINTS

Positive or negative values in their mind-dynamic sense are ener-gyinformation packages. The package is made up of a combination of fundamental anchor-points, from which has been derived the descriptive phrase of *value norm anchor-points*.

You may not be familiar with this phrase since it has not yet come into widespread usage. Our waking intellects are nestled within a cocoon of installed values, which serve as anchors for reality. It is *through* these that our perceptions of past-present-future reality are filtered to make what is perceived somehow fit into the context of the values comprising the cocoon. The value cocoons channel intellect capabilities into different value systems, which then turn out as different mind-sets.

All mind-sets form around and are *anchored* in a centralizing set of perceived positive and negative values, which, for the *resulting* mind-set involved, constitutes what it perceives as right or wrong norms. Intellects participating in given mind-sets are then condi-tioned to value these norms—and we thus arrive at the descriptive phrase *value norm anchor-points*. These, then, can accept or reject phenomena the mind-set encounters, in that value norm anchor-points are positively loaded (accept) or negatively loaded (reject).

Value norm anchor-points have a great deal to do with *how* mind-dynamic processes work and with the active or inactive outcomes of the processes. If the individual's mind-dynamic systems contain negatively loaded value norm anchor-points with regard to future-seeing phenomena, then it is quite likely that the individual's future-seeing processes will be inactive or dormant. In this sense, scientific testing should, in some objective way, be able to demonstrate that beliefs (as the *products* of value norm anchor-points) enhance or depress mind-dynamic performance.

Beginning in 1943 and for several years thereafter, parapsychol-ogist Gertrude Schmeidler conducted the "sheep/goats" test, the goal being to see if those who believed in ESP (the sheep) scored better in ESP tests than those who did not (the goats). The results of the testing showed that not only did believers tend to score better but the disbelievers often scored far below chance expectation. Dr.

Schmeidler's evidence was later confirmed by many other researchers.

In that beliefs are one of the outcomes of installed value norm anchor-points, the sheep/goat evidence establishes that positively loaded anchor-points enhance mind-dynamic processes (in this case, ESP processes) whereas negatively loaded ones depress them. Since the same would clearly be the case regarding future-seeing processes, it is well worth the time it takes to review in detail what is known about value norm anchor-points and what is called *anchored adaptation levels*.

The existence of such "anchors" was first theorized by the experimental psychologist Harry Helson in 1947 and further elaborated by Helson and others afterward. Anchors had a brief heyday in psychological research in the 1950s, during which it was determined that we become adapted to (thus anchored in) phenomena of our environments. For example, if we live in a noisy city, we adapt to the noise and literally make anchor-points that filter it out. If we live in a dangerous environment, we positively adapt our danger-sensing mechanisms, but if we live in a nonthreatening environment we deadapt from our danger-sensing mechanisms.

The early research regarding anchored adaptation levels concluded that an anchor could not be changed once it had become embedded in the individual's subliminal subconscious mind-dynamic systems. General psychological interest in anchors waned at this point.

However, anchors were encountered in another field of research, which began specializing in preconscious and subliminal processes— mind-dynamic processes that take place beneath consciousness and outside of volitional will and decision-making. A good working definition of *anchors* appeared in *Subliminal Perception: The Nature of a Controversy* (1971), by the subliminal perception researcher Norman Dixon. Generally speaking, conscious *and* subconscious judgments of a given individual are related to, and dependent upon, the pooled effects of prior experienced stimuli to which the individual has become adapted and thus anchored in (i.e., his or her adaptation level).

This somewhat unwieldy definition of anchors can be better

understood by example. Our adaptation level to the meaning of hot stoves locks in very fast, and our responses become automatic. If we are repeatedly exposed, say, to religious or scientific tenets we will adapt to them, too. More graphically, if we are exposed to ideas that "sex is dirty," "men are beasts," "money is the root of all evil," or "no one can see into the future," the chances are great that we will adapt to those "values" and become anchored in them.

Since anchored adaptation levels can be conceived of as ranging on a scale from ultranegative to ultrapositive, we can consider that negative and positive adaptation "levels" exist—and that like our responses to hot stoves, they have receded to some spontaneous mind-dynamic strata where they thereafter work on automatic pilot. The adaptation level is considered *anchored* to the degree that it is "solid" or inflexible. Certainly not all sex is dirty, nor are all men beasts, and so on.

Likewise, if mind-dynamic cocoons of value norms surrounding intellect are occupied with the-future-cannot-be-seen values, then the adaptation level to future-seeing phenomena and potentials will be negatively anchored.

A Working Definition of Value Norm Anchor-Points

The valuable phrase *value norm anchor-points* has been contributed by the joint work of the criminologist and subliminal researcher Eldon Taylor, and Charles McCusker, a psychologist in the Department of Education at the University of Utah. Both were researching value positions and value level adaptations accompanying social maladaptation with regard to criminals. But the wider implications of *value norm* anchor-points have since begun to be realized, since everyone possesses and functions within the influences of their own constructed values.

A working definition of value norm anchor-points has been outlined by Dr. Taylor in his book *Subliminal Learning: An Eclectic Approach* (1988): Value norm anchor-points are personally and culturally accepted positions between good and bad, right and wrong, and perceived success and failure. Such anchor points are also very sensitive to estimations of approval and rejection. To extend Taylor's definition a little, it is usual to find that once the value points have achieved the state of being anchored in an individual, their workings are not only maintained intellectually but subside beneath active consciousness, where they proceed to function automatically.

A person walking down the street is a collection of value norm anchor-points that are either negatively or positively loaded with regard to what the individual "considers" is bad/good, right/wrong, and so forth—and which, moreover, are probably working automatically. Experience teaches most of us, sooner or later, that extreme caution and diplomacy are needed to "deal" with collections of value norm anchor-points—and learning how to do so is part of the arts and crafts of pursuing life.

Speaking more technically here, value norm anchors appear to be related to state-dependent conditions. For example, adapting to a noisy environment is a state-dependent condition. Disadapting to your future-seeing powers in order to fit into a society that disbelieves in future-seeing is also a state-dependent condition. Behaviorists referred to this as "conditioning," an idea that permitted them to hypothesize that we are completely formed by our environments. There is some truth to this, of course, since conditioning results in state-dependent adaptations.

Value norm anchor-points exist on a scale from ultranegative to ultrapositive. They have one more characteristic that is pertinent to the context of this book, too: they also possess "acceptable margins," or tolerance levels.

Really polarized anchor points, of course, are very narrow when it comes to acceptable margins—as is the case with closed-circuit intellects. They can tolerate nothing save that which conforms exactly to the anchored values. When really polarized anchor-points manifest themselves in people, they are likely to yield extreme beliefs and behavior. Some other value norm anchor-points may have wider acceptable margins, which can manifest themselves as reasonable tolerance—down to and including mindless or indifferent tolerance in which no value margins are apparent at all. But generally, people resist such wide margins and fight to limit them somewhat. Few people exist who can accept everything.

Highly structured and polarized value norm anchor-points are far more common. For example, several years ago an important editor at *Time Magazine* told me that he would never believe in "psychic stuff," regardless of the evidence. If he had to, then everything he had believed and valued would be wrong.

REALITY-ANCHOR DEFENSE MECHANISMS

Whatever else they may be, the mind-dynamic systems of our intellects are *architecturalized.* They are constructed just like a building (we call the construction "learning") into the special forms and functions of that building. The essential building blocks of this architecturalization are mind-dynamic anchor-points, which themselves can be nothing other than particularized energyinformation packages.

Given the analogy of a building, it is understandable that the integrity and strength of the building cannot be maintained unless it is protected from energyinformation packages that would weaken it, possibly even cause it to collapse. Using the analogy of a computer, we can consider our mind-dynamic systems as consisting of designed programs, which can function harmoniously only if viruses are not introduced into them.

Embedded value norm anchor-points surround themselves with defense mechanisms. One of the greatest mysteries is how our mind-dynamic systems, either as architecturalized buildings or designed computer programs, can develop *defenses* to preserve their functional integrity. But that they do so is clearly beyond doubt—and will quickly be evident when you try to challenge anyone's architecturalized or programmed value norm anchor-points.

Some of the *perceptual defense mechanisms* of value norm anchor-points are quite well known, the word *perceptual* being necessary because anchor-points can literally perceive which energyinformation packages must be defended against or accepted.

Although modern psychologists have not attributed independent *thinking* to anchor-points or to their defense mechanisms, it is understood that they operate "automatically." But it is difficult to consider how, for example, perceptual defenses can defend without "deciding" to do so. Anchor-points also "decide" what fits with them and what does not. Any mindlike entity that "decides" is "thinking." In this sense, then, anchor-points and their perceptual defense mechanisms are minds-in-themselves.

Repression is a term psychologists use to indicate a mind-dynamic mechanism that involves the barring or censoring of experiences, memories, feelings, or perceptions with high anxiety-producing potentials. The apparent function of repression is to avoid dealing with "painful" elements of reality. The future may undoubtedly hold some future-painful episodes. The easiest way to avoid interacting with them is to repress future-seeing information altogether—a temporary measure, to be sure, for as we have seen in several examples, the actual episodes do manifest themselves.

Isolation is a mechanism involving the avoidance of perceiving or recalling linkages of related information that might contribute to anxiety—or as we might say, weaken the building or program. Isolation, as a defense, causes the mind-dynamic system to barricade itself emotionally and intellectually against any phenomena that would stir up anxiety. People who believe that the future cannot be seen are, of course, trying to isolate themselves in the certainties of past and present in order to avoid anxiety about the future unknown.

Fantasy formation is a mechanism by which intolerable realities are replaced by some fiction created by the mind-dynamic system. The fiction conveniently "explains" the realities to the system, which has itself created it. Fantasy formations may replace real realities altogether. Since many past predictions turned out to have been fantasies all along (for example, the many predictions in the early twentieth century that the entire world would be communist by the end of the century), we have to assume that fantasy formation defense mechanisms were at work in the "foreseers."

Denial is an anchor-point mechanism that defends the mind-dynamic system against having to deal with invading realities simply by "blinding" the system to them altogether. Denial imposes a mind-dynamic blackout. The idea that the future does not exist blacks out any cognitive access to the future or to parts of it.

Projection is a defense mechanism via which the installed value norm anchor-points attribute absolute correctness to themselves and project wrongness onto others. For example, the projective defense mechanism may believe it is correct *not* to perceive the future and project incorrectness onto those who do—sometimes burning them at the stake or socially degrading or persecuting them.

Why anchor-point defense mechanisms (which block access to real realities) exist in the first place is a great mystery to researchers. But one psychological theory regarding them holds that they exist to protect us psychologically from shocking or deeply traumatic materials or realities. This is certainly one of the known functions of perceptual defenses. But beneath that specialized function, it may be that they exist to protect an unbalanced mind-dynamic system *from its own internal conflicts* and are "developed" to hold in check radical impulses arising within the system itself.

In the psychic sense, but not in the biological one, such conflicts can arise only after positively or negatively loaded value norm anchor-points have become installed, since conflict is always and only a manifestation of stress between perceived right and perceived wrong. In this sense, the more highly defended a mind-dynamic system is, the more circuitlike it will be, and the more vulnerable and victimlike to the erosions of its own conflict and stress. Knowing, or finding out, what is really right and really wrong alleviates such stress and eliminates the systemic mind-dynamic need for perceptual defense mechanisms.

CORRECTING OUR REALITY-ANCHORS ON BEHALF OF FUTURE-SEEING

How, then, do we locate and deenergize reality-anchors and their associated perceptual defense mechanisms? Again, you must resort to image-building and introspection.

All the concepts in this chapter can be diagrammed or sketched. For example, locate a value or belief you would not change for the world. Draw a circle representing it. Then make two lists.

First, list reasons why you would not change the value or belief.

Number these ideas sequentially, and place each number inside small circles inside the large circle. These will represent your anchor-points.

Second, make another list of ways you would defend yourself against changing the value or belief. Number these, and place them in small circles around the outside of the larger circle. These will reveal your defense mechanisms, which "protect" the anchor-points against changing.

I've made many lists of my "unalterable" beliefs and "strong" convictions about future-seeing as I encountered them—and had the dubious reward of seeing the silliest lists possible. I then introspectively addressed each item on the list as if it were an independent thinking entity and asked where it came from or how it had formed. Having done so, I then experienced a memory-dump—a cascade of memory images. In this way, I found many "sources" for positive and negative reality–anchor-points. Among these, surprisingly, were telepathic transmissions from many unusual sources—which has led to the conclusion, already discussed, that social mind-sets can become anchored in us by some kind of telepathic osmosis (as will be discussed in chapter 13).

11

THE LINEAR TIME TRAP AND TIME-LOOPING

How time can be transcended is considered to be *the* major piece of the future-seeing mosaic, since most people (including myself) have believed that they have to transcend time in order to see into the future. I've not been able to discover when the influential and elegant metaphor "time transcendence" came into usage. But as a metaphor it is also a non sequitur, a fallacy. Getting beyond (transcending) time would actually mean leaving it behind or separating from it. This is *not* the goal of future-seers, and it refers more to experiential states of "timeless bliss" or matters altogether beyond or outside of time.

THE TIME PROBLEM

Dictionaries define *time* as the measured or measurable period during which an action, process, or condition exists or continues. A twofold problem emerges if we hold to this as *the* definition of "time" in a mind-dynamic anchor-point way: first, the "during which" periods we can measure exist only in the present in which we are measuring them; and second, coming or about-to-happen events of the future do not yet exist in those present periods. This definition, then, is useless regarding future-seeing—if only because *other kinds of time* must exist if we are to account for spontaneous forms of future-seeing episodes.

The heart of the problem here is that we use only one word, *time*, to refer to different kinds of time. The best (if inadequate) historical review of different kinds of time is found in *The Encyclopedia of Philosophy,* edited by Paul Edwards (1967).

The *Encyclopedia* points up that we utilize metaphors to describe different kinds of time. The most common of these is thinking of time as a stream that flows and through which we advance. This is *motional time.* But another kind of time is *changing time,* in which we perceive that events are changing from the past, through the present, and into the future. There is a *being-in-the-past* kind of time, as well as *being-in-the-present* and *being-in-the-future* kinds of time. Two other kinds of time are seen as *passage-time* and *duration-time.* We also think of time via the verbal tenses we use: was, is, will be.

But all these kinds of time can be linked back to the definition of linear time in which what has, is, or will happen can be measured within the present *space* in which they are being measured. That present space is the Now, and we measure time backward and forward from the Now. The Now, however is a moving frame of reference against which we judge what was, what is *now*, and what will be. The Now is the space place we are in when we observe we are in a Now. In this sense, we have developed the notion that time is something that passes through space, and that space and time are different and separate. This notion also conveys the idea that time is a linear *continuum* "moving" in space.

The notion that the *linear time continuum* actually exists as a thing in itself gave rise to the enormously popular science-fiction idea of "time machines" that could "travel" backward and forward along the continuum. And most of us depend on this falsifying anchor-point metaphor when we try to imagine how to "get into" or access the future.

ESCAPING THE LINEAR MODEL OF TIME

The quickest mind-dynamic way to escape the linear model of time is not to analyze it in thoughts or words but simply to sketch or diagram it *and* all other kinds of time you can conceive of as being possible, such as time-duration, time-passage, and memory-time. Farther along in this chapter I've provided as figure 3 one of my models of linear time, which you might copy out to start stimulating your time image-building processes.

But the linear model of time *is* very pervasive. We can hardly think of time without falling back on it, because that particular model seems the most rational way of conceiving of time. The future-seer needs to account for this pervasiveness—account for why, when thinking about time, we always end up trapped in that model.

Although the *Encyclopedia* referred to above is otherwise excellent in its summary of time, it does not consider two important factors. First, it consistently discusses the various kinds of time as existing *outside* of the human mind. In fact, we *measure* our linear notions of time by what *is* out there. This leads to the notion that time is outside of us, or, conversely, that we are "in" it and moving along within the Now-Present part of the continuum in some kind of time-encapsulated way. That we have different kinds of time in our mind-dynamic processes is not mentioned. The only reference in the *Encyclopedia* to possible mind-involvement with time is a glancing statement regarding *intuition,* which "can understand time better than rational approaches can."

Second, the *Encyclopedia* was compiled in 1967, just before the period when breakthroughs regarding the left- and right-hemisphere functions of the brain were made. Because of these breakthroughs, it was understood that the left hemisphere processes information and thinks of things in *a sequential manner* that is identical to the linear time model. Putting thoughts into a linear sequence is one of the major functions of words and language. Indeed, if you took the preceding sentence, which is composed of sixteen linearized words, and jumbled up those words, your left-hemisphere intellect could not understand the sentence until it had relinearized them.

From the left hemisphere's point of view, then, the linear time model is *the only way* time can be cast into a sequential manner, which, in turn, is the only way the left hemisphere deals with information. Thus, when time is discussed or read about via *words* it takes on some kind of linearizing perspective because this is how the left hemisphere organizes information. Describing the problems of time *via words or word-thought sequential ideas* thus always returns us to the linear model of time.

In extreme contrast, the right hemisphere of the brain hardly ever linearizes anything. Rather, it thinks in "gestalts," that is, mind-dynamic pictorial configurations made up of many parts but so integrated as to constitute a functional unit *but from which a number of meanings can be derived.* This sounds very complicated. But in fact the average comic book is made up of pictures that are gestalts. We can look at the pictures and understand their *meanings* whether or not linearizing words are introduced into them. Indeed, comic books (and movies) are built upon the interplay between right- and left-hemisphere brain functions.

Western literature, however, is cast almost exclusively in words, and most information has to be sequentialized in order to accommodate the purposes of words. The overall result is that our left-hemisphere functions have become strengthened and dominant in this regard, whereas our picturizing, visualizing right-hemisphere functions are seldom utilized. When we intellectually employ left-hemisphere functions exclusively, we linearize everything, including concepts of time, and largely fail to pictorialize anything in gestalt kinds of ways.

No *future-seeing-functional* mind-dynamic escape from the linear time model is possible if you address the issues of time via sequentializing words alone. You can read what has been discussed above and understand it conceptually "in" your left hemisphere. But if functional future-seeing aptitudes are what you are seeking, left-hemisphere conceptualizing alone will not stimulate your time-transcending right-hemisphere capabilities.

The act of image-building the linear and other kinds of time models activates and strengthens the right-hemisphere mind-dynamic processes through which the different kinds of time can "work" without necessarily first becoming linearized. No words here can describe the subtle changes that will take place in your mind-dynamic systems if you do take the time to image-build.

Also, before you read on, you might diagram what has to happen regarding "time" in order for a spontaneous episode of future-seeing to take place. Hold this diagram aside in order to compare it with the discussions to follow. If you let it, your right hemisphere will illustrate something very interesting.

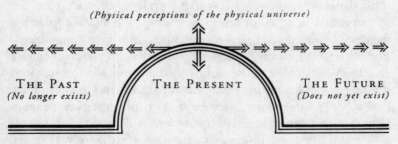

(Physical perceptions of the physical universe)

THE PAST
(No longer exists)

THE PRESENT

THE FUTURE
(Does not yet exist)

*The linear model of time identifies time
exclusively by physical perceptions
of the physical universe.*

TIME CIRCULARITY AND TIME-LOOPING

Linear models of time run into a great deal of trouble when, if you consider them carefully, it can be seen that the actions or processes of *remembering* and *anticipating* are *not* linear. The best way of describing what happens regarding memory is that we retrieve-loop it "up" into our present, and with regard to anticipating we foresee-loop "back" into our present. *Anticipating* is clearly a matter of future-seeing, no matter in what form it occurs or by what methods it is stimulated or undertaken.

The actions of remembering and anticipating cannot be diagrammed with straight lines in the way the linear time model can. And if you take a pencil and paper, remember something, and sketch out what you feel happened as you did so, you will arrive at something like a circular loop.

And in fact, at the greater level of universal matters, *nothing* is exactly linear to the degree that there exist continuous and infinite straight lines of anything. Everything we know of tends to be *circular* in some way—be it human thought, life cycles, a planet, a solar system, a star, a galaxy, and so forth. Linearity, then, is a fabrication of human intellect anchored in the sequentializing processes of the left hemisphere.

THE CURVED NATURE OF TIME

New discoveries of the "curved" nature of time have inspired some physicists to say that at some point we could meet ourselves coming into the past. Once we step out of our fabricated linear time framework, we can begin to learn to recognize that *different kinds of time exist.*

Our biopsychic senses register all that we perceive. But they do not linearize. Rather, they perceive within a circular frame of reference. We physically perceive what is *around* us and *encapsulated* within it. But this encapsulation is, in turn, further encapsulated within what we cannot physically perceive, at which point our psychic perceptions take over. Theoretically, this encapsulating can get sequentially larger and larger until it reaches the boundaries of the entire universe (if those boundaries actually exist).

It is, however, difficult to separate space from the time inherent in it, as Albert Einstein theorized. It was because of this that he and other physicists began referring to a "space-time continuum." The Einstein "continuum" was mistakenly thought by many to mean "linear." But it actually meant the inseparability of time/space and their combined continuous nature. The popular understanding of "continuum" was taken to mean "linearity," which matches the idea that time was linear.

The new advances in understanding what time may be are neatly summarized in Stephen W. Hawking's best-selling book *A Brief History of Time* (1988). In addition to being an excellent history of progressive knowledge in astrophysics, Hawking leads the reader into the "paradoxes" of what should be called *real* time. He establishes very clearly that time is not what we once thought it was— that is, the moment that appears on our clocks, our calendars, and in our Now.

Dr. Hawkings shows that real time consists of multiple dimensional continuua (perhaps as many as eleven). These dimensions overlap and intersect, and "trade" information packages between them. Here we begin to recognize some of the phenomena of future-seeing, which has led many theoretical physicists implicitly to assume that "seeing" the future *is* possible.

In these multidimensions, real time can be seen to "act" in different ways: to flow backward as well as forward, to bend and curve, to cross itself with arrowlike pathways, loop, spin within itself, have anti- and prodirections and inverse and obverse qualities, reflect itself, and so forth—anything but linear.

And if real time is *not* linear, we can finally arrive at the single most important clue that substantiates why spontaneous episodes of future-seeing occur and why conscious control of our indwelling NostraFacs is possible.

The clue is this: if the human species has evolved within a real-time universe, then our very biopsychic nature must "contain" real time–sensing factors. It is completely illogical to conceive that we have evolved completely independently of real time, which characterizes everything else. If we begin to understand things this way, our goal becomes not so much a matter of learning how to *transcend* time as of identifying and learning how to work with our natural real-time mind-dynamic constituents, which permit us to flow with, loop, arch, and go backward or forward along with time's versatile ways. Our memory works this way, literally loop-linking segments of the past with our Now intellect. One of the very few statements many acknowledged seers have agreed upon is that they do *not* transcend time—merely themselves (i.e., their intellect anchor-points).

With regard to this *new* goal, it then becomes important to discover even *one* human time-transcending attribute that exists *outside* the linear-time framework.

TIME-LOOPING

In his book *Four-Dimensional Vistas* (1916), Claude Bragdon (the philosopher of "higher-dimensional existence") used an unfamiliar term, *time-looping*, with regard to his discussions on time-transcending. When I read this book, I had arrived at a particular point in my thinking about future-seeing: that only the existence of a natural Nostradamus Factor in the human species could explain why so many experience spontaneous future sightings. But how this factor actually functioned remained a complete mystery.

My first approach to resolving this issue focused on the ancient past, because *all* ancient "pagan" cultures possessed seers, sibyls, shamans, and oracles—that is, developed future-seers. The ancients must have known of the existence of what I am calling the Nostradamus Factor, which could be "plugged into" for information. But because so much pagan history had been deliberately destroyed, I could not find very much evidence that suggested any methodological development of any human capability in this regard.

This historical search happened to coincide with my own difficulties in understanding what time was and was not. In my frustrations, I finally decided to look up *time* in the dictionary. In doing so I happened upon something that surely gives a clue to the fact that the ancients *did* understand the existence of the future-seeing mind—and, furthermore, added scope to Claude Bragdon's term *time-looping*.

It was quite surprising to discover that our word *time* derives from an Old Teutonic word, *tyme*, which *did not* in its first instance refer to chronological linear time but to a "root which could stretch and extend itself." The concept of this self-stretching, extending root was obviously applied to describe human mind-dynamic processes that the pre-ancients and ancients apparently understood could do likewise. This concept of time has been preserved best in shamanistic traditions and in American Indian lore as well.

On the other hand, our linearizing "time" appears to have been taken from *tyde*—or "tide"—obviously used to describe the repeating ocean tides and the measured events between them, such as the position and phases of the moon.

However, both *tyme* and *tyde* are established upon the root-word *ty* or *ti*, which meant "to extend and to expand."

It was almost shocking to learn that not one but *two* concept-definitions of time had once existed:

1. a chronometric one (*tyde*) that "clocked" phenomena observable outside human organisms but to which many inner biological and psychological phenomena responded as well; and

2. a nonchronometric one (*tyme*) that obviously pertains to the capabilities of seers, shamans, and sibyls. These capabilities "stretch and expand-extend" like roots, and indeed the "root" that goes deep is an ancient metaphor for linking into the deep structures of our other minds.

From *ti* or *ty* have also been derived our words *arch* or *loop*, as found in the concept "to tie." These ancient definitions bring us eerily close to the postmodern idea in New Physics that time possesses "loops" and "arches" that interconnect and tie phenomena in ways that defy *linear* chronometric measurement.

It must be taken for granted, I think, that our ancient and prehistoric predecessors were better at observing and acknowledging human mind-dynamic phenomena than we are today, with all our standards and mechanisms against which we judge, *not observe,* our behavior. It is almost impossible for us to conceive of a lost age of awareness in which one idea of time referred only to measurement of physical phenomena and a second idea of time referred to what went on inside our many levels of consciousness in rootlike extending-stretching-arching-looping ways.

The mind-dynamic association of these "inside" capabilities with "root" is obvious. Roots go *deep* and beneath—but are also that upon which the "above" is founded and given sustenance—and, more pointedly, *will be* founded. The ancient mind-dynamic metaphor, then, is exact and obviously refers to what we today call the subconscious and the deep structures I have emphasized herein.

We must now note the following: physicists today are in the process of demonstrating that time is curved and circular, extending and contracting, curved, looped, and so on. From this they are postulating that there is no reason that the future cannot be seen thereby. These developments actually begin to bring our understanding into the proximity of the ancient usage of *ti,* the human, deep-mind, rootlike function that can also extend, contract, curve, loop, and more.

Assuming our future-seeing mind loops into multidimensional time continuua, what kind of information packages does it loop-link into?

REAL TIME AS MEANING—NOT AS MEASURING OR COUNTING

If there exists a real kind of time that expands and extends (and can probably also contract), and within whose expanding, stretching, and contracting we exist, then we have to search for a mind-dynamic function in ourselves that can do likewise and that *produces information.* It is important to consider this because conceivably we might stretch-expand into time and not know it unless we arrive back, so to speak, with ultimately verifiable information.

Our biological nature *is* operating along a linear timeline, along the birth-to-death one. But there is an aspect of ourselves that clearly utilizes processes that are not linear time–like and that also extend and expand (and contract). This aspect consists of our abilities *to perceive meanings*. This is the precise definition of our introspective (psychic) life, within which we consider the *meaning* of things.

The perceived meaning of things expands and extends the overall functioning of our mind-dynamic systems and literally does so in ways that can be described as rootlike. Little else about us can do this. Even our capacities for reason and logic are totally dependent on our capability to perceive meanings. The failure to perceive meanings *limits* reason and logic and thus the scope and functions of intellect. The failure to perceive meanings also has something to do with how our value-meaning anchor-points are architecturalized.

Our perception of things as things does not do much to establish their *meaningful relationships to other things*. It can even be said that true realities can be established only by perceiving the relationship-meaning between things. In this roundabout way, we arrive back at the original Latin definition of *intellectus* (perception of relationships) and *intuitus* (perception of meanings).

Intellectus-intuitus, then, loop-links things together—simply because meaning exists *between* things, whereas a thing in itself can have no real meaning of its own. This is a very important realization in the context of future-seeing, because once we can perceive the meanings that interconnect things, we can almost automatically intuit the future (and past) implicit in the meanings.

Most people, for example, have been made aware of the ozone hole, which, if it continues to enlarge, will no longer block harmful, cancer-causing ultraviolet radiations from the sun. The ozone hole has come about because of increases of industrial atmospheric pollutants that destroy ozone molecules.

Take a piece of paper and write out "ozone hole" on the left and "industrial atmospheric pollutants" on the right. Consider the possible meanings of the two combined.

Now, between the two, write down the year 2010. Then take your pencil and draw loops that link "ozone hole," "industrial atmospheric pollutants," and "2010" together. You must physically draw this out. Otherwise your right hemisphere will not be stimulated into image-building functioning. Now, watch the mind-pictures forming "in your head."

Three separate meanings have been looped together in this illustrative process (which can involve two or more meaning-topics, regardless of what they are). You may not believe what you are "seeing" (a matter for your anchor-points to sort out), and you will have to wait until 2010 to find out if your mind-images were correct ones. But if you attempt this diagramming, loop-linking process enough times, you will begin to sense your *psychic* future-seeing "roots" stretching, extending, and expanding. And many individuals will become more able to "intuit" something of the future by utilizing the meaning–image-building process.

There is no further way to discuss time-looping in words alone, and only the act of sketching and diagramming will make the issues clearer.

With all the *inner* pieces of the future-seeing mosaic that have been discussed in this book so far, we are now in position to summarize them via the "laws" of future-seeing.

12

THE LAWS OF FUTURE-SEEING

As Albert Einstein observed, God does not play with dice—meaning that the universe is not held together by chance. And if the universe is not held together by chance, then the changes going on in it do not proceed by chance, either. Everything that is and that changes must be governed by laws, even though humans do not know what all of them are.

If everything is governed by some kind of laws, then future-seeing itself proceeds by specific laws that are applicable to the mind-dynamic processes by which time is looped and future events foreseen. We know of three kinds of laws: fundamental laws that govern the existence of things, process laws that govern why and how things change, and moral laws that humans establish to govern their social behavior.

The first two kinds of laws are natural ones. But the third kind arise from human mind-sets and can, in a certain sense, be considered artificial—because we can change them, whereas the first two kinds of laws cannot be changed. We can only learn how to *work with or among them*.

FUNDAMENTAL LAWS OF FUTURE-SEEING

In my opinion, the foundation for a working set of NostraFac laws should begin with either of two *observations*, which are interchangeable. My preference is as follows.

NostraFac Law 1

THE FUTURE ALWAYS FORESHADOWS ITSELF. This is debatable, of course, depending on the mind-set you are part of, who you are, what you believe, and your powers of observation. But historians are very good when it comes to "discovering" foreshadowing when they "autopsy" history in retrospect.

NostraFac Law 2

FUTURE EVENTS ARE FORESHADOWED VIA SPONTANE-OUS NostraFac EXPERIENCES. Whether you agree with this depends frankly upon the educational contexts that have formed your intellect reality-points and their powers of observation.

If these two laws are acknowledged, then they lead directly to the third law, which involves the element we call "time" and needs to be given some kind of priority consideration.

NostraFac Law 3

DIFFERENT KINDS OF TIME MUST EXIST. Whatever individual attitudes and beliefs may hold in this regard, this law must be taken as demonstrated since advancing physics and astrophysics have already established the high probability that different kinds of time *do* exist. And if different kinds of time do exist, then as bio-psychic life-units we must somehow be naturally incorporated into them. Thus, if not by direct observation, the fourth law can be deduced by implication.

NostraFac Law 4

ALL LIFE-UNITS EXIST WITHIN A SPECTRUM OF DIFFER-ENT TIME REFERENCES. In this case, "life-unit" is taken to mean anything with form, or a self-integrity context, whether or not we can perceive that form with our delimited powers of perception. The first definition of "form" given in most dictionaries is "the shape and structure of something as distinguished from its material"—which is to say, from its matter. Thus, this definition has led many to assume that even our thoughts have form, since they have shape and structure even though those are quite intangible when compared to material shapes and structures.

In any event, the "time" of our physical bodies is, as we know, quite different from the "time" of our thoughts, and so the concept that different kinds of time exist is quite credible. Since by observation NostraFac experience must be based in capacities that loop a future event into the context of the present time, we are therefore obliged to assume that different kinds of time must exist. This line of thought leads directly to the next law.

NostraFac Law 5

IF ALL LIFE-UNITS EXIST WITHIN DIFFERENT TIME REFERENCES, THEN THEY MUST POSSESS MONITORING SYSTEMS RELEVANT TO THOSE DIFFERENT REFERENCES. This law is practically self-explanatory. But one factor bears reiterating. If we did not possess a system that is occupied with monitoring the kind of time that is enfolding and unfolding the future, then we would never experience spontaneous forms of future-seeing. Since long-standing human experience demonstrates that we do have such experiences, then they must "arise" from somewhere: to wit, from within some kind of submind-system whose principal function is as indicated. If we assume the existence of an independent future-seeing mind involved with a different kind of time that enfolds and unfolds the future, then we can arrive at the next law.

NostraFac Law 6

THE INDEPENDENT FUTURE-SEEING MIND MUST POSSESS ITS OWN MODES OF PROCESSES, ITS OWN "LANGUAGE," ITS OWN REASON AND LOGIC, AND ITS OWN GOALS OR PURPOSES. These goals and purposes, to be sure, must be related to its principal function, which apparently is to be in tune or in harmony with the matters that it perceives—which are essentially aspect-events in the future that will involve the life-units. Furthermore, these goals or purposes *must* be anticipatory and

self-sustaining in nature, which is to say, creative rather than destructive. If this be the case, as can be shown, then we can arrive
at the next law.

NOSTRAFAC LAW 7

THE FUTURE-SEEING, SELF-SUSTAINING MIND "WISHES"
TO ENSURE THE SELF-SUSTAINING NATURE OF THE EN-
TIRE LIFE-UNIT OF WHICH IT IS A PART. Two observable
factors lead to estimating the accuracy of this premise. First, the
large majority of spontaneous future-seeing "warnings" are apparently designed to remove the life-unit or associated life-units from
harm's way. The fact that we have not learned the future-seeing
mind's "language" in no way detracts from the fact that its principal goal is to *interrupt* trends or activities that eventually will place
the organism in some kind of difficulty, especially of the terminal
kind.

But second, it is hard to conceive of a self-sustaining form of any
kind that is completely and irrevocably self-destructive, since being
so would automatically cancel self-sustaining goals. Indeed, we can
witness self-sustaining warnings even within those people who are
negatively anchored with regard to future-seeing.

Other fundamental laws may exist, but beyond this point we appear
to enter the realms of *process*, via which the future-seeing mind
interacts, or tries to interact, with other parts of mind-dynamic
systems or our entire biopsychic systems.

THE PROCESS LAWS OF FUTURE-SEEING

I am much indebted to Peter Lemesurier who, in his remarkable
book *The Armageddon Script: Prophecy in Action* (1981), isolated
some of the process laws important to future-seeing. Those laws are
marked with an asterisk in what follows here.

NostraFac Law 8

THE FUTURE-SEEING MIND UTILIZES A "LANGUAGE" PECULIAR TO ITSELF BUT ON OCCASION ADAPTS THAT LANGUAGE TO CONFORM TO THE ONE USED BY OUR PRESENT-TIME REASON-LOGIC INTELLECTS. So far as I can tell, the future-seeing mind presents its information primarily in a pictorial or image-built way (and secondarly via gestaltlike feelings, hunches, or gut feelings). In a way this is unfortunate, for to comprehend its language we must learn to *decode* the images or feelings. We have become very inept at doing so, compared to the ancients, who had many achieved disciplines that permitted a fuller recognition of the future-seeing mind's "language."

Images constitute a *universal* form of language, as contemporary sign-makers have lately discovered. Images also are an archaic form of language. Psychologists, such as the eminent Carl G. Jung, have shown that the human species probably has possessed the same image-built archetype "vocabulary" since time immemorial. How the images are interpreted, though, has differed from mind-set to mind-set. Images also contain maximal meaning in minimal space and time and are universally recognizable to any human, unless they intend to portray abstract thinking. But then even *some* abstract images, if they are communal enough and not too highly specialized, are recognized for what they intend to portray.

Our deep-structure future-seeing minds must be very old, since it can be shown that they were widely operative at the beginning of our recorded history and presumably before that. The fact that the future-seeing mind is principally adapted to utilize this old, and proven, universal form of language does more than just suggest its immense antiquity, leading back into archaic and prehistoric times.

On the other hand, what we call our rational and logical intellects are formed as a result of relatively recent materials, primarily architecturalized around culturally fashionable value norm anchor-points. Here, we come to a very important point. If the future-seeing mind *did* opt to use *only* terms or images that arise out of current and fashionable anchor-points, then *meaning* would be jeopardized.

Thus, the future-seeing mind apparently opts to use images and feelings that relate to greater and more precise meanings, avoiding words or images that are too individualistic. If it did not do so, it would not be able to cause us to foresee the future at all. It would have to confine itself to the contexts and limits of individualistic value-meaning anchor-points. And, as has been shown, it is these that inhibit rather than enhance our "normal" powers of future-seeing.

NostraFac Law 9

THE FUTURE-SEEING MIND AND OUR OTHER MINDS DO NOT COINCIDE, ESPECIALLY AS REGARDS TIME VISTAS. This law is, I think, largely self-explanatory by now. But since it reflects a process law as well as a fundamental law, it should, in its process category, be remarked upon. We normally try to convert our impressions to coincide with the linear, moving timeline we use to set up our clocks and calendars. Since, by observation, the future-seeing mind can be seen as responding to some kind of universal "time" or "time-looping," we can expect process difficulties if we try, *as a first order of business,* to correlate future-seeing information exclusively in terms of the linear timeline.

*NostraFac Law 10

VALUE NORM ANCHOR-POINT INTERPRETATION IS INCOMPATIBLE WITH FUTURE-SEEING. Peter Lemesurier calls this the law of divided functions, and his point is well taken. We can certainly envision process difficulties if we try to interpret future-seeing information in the light of value norm anchor-points, which themselves *cannot* "see" beyond the limits and contexts that make them what they are. This kind of interpretation tends to make future-seen information incompatible with, for example, the anchored realities of closed-circuit intellects. Large chunks of meaning usually have to be lopped off to achieve compatibility, and the whole meat of the future-seeing information-set can be lost thereby.

If the value norm anchor-points could already foresee the events presented by the future-seeing mind, then there would be no reason for the future-seeing mind to intervene spontaneously. As it is, the future-seeing mind exclusively seeks to alert us to future factors whose essence and possibility lie *outside* the scope or expectations upon which our value norm anchor-points are focused. If we should try to reduce the future-seeing information into a form that fits only our *anchored expectations*, then we will have lost the most important ingredients of the seeings—to wit, their alerting us to what we do not and cannot expect via our rational and logical mind.

This one law explains why, in most cases, the future-seeing mind tries to deposit its information during some altered state in which the rational-logical mind is "down."

*NOSTRAFAC LAW 11

PRECONCEPTION AND FUTURE-SEEING DO NOT MIX. Lemesurier gives this as the law of prejudicial interference. His isolation of this law is identical to my own. Basically, it means that if we try to analyze future-seeing information in the light of our preconceptions, then we will experience process difficulties, usually obvious only after the fact.

The above two laws lead automatically to the next two.

*NOSTRAFAC LAW 12

THE MOST OBVIOUS INTERPRETATION IS LIKELY TO BE THE WRONG ONE. Again, Lemesurier and I agree. He states this law as the law of thwarted expectation, but I think this phrase, although elegant, confuses the issue a little. What is actually meant is that if we *interpret* a future-seeing information-set we are doing so within the realms of our "local realities." Since the future-seeing mind apparently wishes to let us know of some future event existing outside our local realities, then any interpretation derived from those local realities is likely to be wrong.

NostraFac Law 13

THE RATIONAL-LOGICAL MIND USUALLY REJECTS THE "INCREDIBLE." At this point we encounter mental phenomena based in our perceptual defense systems. That rational-logical minds possess *defenses* is well understood, and that those defenses are serious business is also known. But that these defenses are architecturalized from within given value-meaning anchor-points is not very widely realized. The "duty" of these defenses is to protect the *values* inherent in them, as has been discussed earlier.

The major point here is that what is deemed rationally and logically incredible will also be deemed as unreal. This phenomenology, then, represents the ultimate process difficulty with regard to future-seeing—for it tends to obliterate the work of the future-seeing mind in more ways than one.

NostraFac Law 14

WHEN REASON AND LOGIC ACCEPT FUTURE-SEEING, THEY TEND TO FACILITATE THE ARRIVAL OF FUTURE-SEEING INFORMATION INTO WAKING CONSCIOUSNESS. Obviously we are talking about *integration* here, or the intellect-bridge to the future-seeing mind. But we cannot talk of integration without also mentioning what is integrated with what. Intuitus-intellectus integrates with the deep-structure mind. The deep-structure future-seeing mind cannot integrate with intellect if there are barriers against realizing its existence.

Three additional laws also suggest themselves. But these seem to reflect mixes of fundamental and process principles.

NostraFac Law 15

VIRTUAL TIME IS PROBABLY ROOTLIKE IN NATURE, AND THE HUMAN BIOPSYCHIC LIFE-UNIT MUST CONTAIN A ROOTLIKE TIME-MONITORING SYSTEM THAT IS DIRECTLY LINKED TO VIRTUAL TIME. In the chapter dealing with time-looping, I have done my best to convey the existence in our deeper minds of rootlike time and also the existences of mind-dynamic systems that are compatible with it. True time, however, must also be variable time, and it exists only within or because of the relationships of given phenomena.

The perception of *relationships* extends our time-seeing capabilities, for in seeing-sensing relationships certain aspects of our consciousness can extend and enlarge into their meaning. Something like this was conveyed by the Latin *intellectus* and by the Old Teutonic term *ti*. Perceived relationships permit us to loop-link into their meanings, and our awarenesses are thus extended thereby. Perceived relationships also enable us to predict and forecast.

NostraFac Law 16

VIRTUAL TIME AND CYCLIC TIME ARE PROBABLY SYNONYMOUS. The new field of cycles study has established that events naturally time themselves on a recurring or repeating basis (as cycles, discussed in part two). We can compare the crests and troughs of cycles with our clock and calendar linear dating systems.

Again, we are in the presence of relationships of phenomena and not that of the phenomena themselves. Since cyclic time is variable, it closely resembles the variable relationship-aspects of what I have called *virtual* or *true time*. In any event, cyclic time and true time are loop-linked by relationships between phenomena.

NostraFac Law 17

VIRTUAL TIME, CYCLIC TIME, AND ASTROLOGIC TIME ARE PROBABLY SYNONYMOUS. At its most basic, astrology is the study of the relationship-meaning of cyclic recurrences that respond and interact with the cyclical and predictable motions of the planets and stars—which will be discussed in chapter 15.

Thus, the relationship-meaning of cyclic recurrences can be chronometrized by the motions of the planets and stars themselves. True time, as the timing of cyclical relationship-meanings, is therefore embedded in astrological time. The three are probably synonymous—as pertains to our solar system.

You can see that any intellect that has failed to encode reality-anchors concerning future-seeing's first seven fundamental laws probably possesses no reality basis regarding foreseeing impulses that originate from his or her future-seeing mind. But beyond that, failure to observe the process laws will derail anyone's attempts to see into the future. Instead, that future will be interpreted in contexts permissible only to existing reality-anchors.

Closed-circuit intellects, for example, can easily disregard any future-seeing impulse and end up "seeing" a fantasy formation that fits in with the preconceptions that characterize their mind-dynamic closed circuits—as we shall discuss in the next chapter. Some mindsets may never foresee at all, or if so, only by lucky chance. The reality-anchors of permanent optimists will deroute any impulses carrying future-negative information, and permanent pessimists will deroute impulses carrying future-positive information. Mind-sets that believe they possess *the* truth will repel any impulse information that suggests they do not, and those who want the future to turn out according to their desire will repel information that indicates otherwise. It is easy enough to see why so many failed predictions have come about.

You may want to study these laws very carefully and, as you do, inspect your own reality-anchors in light of them. The most productive way to integrate these laws is to diagram or sketch each of them, because image-building both renovates antagonistic anchor-points and helps strengthen overall image-building capacities.

You can experiment with future-seeing along the lines of these laws. Select a topic that interests you—the rate of increasing planetary pollution, for example. Use each of the laws to determine the relationship of your own reality-anchors to whatever topic you have selected. Undoubtedly you will feel some future-seeing impulse, but check it against each of the laws. When you feel mind-dynamic confusion or conflict of some kind, you may assume that the impulse has been generated from an artificial reality-anchor.

Eliminate that impulse as a possibility. If you experience an impulse that does not result in mind-dynamic confusion or conflict in the light of *each* of the seventeen laws of future-seeing, make the prediction (in writing) and then settle back to await the outcome. As your intellect-bridge builds in positive reality-anchors for each of these laws, you will come that much closer to correct future-seeing.

The remaining pieces of the future-seeing mosaic consist of *outer* phenomena, and inner future-seeing processes must achieve balance against them.

Beyond the future-seeing process laws, individuals may not possess adequate information about *what is* outside of them and thus not really understand how it *can, will, or will not change* into the future. Lack of adequate information about various outer matters constitutes one of the basic pitfalls for the aspiring future-seer. These outer phenomena are discussed as fully as possible throughout part two.

P A R T **TWO**

THE OUTER PHENOMENA OF THE

FUTURE-SEEING MOSAIC

The future always *foreshadows itself.*

Virtual time exists.
Our outer patterns of expectations can prevent us
from entering it.

13

TELEPATHIC OSMOSIS AND PATTERNS OF EXPECTATION: TWO PITFALLS OF FUTURE-SEEING

Future-seeing *and* predictions/forecasts are products that emanate from mind-dynamic processes. But they may not be the same product or equivalent to each other. If we hold that our innate future-seeing mind *does* perceive the future, then we have to account for why so many predictions and forecasts turn out wrong.

Mixups in our inner mind-dynamic systems can account for a lot of predictive error. It is easy enough to see that impulses originating in the future-seeing mind have to run a veritable gauntlet of mind-dynamic obstacles in order to arrive in waking intellect consciousness. The possibility of mind-dynamic error is very great, as the impulses are processed through the gauntlet.

Many of these error-possibilities can be avoided if the laws of future-seeing and time-looping processes are carefully observed. But even so, aspiring future-seers are apt to encounter two additional subtle pitfalls. And it is these that bridge our inner phenomena with phenomena outside of us and that have never been described.

The first of these is a peculiar telepathic osmosis that exists between the seer and the public.

The second has to do with the actual extent of the seer's knowledge with regard to what exists and how it changes. Both of these can cause seers' foreseeing systems to "crash"—without a clue as to why.

The Seer-Public Syndrome

The seer-public syndrome is an attribute of future-seeing that has never been described before. It is composed of three interlocking factors: first, the public is always interested in learning what the future holds and wants predictions; second, it looks to various kinds of future-seers to provide them; and third, the broad public wants the future to turn out well. To satisfy this want, future-seers are obliged to predict that it will; but certain sectors in society want success regarding their future and want the future of competitive or contrasting sectors to fail. Partisan future-seers emerge to satisfy these particular wants.

The "transmission" of these wants among the public, and from them to the seers who emerge to predict their fulfillment, is not obtained by straightforward communication. The public seldom goes to a foreseer and tells him or her what to predict. Like in many other areas of human interaction, implicit nuances are coded in many ways, and sensitive people simply "know" or "get the idea" of the right thing to do for their "customers."

Pessimistic foreseers predict on behalf of pessimestic sectors of the public; optimistic ones predict for the optimistic sectors. It is a well-known fact that pessimism and optimism are psychologically infectious through direct routes of communication and through psychic routes, although these are little understood. Thus, a form of telepathy envelops the need for want-gratification, which can encapsulate the public and their seers.

In this sense, then, various kinds of "telepathic osmosis" link future-seers and their publics via which both absorb the mind-dynamic expectations of each other. The existence of this telepathic osmosis can be identified by observing that the predictions of want-fulfilling seers are *valued*, and predictions of those who do not fulfill the want are *devalued*.

It can at least be said that the public *does not want* certain kinds of predictions. When this is the case, many future-seers will not make those kinds, even though they have no awareness that they are avoiding making them. Predictions that do not confirm public anticipation of the future are shunted into obscurity. Public interests usually do not want to foresee bad times ahead, while good-times-ahead predictions always have good currency. If future-seers are to engage the interests of the public, then the seers are more-or-less obliged to provide the predictions that will engage that interest.

In the sense just outlined, it can be said that public interest in or demand for predictions actually *causes* future-seers to emerge and that they *do* have a social role to play. It is this that explains why societies are never without future-seers (even though many skeptical attempts have been made to eradicate them) and why the predictions of so many of them flop when the real future does come about.

Briefly put, society *does* have expectations. I. F. Clarke, a professor at the University of Strathclyde, has compiled a history of these expectations in his revealing book *The Pattern of Expectation 1644–2001* (1979). He notes that one of the more obsessive preoccupations of any society is the search for the "true shape of things to come." This socially obsessive expecting gives rise to future-seers of all kinds—novelists, scientists, social planners, psychics, futurologists, and so on.

But, as Professor Clarke points out, a large part of these expectation patterns give rise only to a literature of fantasy and imaginative extremes—characterized, for example, by the prodigious "future-seeing" outputs of the noted authors Jules Verne and H. G. Wells. Very few social expectation patterns are ever fulfilled, at least in the ways they are anticipated. What expectation patterns and their allied future-seers do, though, is erect basic stereotypes about how the future will unfold in ways that confirm the expectations of the audiences of the present.

None of this is future-seeing in the true sense of foreseeing what really will happen. Nonetheless, this kind of "foreseeing" always looms large in the public mind, and many "seers" are summoned into predictive activity to help confirm the "truth," which is assumed to be inherent in the stereotyped expectations. The point being made here is that aspiring seers can, by telepathic entrainment, be part and parcel of this subtle but fantastic process. Their attempts to predict can be distorted accordingly, or fail altogether.

KNOWLEDGE-FAILURE DISTORTS FUTURE-SEEING

As we have seen, spontaneous future-seeing impulses can, in ways we call "psychic," deposit information into the intellect that transcends its knowledge limits. This has led to the assumption that "pure" psychic insight automatically and correctly can see the real future. The assumption is fortified by the fact that psychics occasionally do make correct predictions, the *details* of which transcend their knowledge limits. So, the assumption has led to the diligent search for *pure psychic insight*, which is imagined by many to be a thing-in-itself—a precise mind-dynamic power. A psychic, if he or she really is one, is supposed to be able to predict accurately what is to come.

However, if the whole predictive outputs of given psychics are analyzed, the ratio of their successes to their failures is very low. The successes achieve high visibility. But the failures sink into obscurity, and the assumption that pure psychic insight can foresee correctly is artificially maintained.

Careful analysis of correct and failed predictions shows that psychics are most successful when they have extensive knowledge about what they are predicting. The highest rate of failures is encountered when it is obvious, even in the predictions, that the psychic is pulling his or her foreseeing out of thin air.

The extent of psychics' knowledge therefore plays a significant role in predicting. This becomes entirely logical when we realize that even psychic information must be analyzed through intellect-processes that can be closed-circuited with regard to given areas of knowledge. Lack of overall knowledge therefore constitutes a significant future-seeing pitfall inherent in the future-seer him- or herself.

To illustrate this particular pitfall, in 1980 Joe Fisher (a feature writer in England) and Peter Commins (a Toronto industrial designer) published their book *Predictions,* which advertised that "The countdown to the year 2000 has begun" and that "*Predictions* tells us what to expect."

After assuring the reader that they were acclaimed and successful, the authors asked several of the "Modern Psychics" to look into the future and make predictions "especially for this book." Some dozens of forecasts by the modern psychics are given as chapter 7 of *Predictions,* and in this way readers in 1980 and onward were informed about "what to expect." For example: devastating volcanoes will change the face of the world between 1980 and 2000; some form of nuclear war will break out within ten years (1980–90); Quebec will secede from Canada no later than 1985; by 1987–88, airplanes will cross the Atlantic Ocean in less than twenty-five minutes; the United States will establish, by the early 1990s, a space station that will house several hundred people; by 1985, all the world's dictators will be either dead or hiding on obscure islands; the Japanese economy will break down between 1980 and 1984; ocean farming will become a most popular and profitable venture by 1986; and the next pope will be assassinated and cardinals will rule the Church until the papacy is no more in 1989.

The majority of predictions applied only to the 1980s, few being given for the 1990s. The combined success percentage for the 1980s predictions is very low (about .01 percent). One of the post-1989 predictions leads us "to expect" that a woman will be at the "head of world government between 1991 and 2000." This prediction may have flattered the telepathic-osmosis expectations of the feminist social sector. But very little real knowledge existed in 1979 that suggested that a world government would be in existence by 2000, or that a woman would head it. Such knowledge still does not exist as of 1993.

Only one of the "Modern Psychics" touched upon what might well prove to have been the major political event of the last two decades of the twentieth century. This psychic was asked to focus his psychic "eye" on the year 2000. Among other brief (and, as it has turned out, inaccurate) predictions, he mentioned in passing that the Soviet Union will "have to westernize to keep the masses happy" and that Russia will no longer "be red but more of a fine shade of pink."

This turned out to be a correct psychic prediction and, indeed, as of 1992 the pattern of expectation exists in the West that the former Soviet nations will "westernize." But if by that term it is meant that those nations will completely adopt Western free-market capitalism as their chief economic infrastructure, knowledge existing now may be interpreted as indicating otherwise.

None of the "Modern Psychics" made any mention of the onset or development of one of the most significant events that would come to figure greatly not only during the twenty-year period but in history: the emergence and deadly progress of AIDS.

The point I am making is not intended to hold the "Modern Psychics" up to ridicule but to show that they fell into the pitfalls of their own lack of knowledge. As professed psychic seers, they were *supposed* to make the kind of predictions they did. And they went ahead and made them—in the absence of what should have constituted their *first* role.

Before making predictions they should have first *understood* numerous knowledge frames of reference appropriate to what they predicted. As an example of what such understanding might be constituted, if for some reason the Vatican fell into the ocean, still the *mind-set contexts* of the Church would *not* "be no more" for a long time to come. Neither the pope nor the cardinals are *the* Catholic Church. They come and go. The Church is huge, dispersed throughout the world, and would reconstitute itself until such time as Catholic mind-sets were no more. Catholic *mind-set belief* is the Church, as it was in the past and will continue to be in the future. For Catholic belief to "be no more" would probably require five hundred years of deliberate effort on the part of those who set about by abject force to make it no more. The pitfall of understanding-failure is apparent in the prediction itself.

The pattern-of-expectation fear that nuclear war could occur was prevalent in 1980 (when the predictions being discussed were published). Many ostensible psychics flattered this particular telepathic osmosis by offering "hot" predictions that confirmed the public fear.

But a good grounding in international developments gave ample evidence that the world's superpowers *had realized* that nuclear conflict was mutually destructive—and all of them were backing away from it. This particular prediction reflects lack of knowledge in this area.

The prediction that by 1985 all the world's dictators would either be dead or in hiding is patently silly—if knowledge of human nature is considered. The prediction that the Japanese economy would break down between 1980 and 1984 reflected only American hope and expectations and was not in the least grounded in a knowledge of economic affairs. Not only did the Japanese economy not break down, it *grew* to ominous economic proportions. The prediction that ocean farming would become a most popular and profitable venture by 1986 reveals a complete lack of knowledge about costs of implementing such farming versus profits to be made from doing so.

Likewise, the prediction that in early 1990 the United States would have established a space station housing several hundred people was made in the complete absence of any knowledge regarding the formidable costs involved—which would presumably be more than the national debt for a hundred years to come. The prediction that by 1987–88 airplanes could cross the Atlantic Ocean in *less* than twenty-five minutes is surely a fantasy-figment—unless teleportation had been discovered, developed, and refined by those years, in which case airplanes would not be needed at all.

All these predictions, as well as 98 percent of the others published in *Predictions*, have two things in common. They do reflect telepathic-osmosis patterns of expectations *and* the lack of knowledge of existing factors inherent in the psychics who made them. They also run counter to several process laws of future-seeing—especially nos. 10, 11, and 12.

Here are two subtle pitfalls the aspiring future-seer can expect to encounter. The way around these pitfalls concerns the matter of future-seeing *feasibility*.

FUTURE-SEEING FEASIBILITY

There is little doubt that most of the predictions and forecasts published in *Predictions* could occur at some indecisive time in the future. But *when* they might occur is a matter of their feasibility.

It is the duty of the aspiring future-seer *in the present* to attempt to foresee beyond what is feasible in the not-yet-known future. But knowledge-feasibility has a central role that tempers and refines pure psychic insight. Certain things can happen because they are feasible. But certain things cannot happen because they are not feasible. In this sense, then, foreseeing breaks down into two categories—foreseeing the completely unknown and unexpected, and foreseeing the feasibility-unfeasibility change-potentials inherent in what already exists. In the latter case, only adequate knowledge will serve the foreseeing effort.

Observing the laws of future-seeing will aid aspiring future-seers in this respect. But noting the existence of patterns of expectation, telepathic osmosis, and lack of knowledge will serve the feasibility requirements of many predictions and forecasts. Where matters of feasibility are concerned, any aspiring future-seer who cannot show the feasibility grounds for making certain predictions about what already exists is quite likely to tote up a long list of failed foreseeings—which have, indeed, been pulled out of thin psychic air.

NostraFac alerts of the first three kinds are spontaneous, and many do not pay attention to them because they think the warnings refer to events that *are not feasible,* and even so would require unusual decisions and actions. Aspiring future-seers seeking conscious control of predicting, however, often do the reverse. They make predictions that refer to events that *are not feasible,* but many will respond to the predictions in unusual ways if they are published or talked about. The aspiring future-seer would want to make responsible predictions, and so feasibility and responsibility are somewhat linked. The line between them is sometimes very narrow.

Save for a few rare instances, the popular idea that psychics, for example, can automatically and correctly interpret what they foresee without the benefit of any feasibility-knowledge has not held up within the scope of my three-decades-long research. Indeed, feasibility studies enhance not only the capabilities of aspiring future-seers but also the accuracy of their predictions and forecasts. The limits of existing information may be encountered by aspiring future-seers, in which case they are obliged to predict beyond those limits. But existing knowledge cannot conflict per se with future-seeing and, in fact, will enhance and refine many predictions and forecasts.

Most people realize that patterns of expectations (with their psychically contagious peripheries of telepathic osmosis) do exist. And some even realize they are just so much hogwash. If you set about trying to identify these, you will find that your future-seeing reality-anchors will benefit. We know, for example, that political candidates may speak expectational hogwash and deliberately try to instill appropriate telepathic-osmosis beliefs in potential voters.

But your local environment (your home, lovers, job, recreational facilities, and so forth) is also possessed of telepathic osmosislike patterns of expections. In my experience, the effects of telepathic osmosis easily fade when they are identified. The truth of patterns of expectation must be judged against their feasibility. If you make lists of what you can identify as telepathic osmosis, rereading them every once in a while, your intellect will get the idea and begin to edit it out automatically. Your future-seeing mind will "feel" enhanced thereby.

The laws of future-seeing, knowledge of patterns of expectation, and the existence of telepathic osmosis proved to be of great benefit when I undertook to confirm the status of my own future-seeing efforts during the course of 1990. I have waited until this juncture to describe that effort and its results so that you could acquire the background better to understand the difficulties and hurdles that befall the lot of any aspiring future-seer. A description of that project now follows.

14

AN EXPERIMENT TO CONFIRM TIME-LOOPING

A fairly obvious and important question has emerged. Assuming that a future-seeing synthesis can be mind-dynamically constructed in an individual (such as myself), can he or she make conscious use of it actually to foresee the future or even *some* aspects of it?

If successful, that individual would be demonstrating NostraFac experiences of the fourth kind—intuitus-intellectus *controlled* future-seeing.

This was something I had to answer for myself. There is nothing like a successful prediction to get one thinking of the potentials of future-seeing hidden in us all. I had researched future-seeing since 1962 and by 1988 had arrived at the conclusions that form the text of this book. I had not, however, tested them.

But the success of the Berlin Wall forecast narrated in chapter 1 inspired me to mount the needed test. I decided to make the personal effort to align all my inner mind-dynamic systems, obey the laws of future-seeing, and acknowledge the existence of outer factors that might impinge. The result was a year-long foreseeing project. I called it the "American Prophecy Project"—which was actually an experiment to confirm time-looping.

THE AMERICAN PROPHECY PROJECT

The principal goal of the project was to combine with intuitus-intellectus *sensing* all predictive and forecasting techniques with which I had acquired some familiarity. Chief among these techniques were trend analysis, cycles analysis, and astrological analysis. The reason for integrating these with my intuitus-intellectus processes was very specific. The existence of *outer factors* is implicit in trends, cycles, and astrological correlations.

Trends, cycles, and astrological correlations all figure in the feasibility background for making predictions and forecasts, and all give some indication of how things are changing *into the future*, and so "change-routes" are implicit in them and they serve as a cognitive basis for information about outer keys that may otherwise be lacking in the future-seer.

Information about trends is available in the media on a daily basis and from numerous other sources for longer-term analysis. I depended almost exclusively on cycles projections published by the Foundation for the Study of Cycles, which was founded by Edward Dewey in 1941. The Foundation is the world's center for multidisciplinary cycle research and education. My familiarity with astrological correlations arises from my study of that subject beginning in 1962. Astrology is a difficult topic, but it is an undeniable outer key to successful future-seeing and will be discussed as such in the next chapter.

Since in a formal experimental sense it would not do to claim that "I had made thus-and-such a prediction" after the fact, I understood that I had to *publish* the predictions and forecasts in advance. No active premonitions registry existed with which I could register my experimental predictions. I developed a mailing list and began sending the predictions gratis to their surprised recipients. The dates on the predictions, plus the postmarks would attest to when the predictions were issued.

I soon had over five hundred requests to be on the mailing list. Two months into the project, I began mailing a monthly newsletter that summarized collections of forecasts, with updates on earlier ones. All copies of the published newsletters were registered with the Mandatory Deposit Requirements of the Library of Congress as ISSN number 1050-0537. The linear-time window of the project covered the thirteen-month period between November 1989 and December 1990.

The next question to be resolved in advance was how many

correct predictions were needed to constitute the project's success. The normal statistical approach used to gauge success is to average successes (the "hits") against the failures (the "misses"). The statistical method can be used to tabulate quantitative results, but the benefits of using it with regard to tabulating qualitative factors are very unsatisfactory.

The precise *goal* of the project defined the parameters for its success. The goal was to determine if the time barrier could be penetrated *at all* by using a multidisciplinary mix of inner and outer "penetrating time-looping techniques." In this sense, the only result necessary would be achieving as little as *one high-quality penetration* of the forecast date-timed type. Any additional successes would merely give additional support to the efficacy of the multidisciplinary mix.

Additionally, any successful prediction that could have been intellectually derived exclusively from trend or cycles analysis could not constitute the type of success being searched for within the scope of the project's goal. The success, then, had to be one that could not have been anticipated by any known means and to reveal an event so unusual that it fell outside of patterns of expectations and contrasted highly with existing knowledge. I therefore aimed at predicting only the completely unexpected and unanticipated in order to foresee a true time–penetrating event that defied all other explanations.

During the life of this one-year project, more than eighty predictions and forecasts were made. All were specific enough to be judged against subsequent media reports and other verifying sources. A selection of faulty and true penetrations of the time barrier may be offered as follows:

GEOPHYSICAL EVENTS. The project made an effort to forecast significant geophysical events, such as increases in earthquakes and volcanic eruptions. The success rate regarding these is quite low—indicating that there is something yet to be learned in this regard.

WEATHER ANOMALIES. The project forecast only one gross weather anomaly on November 15, 1989, specifying a period between March 19 and April 21, 1990, and indicating the likelihood of extremely unusual weather and extensive flooding. As it turned out, that period was noted for over two hundred tornadoes in the United States, accompanied by severe floods even in areas where flooding is rare. Forecasting weather was abandoned when it was understood that the chances of short-term weather anomalies are very high. Statistically, they can be expected at any time, thus taking this type of forecasting outside of the project's goal of predicting only the completely unexpected.

EXTRAORDINARY ECONOMIC CHANGES. One of the first efforts the project made in December 1989 was to consider and forecast general economic situations for the year 1990. The combination of multidisciplinary approaches utilized signaled a coming severe economic disruption. At the time, all leading economic indicators were good and continued growth was expected. I consulted with four economic predictors I know, who advised that I should not damage my project by predicting the onset of adverse economic circumstances during 1990.

In this case, I foresaw a significant economic downturn coming, but this foresight contrasted highly with economic patterns of expectation and with the buoyant telepathic osmosis of the world. Astrological correlations for 1990, though, clearly showed difficult economic times immediately ahead. Beginning in December 1989, I went ahead and published several forecasts that the United States was entering a recession and that its effects would be apparent by August 1990. The existence of the recession was not officially acknowledged until November 1990, though a backtracking of leading indicators revealed that it had begun in August. This was probably the project's most important and significant long-term forecast.

EXTRAORDINARY SOCIOPOLITICAL ACTIVITY.

Worldwide social disruptions. On December 7, 1989, the project forecast a sudden increase of social disruptions worldwide during a six-day period between December 21 and 26, 1989—disruptions that would take place contrary to international expectations that the world would settle into peaceful amity because of the collapse of communism. Among other notable events of social unrest that awakened during the forecasted period, 650,000 Yugoslavian workers staged a massive strike on December 20; the Lithuanian Communist Party revolted and declared itself independent of Moscow rule; and in India, Hindu-Muslim violence erupted leaving over one thousand dead. Violent social upheavals occurred in Sri Lanka between December 20 and 25 with large costs in lives, and Tigrean rebels in Ethiopia captured military bases and towns. A wave of letter-bombs was experienced in the United States, and the invasion of Panama took place on December 22.

Economic failure in Russia and the Soviet Union. Prior to March 1990, the economic outlook for Russia and the Soviet Union was riding high. The media were specifically stating that Russia's successful entrance into world affairs would take place quickly and positively. On February 7, 1990, the Kremlin had renounced the one-party system, and for this date the project constructed a new Russian horoscope, termed the *interim transition chart*, whose aspects would indicate the future of Russia until some time when it became officially reconstituted.

From this horoscope, and with other multidisciplinary factors, it was possible to predict a period in Russia notable for the fracturing—not consolidation—of the former Soviet Union. The project predicted excesses of all kinds, lack of control combined with over-optimism, unproductive draining away of otherwise worthwhile energies, sudden eruptions of social unrest, and the high probability of increases in diseases and starvation. After this multifaceted prediction was published in March 1990, the former Soviet Union descended into a state of virtual anarchy accompanied by endemic food shortages.

The resignation of Margaret Thatcher. During the life of the project, I kept hoping for at least one successful forecast whose outcome would be so unexpected as to be completely unthinkable, whose details would take it completely outside of any known trends or expectations. In working (during March 1990) with Mrs. Thatcher's natal horoscope and the active horoscope of Great Britain, it became apparent that she and England would undergo a sudden, important, negative change around the first week in December 1990. In March 1990, Margaret Thatcher was at the peak of her career as prime minister, the position she was expected to maintain for the foreseeable future.

I did not know what the negative situation would be, so I turned the problem over to my mind-dynamic intuitus-intellectus and went about other matters while awaiting it to cough up its answer. It coughed up an astonishing answer indeed, and in the project's April 1990 newsletter I published the forecast that around the first week of December 1990, Mrs. Thatcher would suddenly be asked to step down as prime minister to prevent the fall of the Conservative Party. The actual outcome: during the final days of November 1990, Mrs. Thatcher *was asked to step down to prevent the fall of the Conservative Party*—which she did, to the surprise of the whole world. This particular forecast, so rich in detail and its date-time window, constitutes a true time-looping and correct foreseeing of the unexpected and unanticipated.

SCIENTIFIC FORECASTS. The project did not undertake to foresee scientific development, since these usually are too closely related to trends already known. It did, however, make two quasi-scientific forecasts that came about inadvertently.

The emergence of a new disease cycle. In surveying various sets of recurring disease cycles of the past, it became apparent that at least three of these were in the process of peaking during the course of 1990–1995. In our medical times, *increases* of diseases seem unlikely, because most forms of them can be prevented or medically treated before they reach epidemic or endemic proportions. In April

1990, the project began forecasting the immediate upswing of diseases, increasing until at least 1995. The following month, the media began reporting on the completely unexpected upswings of tuberculosis, rabies, pulmonary pneumonia, syphilis, and the Plague—all diseases thought to be under control. Tuberculosis was generally thought to be eradicated in the Western Hemisphere.

Since then, cholera has made a vital upsurge in Latin America and in some sectors of the United States, including Florida and New Jersey. Significant flu epidemics were reported during 1990, continuing into 1991. A serious epidemiclike upsurge of measles is occurring sporadically. The Center for Disease Control in Atlanta has begun issuing advisories to clinics, hospitals, and doctors to be on the lookout for symptoms of the relevant diseases that may have fallen outside their clinical experience.

The Hubble Telescope. On April 16, 1990, a media representative requested that the project make a prediction regarding the Hubble Telescope, which was to be launched into space on April 24, 1990. Astrological correlations for the day and time of the launch indicated that it would result in partial failure, due to a complex of reasons including the interference of unscrupulous people, technological infighting, and errors in construction. The project issued a special bulletin to this effect.

The outcome of the launch was the failure of Hubble's most strategic functions, and later investigations reported that the failures were attributable to an unconscionable lack of organization and certain technological misrepresentations of contractors.

ECONOMIC INDICATORS AND THE DOW. The project made six attempts to forecast shifts of the Dow-Jones Industrial Average on specific days, far enough in advance to rule out trend analysis. All six forecasts were correct. The project also made attempts to predict trends of the economy embedded within the recession. The resulting data suffered from predictive "distortions," which can be accounted for by patterns of "recovery" expectations to which I was

not then immune, but which have been corrected—as will be discussed in the economic predictions ahead.

*FORECASTING THE FALL OF THE MODERN-CONTEMPO-
RARY ART MARKET.* The project forecast in December 1989 the
decline and failure of the modern-contemporary art market during
1990, and it did so in spite of the increasingly high prices such work
was pulling down at auctions. The failure of this market began in
mid-1990 and thereafter became more pronounced. *Art & Antiques*
(February 1991) refers to this failure as an auction-house
"bloodbath."

In summation, then, if not all the project's predictions and forecasts were "right on," a high number of them fell outside chance
expectation, defied trends and patterns of expectation, and escaped
from telepathic osmosis impingements. The areas of weakest predictions proved to be just those regarding which I had the least
knowledge of existing information. No one, for example, under-
stands exactly why earthquakes occur or why volcanoes become
active. And so this kind of information is also missing in my research
of those two phenomena.

15

CORRELATIVE ASTROLOGY AND FUTURE-SEEING

A great deal of confusion has characterized both the history of
astrology and different understandings about what it is. From

the recorded beginning of history up through the European Renaissance, astrology was paramount in shaping many human affairs. But Modern-Age mind-sets rejected it because no scientific basis existed that supported the fundamental claim of astrologers from time immemorial: that the distant planets affected terrestrial life and "caused" events. The planets were "too far away" to affect terrestrial affairs, and so there was no need to investigate astrology scientifically.

Among its supporters, though, astrology is called an "art" when an individual's natal horoscope is used to "read" his or her psychological and motivational profile, a "craft" when horoscopes are used to "divine" the future, and a "science" when it can be shown that planetary relationships repeat themselves, like cycles, and that phenomena on earth repeat themselves "in tune" with the planetary relationships.

Most people are familiar with "birth signs," especially their own—the birth signs being the twelve divisions of the zodiac beginning with Aries and ending with Pisces. The sun is "in" one of these signs at the birth of the individual, and he or she is supposed to manifest astrological characteristics and qualities attributed to the sign. This is called "sun-sign astrology," and when most people think of astrology, this is what they think it is. Since average astrological columns found in daily media draw attention only to sun-sign astrology, it seldom dawns even on scientists that the larger perspectives of astrology are a far different matter.

Since only these larger perspectives are meaningful to future-seeing, the basic elements of average astrology will not be discussed, save as they apply to future-seeing. (Several good books on basic astrological principles are recommended in the bibliography—especially those by practicing Jungian psychologist, Dr. Liz Greene, also an accomplished astrologer, who in her 1986 book *The Astrology of Fate* discusses the clinical uses of refined astrology.)

WHY ASTROLOGY EXISTS

One of the best ways to begin understanding astrology is to examine what people have historically hoped to use it for. In this light, it is important to note that astrological profiling for individuals began only during the mid-nineteenth century. Prior to that, and throughout history, astrology was principally used for one purpose: to help foresee *changes* in the future.

Change may be seen as random from our local viewpoints as individuals who are perhaps lost on the undulating surface of this great ocean. But if change were *random*, then absolute chaos would reign. Since this absolute chaos is nowhere visible in the nonlocal sense, we must assume that we live in a universe of ordered and patterned change. Hence, if the patterns can be identified, then the nature of change-impetus can be foreseen.

THE FUNDAMENTAL ELEMENTS OF ASTROLOGY

The study and predicting of change-impetus patterns constitutes the historical basis for astrology. The historian of astrology John Anthony West, in his informative book, *The Case for Astrology* (1991), which every potential future-seer will want to read, indicates that astrology is based on a simple, two-part premise: first, that correlations exist between celestial and terrestrial events; and second, that correspondences exist between the positions of the planets at birth and the human personality.

A third premise must be added, however: the correlations and correspondences range along a scale from destructive activity (disruptive) to constructive activity (calming); and once the correspondences and correlations are "set into motion" by their planetary counterparts, they then follow their mutual activity to their *predictable* outcomes.

"Celestial events," of course, refer to the planets in their moving relationships to the sun, moon, fixed stars, and other celestial bodies. If the three hypotheses are correct, and if the aspiring future-seer can identify the correlations and correspondences, then astrology becomes the great future-seeing workhorse that many of its past advocates have claimed. The accuracy of the three premises is evident to anyone who undertakes an in-depth study of the "queen of the predictive arts," as it is often called.

THE NEW ASTROLOGY

The fundamental scientific objection to astrology held that the planets could not have any effects on earthly phenomena because of the great distances involved, the absence of a "medium" through which the effects could be transmitted, and such effects would in any event be so small as to be negligible or nonexistent by the time they reached the earth. These arguments against astrology can prevail only to the degree that *they* are correct.

Thus, the case on behalf of future-seeing astrology rests completely on whether *any* celestial phenomena correlate with *any* changes on earth. And in this instance, the case on behalf of astrology begins to accumulate when one acknowledges that the moon and the sun are great chronometers of various earth changes and that phenomena on earth clearly correlate with them.

Both the moon and the sun exert physical tidal forces on the earth, and all life-forms on earth respond in some fashion to these and also to other more subtle moon-sun "inspired" changes.

ASTROLOGICAL "ATTRACTION" AND "REPULSION"

All traditional astrologers held that a universal principle of attraction and repulsion exists and is present in both living organisms and nonliving matter. This universal principle was generally referred to through the catchword *magnetism*, and it was held that this magnetism "occupied" the entire universe. It was the "attraction" of this magnetism that collected certain phenomena into their given forms, and it was the "repulsion" that accounted for maintaining the separation of them.

Any changes in this magnetism would also correlate with changes in the attraction-repulsion ratio or balances. It was held that the attraction-repulsion ratio or balances accounted for the given order and forms of all things and that changes or magnetic fluxes in the attraction-repulsion balances resulted in calming or disturbing effects.

In other words, it was assumed that all things not only were internally possessed of their own magnetic balances (which made them what they were) but that these internal balances could be altered by calming or disruptive fluxes that took place in the external greater magnetic whole. The tidal attractions of the moon and sun that affect the earth had to be admitted by modern scientists. But they departed from the traditional astrological premises by denying (ca. 1746) that magnetism was associated with living organisms. If living organisms did not possess magnetism, then, they were impervious to all changes in the calming or disruptive greater magnetic fluxing.

MAGNETISM

In modern times, the term *magnetism* came to be associated exclusively with magnets with their two north-south or attracting-repelling poles. And so when the term is used, most people think of two poles. But it is important to keep in mind that *magnetism* is simply a word or term and has no intrinsic meaning beyond how it is used. A brief but penetrating history regarding the history of magnetism and various forms of it has been given by Buryl Payne in his book *The Body Magnetic* (1990), to whom I am indebted for his easy-to-read clarity.

Implicit in the astrological premises was the concept that magnetism existed as a *universal principle*. It was viewed as a kind of "substance" that inhabited the entire universe, including the spaces between planets and stars. In contrast to this, one of the chief premises of the modern mechanistic sciences held that the spaces between the planets were "empty." This premise denied the existence between the planets of the astrologer's universal substance through which planetary effects could reach the earth and act to bring about either calming or disruptive effects.

During the 1940s, however, scientists began confirming that at least hydrogen molecules exist in the "empty" spaces between planets. Later, other kinds of particles, such as neutrinos and cosmic radiations, were found to be cascading through the formerly empty spaces. The existence of interplanetary and cosmic magnetic fields is now established, these roughly equivalent to the traditional astrologer's universal-substance principle within which attraction-repulsion takes place.

The case *against* astrology again became considerably weakened when it began to be confirmed (ca. 1930) that organic organisms *do possess integral magnetic fields* that are susceptible to various kinds of magnetic and electromagnetic changes external to them. As the Russian researcher A. S. Presman (one of the foremost scientists at Moscow University) indicated in his book *Electromagnetic Fields and Life* (1970), although the electromagnetic spectrum was once thought to have no influence on living systems, it has been confirmed that most of the external factors that have been implicated in the evolution of life are electromagnetic in nature.

One of the problems here, though, is that although we use the term *electromagnetic* as if it were one thing, no actual interdependent relationship between electricity and magnetism has been established. Magnetism (in various forms) and electrical phenomena are known to exist, and they have certain relationships. An electrical current can generate a magnetic field of a particular kind, but organisms also produce magnetic fields that are not electrical in nature, even though electrical currents applied to a biological organism can have dramatic calming or disruptive effects.

It has also been confirmed that other types of fields exist around the biological body that cannot conveniently be labeled either electric or magnetic but that indirectly are related to both of them. Biological organisms, then, possess intrinsic fields (called *biofields*) that interact with electrical, magnetic, and gravitational fields or forces.

The purpose of this discussion has been to show that all the fundamental scientific objections to astrology have been vanquished—not by astrologers but by progress in the sciences. The cutting edge of the new knowledge now holds that "subtle fields" occupy the entire universe and indeed act as some universal principle that interconnects all that is. These fields exist in some kinds of ratios or balances, and when these are "fluxed" by nonlocal celestial or local terrestrial magnetic events, the fluctuations propagate throughout the whole. The exact mechanisms that account for all this remain very much a mystery.

The planetary revolutions around our sun constitute an example of nonlocal magnetic events. Any planetary motions that calm or disturb the ratio of balances regarding the sun can be considered merely as astronomical effects in their physical sense. But when these effects in turn correlate with calming or disruptive effects among living organisms and nonliving matter on earth, the situation begins to fall within the nuances of astrology, whose purpose is to analyze and predict what the effects will be.

ASTROLOGICAL EFFECTS

Although a conjunction of Mars and Saturn will correlate (cause?) an increase of solar flares, from the physical point of view there is no easy explanation available why this conjunction should also correlate with sudden escalations in violence, warfare, and aggressiveness on earth. Astrology has never interested itself in how this can be but through the ages has only noted that the correlations do occur. And since they do they can be predicted if it is known in advance when Mars and Saturn will periodically conjoin.

The only feasible explanations are that planetary magnetisms do exist; that the planetary magnetisms of all the planets in our solar system are somehow interrelated; and that these interrelationships flux the ratio and balances of calm and disruption which then have correlative and corresponding results on the earth.

It is now completely accepted that earth possesses a geomagnetic field (sometimes referred to as the geoelectromagnetic field). This field is variable, like (as Buryl Payne describes) the surface of the sea, with little waves on top of bigger waves, with tides that come and go, and can be tranquil or stormy. The smallest changes in this field are called *micropulsations* and, as it turns out, are close in frequency to some brain rhythms. The largest of these changes are called *magnetic storms*. The geomagnetic field penetrates everywhere and extends out beyond the planet to some point that has yet not been mapped.

But practically the whole of earth's geomagnetic field on its surface has been mapped, and disrupting and calming fluxes in it are constantly taking place. Humans also possess a biofield that is embedded in earth's geomagnetic field. Changes in the latter bring about chemical and mind-dynamic (psychic) calming or disruptive effects.

A classic example of such magnetic effect-changes is when the sun erupts in sunspots or flares and an increase of solar plasma (composed of solar particles) then emerges from the sun. About eight hours later the "wind" of these particles begins colliding with earth's geomagnetic field, ultimately enveloping all of the earth. A magnetic storm is now occurring around earth, and within minutes the calm of the earth's field can be disrupted. Large voltage surges in telephone wires can occur. Radio reception disruptions can ensue, and computers and other sensitive equipment may malfunction.

The magnetic storm produces micropulsations, some of which are close in frequency to our brain rhythms. People may develop headaches, have insomnia, and begin demonstrating erratic behavior. At this point, the distinction between biological and psychic behavior becomes blurry, and in the worse cases someone may become aggressive or start a war. Planetary positions apparently trigger solar eruptions, which can in turn trigger changes in the human mind-dynamic systems, animals, and plants.

The sun, of course, has its own patterns of activity. But the planets revolve around it. These are held in their orbits by gravitational and magnetic circumstances that were once thought to be understood but are now known not to have been. Presumably, the planets have achieved their orbits within the sun's magnetic field, which exists outward to some indefinite point far in space. It is reasonable to assume that the sun's magnetic field is susceptible to the orbiting of the planets and that certain alignments (in astrology, certain aspects) of them "contribute" to calming or disruption of the solar body.

A number of studies have shown that these alignments or aspects correlate with an increase on earth of accidents, heart attacks, blood disease, and admissions to hospitals. The Crimean Medical Institute in the former USSR analyzed hospital records for thirty years. The study revealed that the highest frequencies of hospitalization due to schizophrenia coincided with geomagnetic fluctuations which in turn correlated with unusual solar activity. And this solar activity correlated with specific planetary positions.

That there are energetic interactions between earth phenomena and the motions of the planets and fixed stars has been confirmed many times, with regard not only to organic but to inorganic processes. The disruption of telephone lines and computers are just two inorganic examples. But various biochemical processes take place for better or worse depending on the position of the planets. The rotations of the planets, activity of the sun, and relationship of the planets to solar activity unquestionably affect colloids and precipitates, water, and the rates of other chemical interactions. It has now been proven statistically that the moon and solar activity affect albumen, the organic colloid that helps blood to clot.

THE ASTROLOGY OF CYCLES

The study of cycles has confirmed that all cyclic activity on earth occurs in tempo with specific kinds of *extraterrestrial* (read "astrological") phenomena. As has been confirmed by work at the Foundation for the Study of Cycles, epochs of peace and war coincide with particular planetary arrangements, as do weather patterns, including wet and drought cycles. Volcanic and earthquake activity increases and decreases in accord with particular planetary arrangements. Disease epidemics come similarly into existence, as do growth and decline cycles. Political and philosophical empires come and go in accord with planetary arrangements, and, believe it or not, certain planetary arrangements also coincide with changes in clothing fashions.

In other words, today we have several forms of neoastrology without designating them as such. Scientific advances that have revealed that the positions of the planets do correlate with phenomena on earth cannot and should not associate themselves with traditional astrology. These advances have been made under their own steam, and there is no real need to compare them with the astrological assumptions and presumptions handed down since antiquity.

ASTROLOGY AND TIME-LOOPING

Though one might say that nothing in the future can be perceived by any means, we *can* forecast with accuracy what the future motions of the planets will be. Since the positions and motions of the planets correlate with *meanings*, the feasible meanings of their future positions will be approximately, or exactly, similar to their meanings in the past.

In human terms, we know that if we can be certain of *one factor*, that certainty sets forth a series of meaning-deductions from which approximate-to-exact causes and effects can be further deduced.

For example, conjunctions of Jupiter and Saturn take place on a predictable schedule. Increases of upsets in economic factors have also repeatedly occurred in the past in "rhythm" with the past conjunctions. One of the "meanings" of the future conjunctions, then, is increases in economic upsets, whose feasibility can be deduced and anticipated with some confidence. With the future conjunction as a point of focus, NostraFac impressions can contribute specifics and details of the upsets.

It is at this point of understanding that astrology becomes the superlative foretelling methodology that has always been its precise claim in the past. The only fly in the astrological ointment is the human factor—for much depends on the astrologer and his or her capabilities, not only with regard to astrological expertise but also with an innumerable number of phenomena outside that expertise.

The "fly" obviously has much to do with the value norm anchor-points that architecturalize the realities of the given astrologer. He or she will *interpret* astrological meanings *through* his or her value norms—which is to say, through preconceptions, preformed expectations, beliefs, and limited or far-ranging viewpoints. It is because of this tendency that astrology is usually referred to as an "interpretative" science or art. But this simply means that the inexperienced astrologer will interpret a lot, whereas the more achieved astrologer will interpret less—which again places us within astrology's dilemma-aura of approximate-to-exact practice.

In any event, if the future placements of the planets "inspire" the intuitus-intellectus emergence of meaning patterns and thus inspire the emergence of specific meaning-phenomena that correlate or correspond with the same situation in the past, then *knowing* the future positions of the planets *loops time* for us—which is to say, a meaning-loop to the future comes into existence, from which approximate-to-exact deductions can follow.

For example, I can assure the non–astrologically informed reader that specific "alignments" between the two planets Mars and Saturn *always* correlate to the appearance of negative (destructive) phenomena on earth. Because of this, astrology's traditional lore has branded those two planets as "malevolent." Likewise, conjunctions of Jupiter and Saturn always correspond with certain kinds of economic indicators. We are referring to astrological change-patterning here, which manifests itself on earth as observable and confirmable cyclic activity.

Why any of this should be is, of course, a complete mystery—until it is realized that the universe is infused and interlinked with "energy." In this energy, patterns with what can be called destructive and constructive harmonics *must* exist, which leads rather naturally to the concepts of harmony and disharmony or, as it was termed during the Renaissance, the astrological "music of the spheres."

Thus, astrology can time-loop us with the future, and we can foresee calming or disruptive times ahead depending on which planetary configurations will take place. These astrological phenomena are *outside* of our inner mind-dynamic systems and thus consist of outer information that can contribute to future-seeing precision.

Astrological information needs to be compared to how given-state affairs will be at the time of the planetary aspects. We know that things in the Now are always in the process of changing into the future. Nothing ever really stays the same. And so things must change for better or worse into the future. Their future-seeking paths, so to speak, are what I have termed *change-routes*—collectively called the Furnace of the Future.

16

CHANGE-ROUTES INTO THE FURNACE OF THE FUTURE

*C*hange-route is a term I have adopted to facilitate intuitus-intellectus participation with the natural future-seeing potentials of our mind-dynamic systems. Basically, the term refers to the way things go *while* or *when* they are *in process of changing*. A change-route is also a *direction* along which energyinformation moves as it emanates from a "cause" and ultimately manifests itself as an "effect." What happens *between* the cause and the effect is change, and the direction in which that change goes into the future is its route. The type of energyinformation that flows along the route determines what the effect will become.

For example, we can conceive that the footpath or highway between two towns is the route between them. The first town, as cause, sent eggs and milk along the route to the second town, and the effects that transpired in the second town were positive. In this instance, the change-route had future-positive effects. Later, illicit drug centers formed in the first town, and soon the change-route was being utilized to send illicit drugs to the second town. Future-negative effects then occurred in the second town.

From the future-seer's point of view, only two basic kinds of energyinformation exist: those that produce future-positive out-comes (effects) and those that produce future-negative ones. A cause, by itself, often cannot be seen as either positive or negative at first, and effects by themselves are often misinterpreted either way. The reason for this confusion is very simple: we can perceive causes and effects *only in the present*. It is only by perceiving the change-routes that are emanating from them, changes that prefigure future outcomes, that we can foresee something of the future. The ability to sense or see change-routes is a very crucial one to aspiring future-seers.

To expand briefly on this theme, change is what links causes with their effects, or vice versa. Since we normally focus on causes and effects in the way we consider two poles that are apart, we tend to miss what exists between a cause and an effect. What happens *between* cause and effect is a transformation of some kind. But that term does not usually suggest the *way* or *route* via which the trans-formation takes place.

Most of us have been taught that we live in a cause-effect universe. But this is true only as regards our perceptions of the present, and most of our nomenclature has been evolved to identify things in the present. But actually, as many physicists have speculated, it may be more true that there are no exact causes and effects—only an endless, multileveled "ocean" of changes, some of which we intellectually conclude are "causes" and others of which are "ef-fects." In any event, causes result in effects, which themselves be-come causes that produce effects, and so on ad infinitum. In sort of a metaphysical way, effects-causes spawn each other and, since ancient times, this has given difficulty to determining what cause is.

A cause has traditionally been thought of as that which produces something and in terms of which what is produced (its effect) can be explained. But in all cases this appears to be only a relative distinction, because philosophers have taken for granted that no new something can be produced out of nothing, by a cause.

The most general idea of a cause, then, is that which produces, and thus accounts for, some change. And in modern times many scientists have insisted that as a concept, *a cause* is worthless. Many writers have noted that the word *cause* seldom occurs in the vocabulary of physicists. These otherwise tend to refer to "concomitant variation," "variable" or "invariable sequence," and so on—in other words, to chains or sequences of changes that appear to be relative to each other and that I have opted to call *change-routes*.

Locating and focusing on change-routes permits the future-seer to identify dynamic way–like development paths between what we call causes and effects. Such focusing permits time-looping, in that identifying change-routes permits a perceptual linking to both its "causes" and its "effects." This may be difficult to understand at first, but we often sense that something is going to change before we realize what the causes and the effects of the change are.

Sometimes change-routes can be perceived intuitively, or, if one's reality-anchors permit, by correct intellect judgment of what is happening in the present. But astrological techniques can enhance the process. As a case in point, we can review the horoscope of the late, great USSR. A nation, like an individual, has a "birth," and a horoscope can be erected for it. The USSR was formally "born" when Lenin's Bolshevik Revolution overthrew the Kerensky government on November 7, 1917, and declared Russia to be communist.

In the horoscope we find the planets, moon, and sun in relationships from which change-routes of the new communist government can be astrologically intuited. Saturn and the moon are in conjunction (in Leo), corresponding with extreme authoritarianism of the empire-making kind. The sun and Mercury are also in conjunction (at 14 and 16 degrees Scorpio, respectively). Astrologically speaking, the sun represents the new Union's lifeline, but in Scorpio together with Mercury, the life was to be secretive and capable of great cruelty. The change-routes into the future of these aspects were strong ones, but quite future-negative.

In the birth horoscope, the nefarious planet Pluto is seen at 21 degrees Cancer, which has a trine (benefic) aspect to Uranus, the planet that correlates to extreme changes and radical undertakings.

NATAL HOROSCOPE OF THE
UNION OF SOVIET SOCIALIST REPUBLICS

7 November 1917

KEY TO THE PLANETS

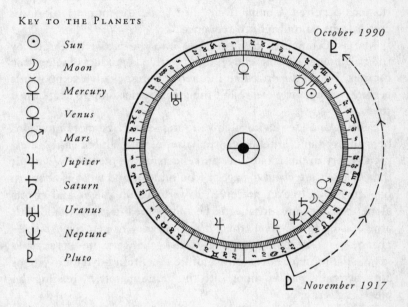

☉	Sun
☽	Moon
☿	Mercury
♀	Venus
♂	Mars
♃	Jupiter
♄	Saturn
♅	Uranus
♆	Neptune
♇	Pluto

October 1990

November 1917

NOTE: *Pluto was at 21 degrees of Cancer in November 1917.*
But by October 1990, it had moved in its orbit to where
it became conjunct to the Union's natal Sun and Mercury.
Pluto, the great disruptor and end-bringer, did its work
in this case. The Soviet Union fell.

The undertakings of the new communist state were to be radical,
secretive, and deadly, and these particular change-routes again indicated future-ngative consequences. Many astrologers predicted the
ominous change-route nature inherent in this horoscope, which, as
we now know, unfolded accordingly.

In astrological parlance, Pluto is the signifier of "death and rebirth." When that planet moves slowly along its orbit to a point where it reaches some significant aspect in a natal horoscope, change-route death and rebirth phenomena will occur. In the case of this national horoscope, in October 1989 Pluto reached the 14th degree of Scorpio, where the life-sun of the USSR resided in its natal horoscope. The expected and predictable death-rebirth phenomena occurred. Communism "died," and the former Union was cast into its painful rebirth sequence.

Marxist-communist change-routes into the future were seen by their adherents as completely future-positive, a product of telepathic osmosis. But in the end their inherent future-negative components became redundantly clear, and the great Soviet Empire abandoned them.

Sensing and identifying change-routes seem to be more functions of intuitus than of intellectus, the latter of which more easily interprets reality in terms of causes and effects in the present. We intuit that changes are *about to happen* (the future), and what is about to happen is hardly ever perceived if we focus on causes and effects alone. But if intuitus-intellectus become joined (as they should with any aspiring future-seer), then it is more easy to perceive: CAUSE–change-route–EFFECT–becoming–CAUSE–change-route–EFFECT and so on, ad infinitum. Any aspiring future-seer's mind-dynamic systems are practically *impelled* along into the future merely by reading the preceding sentence.

The major problem in identifying change-routes, however, is that none of them exist independently of others. To make this more clear, we might consider that *the future* is a gigantic superstructure of about-to-happens. Within this superstructure are layers upon layers of change-routes whose individual energyinformation packages meet and interface with those of others. It is always obvious that many changes can, will, or should take place. But many of these do not, which leaves us with the mystery of why they did not.

The reason why what can, will, or should happen (or happen in *anticipated* ways) does not come about is that for potential changes to become real *a number of change-route factors have to coalesce* in the superstructural future. When all the separate potential factors that are *party* to some supersystem change converge at a given point, only then does the real change get under way.

We can always intuit that things might change potentially. But often the energyinformation of these potentials seems to bleed away into nothing and the potentially real changes remain just that—potential. This probably accounts for why, as it is said, that the best-laid plans of mice and men oft go astray. The necessary change-route coalescing does not take place. *Whether* and *when* future-negative or future-positive change-routes will coalesce can be determined astrologically.

In this roundabout way, it can be seen that change-routes, when they do coalesce, can do so either in balancing or imbalancing ways. And it can be taken for granted that change-route imbalances are always future-negative until such time that balance can be restored.

Even though the entire change-route superstructure of what-is-about-to-happen might well resemble a gigantic and impenetrable labyrinth, it is nonetheless possible to isolate and describe certain specific types of change-routes. You will need to bear these in mind with regard to the predictions for the future that will follow.

What familiarity with the change-route labyrinth I have achieved confirms the existence of least seven different kinds of coalescing change-routes:

1. *Intervention-impact changes.* These are changes that humans have no control over and must adjust to their aftermaths when they occur. Many predictors focus on intervention impacts. Falling into this category of change are predictions referring to California sinking, a big comet hitting earth, the assassination of a president, or the sudden appearance of a new invention that redirects economic and cultural history. Trend-analysis cannot foresee intervention impacts, and neither can they be derived from cycles analyses.

2. *It WILL change because it CAN change.* Whatever can change probably will, since that is the way things seem to work. This is analogous to Murphy's Law, according to which what can go wrong probably will. Cycles analysts are getting

better and better at foreseeing these kinds of changes, since a large number of them are cyclically sensitive. Weather will change because it can change. Politics will change because it can change.

3. *What changes does so because it DOES.* Life cycles fall into this category, since they consist of a series of predetermined changes that take place automatically in stages throughout the cycles. There can be no avoiding of a does-change.

4. *What MUST change MUST change.* Circumstances that reach a specific point and can go no farther then *must change* since nothing in the universe can stay the same forever. The Soviet Union reached an astrological must-change point during the 1980s. The United States is quickly reaching must-change points with regard to its economy and social imbalances. There is no other option with regard to a must-change, save that it must change.

5. *Spirals of growth and decline.* This is analogous to "what goes up must come down." Since there appears to be no such thing as perpetual growth or perpetual decline, any activity will undergo growth and decline—often in cyclical fashion. Those transfixed on the illusion of perpetual growth do not make good future-seers.

6. *STOP and START change.* Simply speaking, certain things stop, while other things start. Sometimes what starts often replaces what has stopped. But sometimes what starts begins something new, for which no past precedent exists. Sometimes things stop even though there is no precedent for their doing so. Stop-start changes are very good at making the past detach from the future. The Industrial Revolution separated the medieval serfdom past from the industrial future—and started capitalism and wage slavery, two things that had never gotten a good start in that past. The evolution of computers started a new future, and with it the age of typewriters stopped and was detached from that future.

7. *Transitional changes.* A transitional change is the period between—for example, growth and decline, and what stops

and what starts. Transitional changes refer to what have been called *paradigm changes*—that is, when one set of realities, mind-sets, and telepathic-osmosis expectations is in process of being replaced by a new set. Some kind of reality revolution is involved in transitional changes. What was encoded as reality before is deconstructed, and transitions to new reality constructions take place. As of this writing, humanity and earth itself have entered a very big transitional epoch (the millennial transition, as will be described), during which the outdated past is about to give way to a new future, which is just now in the process of beginning to encode itself.

With the possible exception of some intervention-impact changes, all of the above change-types have astrological correlations within given limits. The competent astrologer can prefigure and predict change epochs, and sometimes even describe the near-exact nature of the changes. I have already established that astrology is a superior cycles-analysis and time-looping instrument.

All these types of change-routes can be located in the furnacelike superstructural future, and they serve as predictive "maps" for intern future-seers as they try to make their way into its labyrinth of change-routes. All the predictions to follow in this book have been drawn from my understanding of this furnace-labyrinth and its inherent kinds of change-routes.

All the preceding change-routes are lawlike, or quasi-lawlike, in nature, with the exception of intervention impacts. Intervention impacts may occur because of certain laws that it is beyond my ability to identify so far. But as it is, intervention impacts are experienced as "chance" occurrences that take place in the absence of comparative precedent that would allow a lawlike logic to be established for them. For example, comets may collide with earth, but we have no real way of establishing a database that might calculate lawlike comet collisions.

There is one more change-route process, however, which is absolutely a law—and an unforgiving, nonnegotiable, intractable one at that: this is the major, future-negative change-route law of diminishing returns. Any human failure to take note of this "heavy" law automatically results in suffering. I will discuss this law ahead in the context of the first prediction-set—the forthcoming failure of capitalism—since it is in this context that it can best be described.

If you can learn to identify quickly each kind of change-route discussed in the preceding, you may successfully predict for yourself that a lot of telepathic osmosis and patterns of expectations will fall away, ceasing to be the future-seeing obstacles they once were.

I used image-building methods to diagram all the change-routes discussed here. I also began to carry a small note pad around with me. I headed successive pages in accordance with each of the potential change-routes I've described. When I encountered a given situation that I realized must change for either the negative or the positive, I took some time to figure out which change-route pattern was most feasible for it and to figure out why. This is actually a very easy form of future-seeing practice, which has the additional value of adjusting reality-anchors.

For example, I studied the case of Leona Helmsley, who was on trial for tax evasion. Since the trial must have an outcome and must change-route into given about-to-happen directions, it fell into the what-changes-does-so-because-it-does category. The whole situation indicated that the law could not allow Mrs. Helmsley's case, so much in the public eye, to set a precedent for escaping punishment for tax evasion, regardless of her wealth or health or expensive lawyers.

This brought the matter into the what-must-change-must-change category, and since tax evasion of great magnitude fell into the must-stop category, Mrs. Helmsley's future became perceivable. She would be sentenced to a term in jail—which is what happened. If I had not studied the feasible change-routes, I might have fallen victim to the telepathic osmosis syndrome, which favored leniency for her.

Knowledge of change-routes alone increases consciously controlled future-seeing potentials about 75 percent.

17

THE ABOUT-TO-HAPPEN: ASHES-MAKING AND PHOENIX-MAKING

The future is usually defined in dictionaries as "the time to come." This definition may be convenient for lexicographers (who define words), academics (who teach the definitions), and all those who then suppose that the future *actually is* the time to come. And this definition may inspire future-seers to focus their intuitus-intellectus on "the time to come"—as I have seen many try to do.

But any aspiring future-seer whose mind-dynamic intuitus-intellectus is anchored in this definition will have difficulty in producing correct predictions except by mere coincidence.

From the future-seer's point of view, the definitional problem here is that "the time to come" does not fit with what takes place during a spontaneous future-seeing episode. Our Nostradamus Factor alerts us not to the time to come but to *what is about to happen*, whether this be sooner or later. And if we trace our term *future* back to its origin in the Latin *futurus*, we find that in Roman times it meant "that which is about to happen."

There is a considerable qualitative difference between "the time to come" and "what is about to happen." The former definition may be intellectually convenient, but it is infertile when compared to the latter, which arouses anticipation. Such arousal presumably triggers our biopsychic anticipatory systems, without which we might not stay alive more than a day or so. "The time to come" arouses no mind-dynamic links to anything other than our clocks or calendars. "What is about to happen" links us mind-dynamically to just that—what is about to happen.

And what is about to happen is *change*—either minute or great change, but always and only change. And with this more correct definition we encounter the aspiring future-seer's greatest stumbling block. For in going from the theoretical classroom (such as is represented by the first part of this book) into the open field of experimental predicting, any aspiring future-seer immediately has to begin dealing with something that cannot be encountered from the vistas of the classroom armchair—which is to say the Future, as the furnacelike realm of changes that are about to happen.

The meaning of this can best be made clear by analogy. Most of our achieved abilities and disciplines have been founded specifically to deal and work with phenomena that do not change very much. And so what was learned in the classroom can be applied directly to what will be encountered in the open field. For example, a surgeon can be certain that the organs on which he or she will operate will be the same organs that the surgeon studied in school. The methods and rules that an architect or bridge-builder studies in school will be applicable in the field at the sites where the structures are to be erected.

The future-seer has no such luck. Nothing in the future will stay the same as it was during the classroom period. We have become very good at learning how to deal with stable phenomena but have remained very inept at learning how to deal with changing realities along the change-routes of the future.

In attempting to enter into the change-route field of the future, the seer is obliged to enter into what amounts to changes taking place in a rolling tunnel. Further, this rolling tunnel will have subset tunnel networks going off in this or that change-route direction, some of which have dead ends, while new ones are opening up.

Whatever the ostensible future-seer has learned in the classroom has to be constantly recombined in various ways in order to even attempt to negotiate the *moving* labyrinthine networks of these tunnels. The labyrinthine, moving, super-megasystems of change that all together constitute what is about to happen are filled with potential and real changes, with coalescing and uncoalescing changes, with ends and beginnings, with maybes and certainties, with simple and complex changes, with what will and will not happen—and with things the ostensible future-seer might not even recognize because he or she possesses no personal mind-set anchor-points against which their meanings can be judged or even intuited.

The furnace of what is about to happen is the "place" where prices must be paid for past mistakes and miscalculations, the place where the new appears unexpectedly, the place where disparate forces coalesce, or where what has come together in the past breaks apart in the about-to-be.

However, certain general aspects of the about-to-be are predetermined by four universally preexisting conditions that any aspiring future-seer must consider:

1. specific growth and decline cycles will unfold (they are about to be in a preexisting sense);
2. from the astrological point of view, events and situations on earth will correspond to the future positions of the planets, and these correspondences will be constructive or destructive;
3. from the moment they are made in the human realms, mistakes and misthinking in the past-present are thence in the process of acting as causes that will have effects up the about-to-happen timeline: and
4. again in the human realm, correct thinking and decision-making likewise act as causes in process of bringing effects into existence up the about-to-happen timeline.

Human progress is never at a standstill. But human mistakes and misthinking are never at a standstill either. Astrological correlations are never at a standstill. And, as cycle researchers have begun to discover, those correlations are linked with specific cycles of growth-decline and constructiveness-destructiveness in nature and in the affairs of humans.

WHAT IS THE ABOUT-TO-HAPPEN?

The about-to-happen is the working field-reality into which the aspiring future-seer must go after leaving the theoretical classroom—

in the same way that ecologists, after their theoretical training, must eventually go out into working field-realities of ecological problems. As it is, in 1992 (as this book is being written) the immediate working field of future-seers is the *millennial transition epoch*. We have been impelled into this transition not only by our Christian calendar but also by certain situations arising out of the past whose change-routes signal that the future is going to be considerably different from what has happened before.

Certain unfamiliar terms are important in discussing and predicting the about-to-happen during the millennial transition.

THE MILLENNIAL TRANSITION EPOCH. This epoch encompasses the twenty-year chunk of time between 1991 and approximately 2010. It includes not only the end of the twentieth century and the onset of the twenty-first but also the end of the second millennium and the onset of the third. Such transitions are always susceptible to experiencing great change. For reasons that cannot really be explained, human psychology anticipates greater changes during such transitions more than at other times.

FUTURE-NEGATIVE. This term refers to situations and events that will change-route toward destructive outcomes that cannot be avoided or redirected into more propitious outcomes.

FUTURE-POSITIVE. This term refers to situations and events that either may have or can have creative-outcome change-routes if future-negative situations do not intervene.

FUTURE-ABSENT. This term refers to phenomena existing in the past and present but that will go out of existence (stop existing) in the future.

BIG CHANGES IN SHORT PERIODS OF TIME. This refers to

change-routes of a magnitude that produces large effects in short periods of time.

STOP-START CHANGES. This refers to change-routes that will either end or begin.

MIND-SET CHANGE-ROUTES. The sum changes of world-views, beliefs, and assumptions shared by sectors of society that preconfigure how, as a group, they see and interpret "realities" and that largely determine how, as a group, they respond to realities. It is a human right to form and participate in mind-set phenomena, but future-seers are obliged to discuss them in the light of their future-negative or future-positive nature.

CONTEXT. This term literally means "weaving together." In its literary sense, *context* is taken to mean the parts of a discourse that surround a word or passage and can throw light on its meaning. But changes and events are also surrounded by contexts that throw light on their meaning—and extend that meaning into prediction-rich potentials. Mind-sets are also formed within contexts, and, in a direct sense, when the contexts surrounding a mind-set disappear or are altered, so must the mind-set disappear or alter. The more precise meaning of a predicted event or change cannot really be established unless their surrounding feasibility contexts are also predictively considered.

HISTORICAL CONTINUITY. This concept in history studies holds that human history is, in time and duration, made up of an uninterrupted connection, succession, or union of developments and events. Broadly speaking, the theory of historical continuity presupposes that the future is built on the sum of the past and that the sum of this past extends into the future in evolutionary kinds of ways. The supposed evolution of human consciousness falls into this category, and in this case the historical continuity is usually seen in a continuous and positive evolutionary light. I do not debate the merits or flaws of the theory of historical continuity. But it may be pointed up that our supposed historical continuity is actually *not* continuous but rather can be broken by sudden starts and stops. These redirect historical contexts into change-route ways for which no past precedents have existed. The only thing that *is* continuous about our history has been our presence on earth.

SECURITY LIFELINES. *Security* refers to freedom from danger and from fear and anxiety and to the quality or state of being secure both in the given Now and, more importantly, with regard to future-positive certainties. The term *security lifelines* will be used with regard to several change-route contexts in the predictions that follow. But I will use the phrase predominantly in association with 1) the contexts in which the future of the working classes is being discussed and predicted, and 2) those in which the well-being of our planet earth is being discussed and predicted.

THE MILLENNIAL RENAISSANCE. *Renaissance* is taken to mean a point in human historical time during which a given continuity is supplanted by another in supercreative ways. A renaissance forms when new knowledge supplants old knowledge. At such a time, the historical continuity is broken. Specifically, the past is detached from the future, which is redirected into phenomena that cannot manifest themselves so long as the limits of the old knowledge prevailed. Implicit in any renaissance is the fact that old mind-sets oriented in the old knowledge become necrotic and future-negative. These must fail, retire, or simply die away through the laws of attrition and be replaced by mind-sets centralized in the new knowledge. In this book, the term *millennial renaissance* will be used to refer to the period between 1996 and 2008, during which new knowledge patterns will successively replace old ones.

All the preceding terms can be used by future-seers as points of intuitus-intellectus focus. For example, the intellect-concepts of future-negative and future-positive change-routes are particularly meaningful in considering certain situations, such as our ominous ecological problems. These two terms serve as time-looping factors that awaken anticipatory mechanisms dwelling within our Nostradamus Factors. To test this for yourself, you may wish to study the change-route feasibility of some particular ecological situation—or perhaps some situation more local to yourself.

Describe the situation as you intellectually see it. Compare that description to the process laws of future-seeing in order to locate reality-anchor interference. Eliminate this interference. Construct a new description. Again compare this to the process laws of future-seeing. Continue this process until either you realize that your knowledge of what is involved is insufficient (which can be corrected by gaining additional information) or you arrive at some about-to-happen certainty.

Remember to focus on what is *about to* happen, not upon what *is* happening. Change-route impulses will become clearer to you. If you perceive that the change-routes are future-negative, you will now have a chance to intervene. If they seem future-positive, you have a chance to support them. Compare your future-seeing conclusions to the telepathic osmosis that pervades outside of you. Your future-seeing failures are unimportant. Your successes are important. You will find that your Nostradamus Factor, through your mind-dynamic intuitus-intellectus processes, will help you.

THE ASHES OF THE PAST AND THE PHOENIX OF THE FUTURE

The metaphor *the furnace of the future* is, of course, a nice way of referring to that allegorical "place" where the past is consumed until only its ashes remain, from which the phoenix of the future is reborn.

Some periods of history have been very furnacelike, others very ashes-making (future-negative), and still others very phoenix-making (future-positive). The one aspect of the about-to-happen is that *change is never future-absent*. Change-routes of various kinds can be slow or fast. But the fact that change *will* take place is clearly the chief and most dependable feasiblility factor on the aspiring future-seer's worktable. And all changes-into-the-future can be predicted by first determining if they are ashes-making or phoenix-making.

In the general overview of the about-to-happen that future-seers must develop, *the ratio* of ashes-making processes to phoenix-making ones determines whether what is about to happen will generally be future-negative or future-positive. As a rule of thumb, short-term planning, policies, activities, objectives, and goals are usually ashes-making—due simply to the fact that the about-to-happen heads us into long-term changes.

Predictions based on short-term phenomena, then, may be correct in the short term but are very likely to become erroneous in the long term. Additionally, whether correctly predicted or not, short-term change-routes fulfill themselves before they can be redirected in keeping with the longer-term phenomena of the future's furnace. Conversely, if long-term change-routes are foreseen, the human plans, objectives, and so forth progressing into the future can be redirected or corrected in the face of what actually does happen.

Short-term objectives or foreseeing equate to Russian roulette so far as the future is concerned, since they indicate that long-term objectives or foreseeing will be future-absent. The about-to-happen, therefore, always comes as a "surprise" to short-term mind-sets. Living for the short-term Now or the near-Tomorrow is almost certainly ashes-making for the future.

Ashes-making and phoenix-making may begin in the inner mind-sets of humans, but inner mind-sets alone do not prefigure the about-to-happen. The prefiguring comes about as the result of *inner decisions set into outer activity*, as was discussed in chapter 6. The activity prefigures the future, and the activity always comprises outer phenomena for the future-seer. Once set into motion in the outer realms, the activity must then result in either future-positive or future-negative change-routes—simply because the activity *must result in something*. What then happens does so because it must.

Given all the future-seeing phenomena that have been discussed, if the aspiring future-seer can determine the prefiguring difference (or ratio) between ashes-making and phoenix-making phenomena, he or she *will be able* to foresee the future or at least significant aspects of it.

You can, for example, compile lists of activities in progress in the world about you. Determine if they are short-term or long-term activities in orienting scope. By general rule of thumb, assume the short-term to be ashes-making and the long-term to be phoenix-making. The coalescing trajectories of their respective change-routes will become visible to you. Your intuitus-intellectus processes will then "dump" their foresights, and you will be able to make predictions. Be sure to compare your predictions to the process laws of future-seeing in order to eliminate the possibility that your predictions have been unduly influenced by nonfuture-seeing reality-anchors.

At this point, it is necessary to make treks into predicting in order to demonstrate ashes-making and phoenix-making. You can compare your predictions with mine, remembering, of course, that I, too, am only an aspiring future-seer. Advance change-route signals of the millennial transition already identifiable indicate that the furnace of the future will be very hot indeed. The feasibility is very high that many powerful coalescing change-routes of ashes-making and phoenix-making will converge during the millennial transition.

18

MAJOR ECONOMIC CHANGE-ROUTES OF THE MILLENNIAL TRANSITION

On average, most people are interested in what will affect *them* in the immediate future, not in the long term. But what will happen during the millennial transition is important to most of us now, because those who are not past their sixty-fifth year by 1992 have the reasonable expectation of being alive in 2010 and will partake of the events and phenomena of those years.

The intervening millennial transition, then, will be what many of us have lived through, for better or worse, by the year 2010. The superstructure of the transition (or any future) consists of major change-routes along which and because of which what is about to happen *does* happen. Natural cycles of growth and decline mandated by astrological correlations are good examples of these.

For future-seers, a predictive key concerns foreseeing what superstructural conditions will be like around 2010 and having a "backward look" at how they came to what they are. In this sense, I foresee conditions that are largely unrecognizable to our telepathic-osmosis mind-sets in 1992. If this foresight is anywhere near correct, then many great and unexpected superstructural changes will take place.

Unfortunately, many of these changes are ominous. The change-route feasibility for these ominous changes were "coded," or set into convergence, during the twentieth century. The first inhabitants of the twenty-first century will have inherited the future-negative effects of the codes. Many of our present institutions, as the sources of these future-negative effects, will have broken down or been abandoned by 2010.

Thus, in very real ways, by 2010 the future will have detached from the historical past to a degree unprecedented in history. None of this, as predicted, coincides with the general patterns of expectation prevailing at the beginning of the transition. Indeed, great efforts are currently being made to insure that traditions, institutions, activities, and expectations prevailing now pass intact into the new century. The mainstream managers and manipulators of the present are confident that the future will be constructed upon their works. The fact that this cannot happen is confirmed by existing knowledge, which portends differently.

But existing knowledge also confirms that a renaissance of some kind *must* come into existence—if for no other reason than to offset what is failing. The emergence of this renaissance is also mandated by astrological correlations (as will be described) and can be predicted. Its emergence will start up change-routes into the future that are completely absent today. By 2010, and by the force of emergency, people will think about many matters in future-positive ways that are completely different from how they are being considered today.

ECONOMIC CHANGE-ROUTES OF THE TRANSITION

The superstructural change-routes of the millennial transition will involve many significant matters besides economic issues. Ecological matters will take increasing precedence over economic interests. Individuals whom I will term *profuture activists* will appear, who will redefine the purpose of "the economy" and "the ecology" by 2010.

But since economic vistas loom large in everyone's concern, I will begin the following predictive sets by considering the economy.

The Failure of the "New World Order"

Both outer economic facts and economic belief-realities produce change-routes into the future. Those of the belief-realities usually culminate in future-negative ways, as history has shown. If a given economy is seen to be suffering, the future-seer may be relatively certain that economic beliefs have superseded economic facts.

Patterns of expectation (as beliefs) are currently holding that a new world order based upon capitalistic free-market ideals is coming into existence and will characterize the superstructure of the future. This expectation, fortified by strong telepathic osmosis, serves as the unquestioned basis for many books predicting the future.

Among these is the book, widely read in Europe, by Jacques Attali entitled *Millennium: Winners and Losers in the Coming World Order* (1991). Mr. Attali has been special adviser to French President François Mitterand since 1981 and is currently President of the European Bank for Reconstruction. *Millennium* has been endorsed by the popular American futurist Alvin Toffler. Another significant book is *Crystal Globe: The Haves and the Have-Nots of the New World Order* (1991) by Marvin Cetron (President of Forecasting International, Inc.) and Owen Davies (a former senior editor at *Omni* magazine).

The general predictive premise of both books is that a new world order is coming into existence that is largely based no longer on political motives but on worldwide capitalistic free-market economic perspectives. Accordingly, the world will be a more peaceful and prosperous place because it will no longer be ruled on behalf of ideological and military-political competition. Instead, the new world *economic* order will promote the well-being of the trading nations linked into the international free-market enterprise.

Both books, however, predict that larger and sharper divisions will occur between the wealthy and poor of the world, largely because the wealthy are "functionally equipped" to capture free-market systems, whereas the poor are not.

This predictive view of the future seems logical enough to the worldviews of the future that came into existence during the 1960–80s (internationalism and the global village concept) and that are expected to fulfill themselves in the times ahead. But this predictive view is based on four uninspected reality-anchored expectations through which the future is being interpreted:

1. that a new world order *is* coming into existence;
2. that it *will be* implemented as an enormous free-market economic world order;
3. that the essential capitalistic concepts underlying the free-market systems *will continue to prevail*; and
4. that through all of this political motives *will cease* to play a world-shaping role.

If all four of these expectations are feasible enough, then capitalism will go universal and much that is predicted in these two books will probably materialize in the future.

But are these four uninspected expectations correct to begin with? I will predict that they are not, adding that even if they are, as they stand they cannot incorporate in advance any unanticipated phenomena that might redirect the future into avenues of development that have not existed in the past or do not exist today.

As a prediction, the idea that a new world order is coming into existence based on economic realities of the twentieth century is in error. Rather the old *political* world order is in the process of passing out of existence. It is being dismantled if not destroyed.

In this process, economic opportunism can flourish during what amounts to political uncertainty and doubts. During the millennial transition political uncertainty and doubts will increase (as they already are), leading to periods of political chaos. Since economic opportunism can flourish when old political orders disintegrate, it is the present version of this opportunism that is being offered up as the basis for a world that will be a more peaceful and prosperous place.

The functional beliefs and methods of this economic opportunism, however, are deeply rooted in the old political orders that are passing out of existence. I will predict that the former cannot survive without the latter, and since the old political orders are being dismantled, so must their economic expressions follow suit.

The impetus for the new-world-order telepathic osmosis is the notion that now that communism has failed (1989), the American and European democratic-capitalist forms of free-market economy can proliferate unimpeded throughout the world; and that the collective movers and shakers of this economy will form the principal nexus of the new world order. Global economic largesse will be produced by this order, which will benefit all of earth's citizens. The going may be rough at first, due to initial necessities of economic dislocations, but the end justifies the means.

The American version of this pattern of expectation predicts that the United States, as the natural home of the free-market economy, will surge vibrantly into the next century as a leading power of the new order. The European version, as expressed through the founding ideas of the European Economic Community (EEC), has it that the EEC will likewise figure prominently in the great global economic surge now shaping up.

In essence, the meaning of all this is that governance and rule of the world are to be undertaken by economic structures on behalf of those structures. Even more simply put, the rule of the world is to fall into the mind-sets and economic-empire motives of businesses, economists, speculators, corporations, capitalists, and financial innovators.

These, on a worldwide basis, will allegedly agree to making the world a more peaceful and prosperous place. And the advocates of this new world order ask us to believe this is *about to happen*—even though it is clearly understood that the basis of the free-market system is *competition*—competition that can become even more, or at least as, militant as political processes.

The two books mentioned in the preceding, which I take as indicative of the central thinking of the new world orderists, frankly indicate this competitiveness. For starters, they are predicting an *increase* of larger and sharper divisions between the wealthy and poor, or between the haves and have-nots.

But since the wealth of the human world is already held in the hands of about 3 to 5 percent of its populations, the increase in the number of the have-nots can only mean both the increase of Third-World conditions throughout the whole world and the dismantling of the worker middle classes of the developed nations. The wealth of the world is in fact accessible because of workers who agree to make it so on behalf of economic entrepreneurs. And much of the access to this wealth is possible only because of skilled and trained workers who are *remunerated* sufficiently to make it worth *their* while to be functional cogs in the wealth-gathering scheme. These represent the middle classses.

The major change-routes any future-seer would want to inspect in this case concern the feasibility of whether the workers of the world will, during the immediate millennial transition, meekly consent to being numbered among the increasing have-nots, thereby permitting larger and sharper divisions to occur between them and the wealthy. This particular change-route is clearly future-negative regarding the have-nots.

The telepathic-osmosis glamour of the new world order, then, is exciting as regards the already superwealthy (or those who might aspire to becoming so). But the new world order, as expected and described, will culminate in significant future-negative change-routes.

I predict that the middle-class workers of the world will not sit still if indeed it becomes apparent to them that the divisions *are* becoming larger and sharper. When they revolt, as they will, the new economic world order will suffer disruptions. Although there are other reasons for it, as we shall see, the new world order concept could well go down in flames on this one future-negative change-route alone.

But there are additional change-route feasibility questions to be considered. Why *should* the divisions between the haves and have-nots become larger and sharper in the future? If *world* prosperity is to ensue, surely the divisions should decrease.

Surely these questions will arise during the millennial transition— for, as larger and sharper divisions between the wealthy and poor increase, the latter will certainly become more sensitive to them, especially when the future-negative change-routes of the new world order become more pronounced.

The real change-routes into the future belong to the have-nots, the masses who must partake of future-positive lifelines if they are to remain "contented" and not turn socially disruptive. If the new economic world order belongs only to the wealthy, this order will clearly be in the company of the world order detailed in George Orwell's depressing novel *1984*.

Certain predictions can be drawn from this situation and accompanying patterns of false expectation. But these predictions can better be understood in the light of the whole change-route superstructure of the transition. Among other change-routes, ominous ecological matters will intervene in all forms of economy during the transition, as will be discussed ahead. But whether or not the new world economic order will succeed is especially linked to another economic matter to which are attached very compelling change-routes: the probable failure of capitalism itself.

THE FAILURE OF CAPITALISM AND THE CHANGE-ROUTE LAW OF DIMINISHING RETURNS

The formal definition of classical *capitalism* is mounted on the following premise: that it is an economic system characterized by private ownership of capital goods, by investments that are determined by private decision independent of and immune to government controls, and by privatized production, development of natural resources, and distribution and consumption of goods whose prices are determined mainly in a free competitive market.

If we adhere strictly to this formal definition, then it is obvious that little of classical capitalism remains in human affairs, for there is hardly an existing economic activity in any nation into which government controls have not intruded in some form. Indeed, virtually the only truly capitalist venture remaining on earth is the production–free-market trade in illicit drugs—a change-route factor into the future that cannot be ignored.

In its classical sense, then, capitalism has alaready failed. And what remains of it is often severely adulterated by government controls. But capitalist enterprises succeed not only by escaping or defying governmental controls but also sometimes by seconding those controls for their private benefit. Capitalists can take over or integrate with governmental systems to the degree that the bound-aries between them become fuzzy or indistinguishable.

Government-sponsored trade agreements, for example, are en-tered into between nations to protect and equalize private capitalist enterprises. It becomes difficult to distinguish between political and economic motives. But this situation has prevailed in the past. And if, for example, we consider the politicized-economic contest be-tween the United States and Japan, it is unlikely to be abandoned in the future even though new world-orderists advertise that political motives will no longer play a part in the forthcoming free-market world order.

Classical, or pure, capitalism, then, does not exist, since if it and its free-market appendages are not free of government involvements it cannot be called capitalism—unless we want to introduce the strange but true term *governmental capitalism* in whose scope gov-ernmental processes are unduly influenced by capitalist–free-market motives. But in this sense, then, governments would "belong" to the wealthy.

This feasibility gives rise to several future-negative predictions having to do with the governmentally enforced larger and sharper divisions between the wealthy and the poor, the processess of which have already become evident in the United States.

The free-market capitalism (if we still want to call it that) that characterizes the "democratic" developed nations is subject to two important drawbacks: the natural cycles of growth and decline and the law of diminishing returns. Most free-market exponents theo-retically aim at perpetual growth through what is called the man-agement-by-objective method, the major objective being perpetual growth.

This strategy runs afoul of growth and decline cycles and the law of diminishing returns, both of which snarl the free-market theory, profit-taking, and workers' lifelines into the future. The pursuit of perpetual growth permits only telepathic-osmosis optimism allegedly of the future-positive kind—which in turn occludes any perception of real future-negative change-routes.

Economic systems aimed exclusively at perpetual growth (as was the case in the United States during the 1980s) are therefore unprepared to consider or identify future-negative downturns. These, in any event, are of marginal interest to the wealthy, who will remain reasonably wealthy through the downturns. The future-negative effects resulting from the occlusion of future-negative change-routes or the marginal interest in them, though, appear at the worker levels (as is the case in the United States at the beginning of the 1990s).

The perpetual-growth telepathic-osmosis syndrome requires that economic systems pursuing it become larger and larger in order to accommodate expected growth. At some point during the growth, the systems will encounter natural cyclic downturns. But, as well, they will encounter the future-negative change-routes of *the law of diminishing returns*—which is of extraordinary *meaning* to future-seers.

THE LAW OF DIMINISHING RETURNS

In economic theory, the law of diminishing returns is defined as a rate of yield that, beyond a certain point, *fails* to increase in proportion to additional investments. Complementary to this is the law of increasing returns, which refers to a rate of yield that increases from a certain point in proportion to investments.

Both these laws, of special interest to future-seeing, can be lifted out of their economic contexts and superimposed on all of our life's activities. A certain make-break point exists between investments and yields—for example, in love affairs, family matters, career pursuits, philosophical and religious efficiency, mind-set orientations, political and sociological programs, and so forth. We invest in these according to our choice because we believe they will yield future-positive results. Any effort to make things work or succeed, though, is susceptible not only to the law of increasing returns but to the law of *diminishing* returns.

In economics, however, the telepathic-osmosis syndrome of perpetual growth occludes perception of the make-break point existing between investments and yields. This is reflected in the rampant illusion that pouring more money (i.e., investment) into something will correct its yield in continuing future-positive ways. The law of diminishing returns defeats this illusion.

The change-route law of diminishing returns is therefore of enormous *outer importance* to the future-seeing process since it has a great deal to do with the feasibility of what is about to happen. My own research into this matter has revealed that changes are routed *into* the law of diminishing returns because of specific processlike principles:

1. A line of activity is set in motion because it promises to yield certain future-positive outcomes with regard to profit and security. The most logical way to try to ensure the efficiency and effectiveness of this line of activity is to increase it in both intensity and size. The activity then grows, and sustaining the growth requires more investments. And the larger the investments become, the more the growth is expected to increase its yields of profit and security.

2. But the larger the growth and the more the investments, the more the activity's *inertia potential* begins to increase. In physics, *inertia* is defined as a property that remains in uniform motion unless acted upon by some external force. But in terms of investments-in-activities, inertia can be said to come into existence when the ratio of investments begins to be absorbed *by the activity itself*—a state that, in turn, suddenly decreases the ratio of profits and security lifelines of the activity.

3. In a certain sense, the activity begins to cannibalize its own investments and, in so doing, becomes necrotic in terms of yields. Growth suddenly turns into decline because the accumulated inertia cannot easily be resolved simply by increasing the scope of the investments.

4. Major systemic changes are required if resolution is to succeed. But systemic changes demand the one thing growth systems fear the most: restructuring—during which the system may fail completely. And, in any event, the necessity of future systemic changes is usually not encoded in the

activity at its starting point because no one realizes that a
point of inertia will eventually come about.

5. All growth-inertia-decline systems are acted upon not only
by internal but by external factors. Even optimum growth
states can be adversely affected by external factors (such as
natural decline cycles), and such factors can easily super-
impose a state of inertia on such a growth system. In economics, as is well realized, vitalistic profit-making activities
can suddenly suffer inertia-reverses because of sudden shifts
in market-consumer interests. Yields of profits and security
lifelines begin to diminish. The dreaded make-break point
between investments and yields has been "achieved."

The law of diminishing returns, then, appears to activate when a
state of cannibalistic inertia is developed. Small systems can restructure the most easily and quickly, because less is involved to
effect the change. But larger systems are very sensitive to that law.
The larger a system has become, the more difficult it is to restructure—as is the case in the United States today. At the very
least, longer periods of time-abeyance are required to restructure a
large system (if doing so is envisioned at all)—and time-abeyance
is one thing from which yields suffer the most.

Any ostensible future-seer can predict difficulties with regard to
systems that are so large that they cannot restructure *without* experiencing the inertia-effects of the law of diminishing returns. And
the law can easily collapse such a system before it has time to
restructure.

The exact feasibility vista for future-seers at the beginning of the
millennial transition, then, is to judge whether and when mega-
economic systems will reach the make-break point that activates
the law of diminishing returns.

The owners of most free-market mega-economic systems blame
competitors for their difficulties rather than their own ratios of
noncompetitive inertia—as is currently the case between the United
States and Japan.

Management by objective, long the major theory of American
economic "growth," permits the allegedly future-positive vision of

perpetual growth—but it does not permit the perception of future-negative inertia outcomes inherent in the vision itself. The Japanese, since the 1950s, have pursued not the policies of management by objective but rather the policies of management by statistical quality control, as we shall see ahead.

In forty years, Japan, a small nation, has risen from war-torn defeat to become the premier mega-economic power, efficient and competitive. Something of the reverse has taken place in the United States, whose mega-economic governmental systems are failing because of mega-inertias and the law of diminishing returns—immediately reflected, of course, at the worker level in rises in unemployment and other defaults of their security lifelines.

Most capitalist free-market ventures cannot succeed past a certain enlargement of growth without appealing to often substantial governmental subsidies—another factor that interlinks them with political motives. The subsidies are in turn derived from the taxpaying public, who are the first to experience both future-negative outcomes of enlargement inertias *and* the burden of underwriting the subsidies. The complexity of natural decline cycles must be integrated with all this, of which several ecological ones are in the offing during the transition.

I will predict that the change-routes of the millennial transition are headed to increases of mega-economic failures—of capitalism, of the new world order, of many national economies, and to the one correct expectation as given: the increase in the division between the haves and have-nots. Tough economic times for the have-nots are almost certainly ahead, and they will primarily constitute the nature of the transition superstructure.

How, then, will this be dealt with say, in 1996, 2000, or even 2010? Predictions concerning this will unfold ahead in the context of other situations needed to understand them. But certainly the failures will be used to justify the abandoning of their root causes—which, frankly put, exist in the mainstream mind-sets of the twentieth century. By pressures building from developing negative circumstances, these will be forced to end. What is tantamount to a completely new rescripting for the economic future will unfold.

Economic future history will detach from the past in completely unexpected ways.

Any aspiring future-seer can utilize the five points, as given in this chapter, that lead to systemic inertia and thus to the activation of the law of diminishing returns. You can easily locate areas of inertia in micro- and megasystems. Such inertia defeats the investment of additional resources of any kind. Either the system must restructure or its subsequent change-routes will increasingly lead to future-negative outcomes.

If you can spot a verifiable systemic inertia, you will find that you can predict its outcomes. When more goes into such a system than comes out of it, you may be 90 percent confident in predicting that the system is ultimately headed for a crash.

19

THE LATE, GREAT UNITED STATES OF AMERICA?

Americans generally have a vision of their nation as the world's leader in international affairs. And, indeed, many other nations perceive the United States that way, too. A great deal is at stake for the change-routes into the future if the realities of this vision are jeopardized in any truly significant way. In my opinion as an aspiring future-seer, the realities of this vision are accompanied by patterns of false expectations and not a little futile telepathic osmosis.

Other nations that point out that the United States are in jeopardy are accused of America-bashing. But where there is so much smoke, there is surely fire. And in the foreseeing sense, much about America's future depends on whether these fires can be addressed by Americans during the millennial transition.

I predict that the United States will have to suffer irreversible future-negative change-routes during the transition before the requisite national enthusiasm to ameliorate them will emerge in the necessary volume and intensity. The amelioration will result in the emergence of radical solutions that will differ enormously from those twentieth-century factors that set the future-negative change-routes into motion. We are already beginning to suffer some of this, and so this is not real predictive news.

Aside from certain sensitive issues of moral leadership of the world, the basic power of the United States has frankly and squarely resided in its economic and military power. In fact, its military power has generated a great deal of its economic power—and the "emasculation" of its military power has direct implications regarding its residual economic power.

Patterns of expectation are currently holding that this great military power is no longer needed, that it is dinosauric and redundant in a world headed for universal economic peace and well-being. I have already offered my predictions on the feasibility of universal peace. But this still leaves the matter of whether the United States can safeguard its premier position into the future. If this position is to be one principally of economic leadership, then the feasibility change-routes for it are already very ominous indeed.

I invite you to make your own predictions before reading on, to see how they tally up with mine.

For reasons that I have never completely understood, Americans have placed great faith in "the Economy" as a thing in itself. It is for this reason that other nations see us as exclusively money-minded. Money does "talk," of course. But as we have often discovered to our embarrassment, pouring money alone on difficult situations does not ameliorate them and sometimes causes negative new situations to emerge. In my predictive opinion, it is this "pouring" that has led, and will continue to lead, to a number of future-negative "economic" change-routes, some of which are intractable by now.

DEFINING "THE ECONOMY"

The existence of multiple economic definitions seems to have something to do with the abject failure of many economic predictions. Accurate economic predicting is actually quite rare. Because I have not been able to discover an official definition of *the economy* that is widely agreed on (disagreement being more common), I have had to construct my own understanding of what it consists.

We generally think of "the Economy" as a singular entity of some kind, which has to do with the production, distribution, and comsumption of goods that are derived from material resources and the needed services to get them to consumers. However, there are several different forms of it.

In a simple economy, the availability of resources and the consumer demand for them act as natural balancing points that keep the related economic transactions relatively stable and predictable. In this straightforward form of economy, producers cannot alienate their buyers, and buyers and producers alike must treat one another with certain ethical considerations. This is a very old form of economy, and it exists here and there throughout the world.

A second kind of economy exists, which is sometimes referred to as a *transactional economy*. It consists not of trading in products or in services related to that process but of investments, credits, loans, debts, and percentage yields derived from monetary transactions. This kind of economy ostensibly exists to facilitate the operations and expansions of the producer-consumer economy. This economy is hardly ever straightforward or simple, and it has few natural checks and balances. It is especially vulnerable to the visions of management by objective—the objective being profits only.

A third kind of economy is the *banking economy*, which requires *depositors* and whose offered service is to allow the depositors to stockpile their monetary holdings in banks, ostensibly to keep them safe. In centralizing the monetary holdings of their depositors, banks naturally become centers that facilitate loans to the transactional form of economy.

The latter two tiers of "the Economy" are not directly subject to the natural balances of the first producer-consumer tier of economy. But human nature being what it is, if the transactional and banking forms of economy were not subjected to some kind of balancing controls, transactional usury and bank thefts of depositors' holdings would develop.

Prevention of transactional usury and bank thefts requires the emergence of a fourth kind of *regulatory economy*, originally designed specifically to keep the transactional and banking economies in check. In democratic nations, the regulatory economy is usually a function of civic and national governments. Sometimes their role involves stabilizing the lower-level product-consumer economy against the threat of monopolies, which can then benefit from usury tactics.

Civic government functions, however, have monetary needs that are met by various kinds of taxes. A *taxation economy* comes into existence to fulfill this civic monetary need. Taxation makes "the Economy" five-tiered—and obviously very complex.

The economy is further complicated by a sixth kind of economic endeavor that has many varieties: the *management economy*, whose goal is usually to influence all the above economies in ways that benefit vested interests, usually by avoiding or circumventing all the natural and artificial checks and balances on them.

A seventh kind of economy also exists: the criminal economy. The criminal economy deals in all matters that the civic and governmental regulatory economy otherwise forbids. The economic practices of the criminal economy are always covert and hidden and can range from the smallest gang leader up to and including very large and refined illicit systems operating invisibly within all the other economies already mentioned.

The *debt economy* is a special extension of the transactional economy. People who owe money have to pay monetary interest on the amount owed. In healthy economies, debts and their interest-making repayment potentials are somewhat equivalent. The debt load never exceeds by very much the repayment obligations. But a great deal of money can be made by artificially increasing the debt load, because more interest can be achieved. The advocates of the debt economy therefore encourage extensive debt loading, and they usually do so by arranging that any defaults will be bailed out via credits derived from the taxation economy.

The *welfare-state economy* must also be considered, especially when welfare needs or demands accelerate, thereby increasing the size of the debt, taxation, and transaction economies.

Finally, *the capitalist free-market economy* does indeed exist. But it is distinct from the simple economy regarding the production, distribution, and consumption of goods. These two economies are distinguishable because the free-market economy focuses exclusively on ensuring profit-making, whereas the latter may consist only of what amounts to subsistence living.

A wage-earner participates in the natural subsistence economy by earning enough money to fund his or her security lifelines—and under normal circumstances will do what is labor-required to ensure him- or herself. On the other hand, the capitalist profit-maker will embark on no economic venture unless it results in profit-taking, usually in amounts that exceed his or her basic life-security needs. The capitalist profit-maker anticipates extraordinary income, and unless this individual achieves it, he or she may not undertake a particular economic foray. As a particularly sad example, capitalist pharmaceutical companies will not develop medicines that could cure tropical diseases. The specific reason is that the peoples of the tropical latitudes largely number among the have-nots and cannot afford to pay for them. No profit-taking, no medicines—pure and simple.

From the future-seer's point of view, then "the Economy" is made up of a complex network of systemic interlocking economies that clearly extends well beyond the classical definition of "economy."

THE AMERICAN ECONOMIC SCENE

In the original Japanese version (translated by the United States government) of their book *The Japan That Can Say "No"* (1989),

Akio Morita and Shintaro Ishihara discussed certain characteristics of the central capitalistic profit-taking philosophy that have led to the increasing instability of all Western capitalistic businesses and economies. Some of their commentary was unflattering to American business mind-sets, and it is interesting to note that when the American version of their book came out, it was "edited" (read: "censored") in such a way to disturb those mind-sets *less*.

One central critique discussed at length in "*No*" was that profit-takers focus only on immediate profit-taking, not on long-term economic stability. Profit-takers tend only to *plan* ahead for profit-taking—an objective that falls neatly within the scope of the management-by-objective method. And the more immediately those profits can be taken, the better. But this has led, as Morita and Ishihara comment in their chapter entitled "The Decline of an America Which Can See Only Ten Minutes Ahead," to capitalistic businesses' inability to plan ahead for the long term, since they plan only for short-term profit-taking (and then, in my opinion, usually only via the transactional economy).

Morita and Ishihara point out that aggressive planning only for short-term profit-taking prevents longer-term economic planning, say, for ten or twenty years ahead. Plans to establish long-term security lifelines of workers, then, have no real place in such short-term planning and would in fact constitute an inconvenient impediment to it.

To my knowledge, few American mind-sets (economic or otherwise) have any long-term economic plans for the future. Even long-term ecological protectionist groups must combat the short-term profit-taking plans of prevailing capitalist mind-sets. The current economic situation in America is rich in future-negative change-routes, many of which are already coalescing into predictable realities and will continue to do so into the future.

The American economic tendency to work only toward short-term profit-taking surely will seriously jeopardize America's economic future. Short-term profit-taking planning is capitalistic exploitation, pure and simple. And no major economic power can preserve a preeminent place in world economic affairs in the present and future absence of serious planning for long-term economic stability.

The American economic picture during the millennial transition is not good, in light of what has been discussed in the preceding. But since the economies of nations are all by now interlinked in the one-world sense, this picture should be extended by a brief commentary on the world economy.

THE COLLAPSE OF THE WORLD ECONOMY

Before continuing, you might well ask yourself if you understand what the world economy consists of. Most will assume it is composed of the standard definition of the economy's natural processes: resources—their development and their distribution. It is probably true that resources do play a role in the world economy. But the world economy is predominantly composed of the transactional and debt forms of economy.

This fact has been given unimpeachable credibility by the Swedish economic analyst Rolf Osterberg in his book *Corporate Renaissance: Business as an Adventure in Human Development* (a European bestseller currently forthcoming from Nataraj Publishing in the United States). Mr. Osterberg's assessment appears to be correct and is briefly summarized as follows:

The transactional and debt economies achieve profits by increasing the scope of financial transactions to derive "fees." Fees can be enlarged by increasing debt holdings in order to benefit from interest payments on them. The largest debt borrowers in the world are the Third World nations, who allegedly utilize the borrowed monies of the industrial nations to industrialize themselves.

According to international figures published in July 1989, the Third World's total debt burden was conservatively estimated to be in the vicinity of 10 trillion (100,000 billion) U. S. dollars. This is a meaningless figure unless it can be compared to something we can understand. If a million dollars is compared to seconds ticking away on your watch, then it is equivalent to ten months, while a billion is equivalent to thirty years. The Third-World debt burden, then, is equivalent to three hundred thousand years.

Some portion of this gargantuan debt burden is owed to such institutions as the International Monetary Fund and the World Bank, which are financially supported by the industrialized nations. Likewise, the larger portion of this staggering paper debt economy is owed to transactional profit-taking interests (banks, etc.) of the developed nations. As Mr. Osterberg says, in order even to begin to repay portions of the interest on the debt, the developing countries are ruthlessly forced to exploit natural and human resources.

It has long been clear to informed economic analysts that it will be impossible for the developing countries ever to honor their debts—they often cannot even pay the staggering interest, much less settle the principal. The debt-loaning megasystem has temporarily solved this problem via the transaction economy by rolling over the loans into new ones, to which even more interest is added. Not having the money they need to service the principal of the loans, the developing countries have to pay interest equivalent to approximately $25 million *per day* to the loan sources in the industrialized nations. This is exploitation the degree of which far surpasses that which took place during the time of colonial empires.

Since there is no other aspect of the world economy that compares to this $1,250 billion debt hallmark (which is *increasing* daily), it is this aspect that figuratively *is* the world economy. This enormous debt will never be repaid, for there is not enough development or enough resources on earth to repay it. Mr. Osterberg points out that the right thing to do would be immediately to write off these loans and fully accept the consequences.

But, he continues, that cannot be done. The loans represent a large part of the total balance sheets of so many banks that if the write-off were done it would result in a breakdown of the industrialized world's banking systems—and, as a consequence, a breakdown of the world economy. Accordingly, banks and lending institutions continue to list these debts on balance sheets as *assets*, which are now nothing more than just so much debt-economy empty air.

Since the total world's debt economy now far exceeds the world's real resource economy, the vicious circle of production-consumption (economic growth) of resources can *never* be used to bring the world's debt economy back into stability. The only remaining bailout source to cover the empty-air debt-economy is the tax-paying economy—which will naturally be cannibalized in attempts to keep the debt economy somewhat stable.

The taxpaying economy can be as vital as are the taxpayers willing to "contribute" to it. Thus, this solution might be feasible if profit-taking exploiters were not moving the labor needs of their enterprises into the Third World nations, where labor is cheaper than in the developed nations—naturally increasing unemployment in the developed nations. At a certain point, then, the tax-paying economy will fail as the final resource for sustaining the world's debt economy. And at that time, the world's debt economy will collapse.

I predict that this collapse will take place in future-negative, change-route stages, the first of which is already in process as the "recession" of the 1990s, which is affecting nations worldwide. The United States has the dubious honor of being the centerpiece in this world debt economy. At the start of the twentieth century, America was the world's largest creditor, whose munificence in lending now cannot be repaid by *its* debtors. As a result, the United States have had to borrow and consequently are now the world's single largest debtor in the scheme of the global debt economy.

It is doubtful that increases in transactional and debt economies are going to serve as permanent bandages to this enormous and ominous situation. Thus, it is well within predictive feasibility to estimate that the failure of the world economy will be completely visible by 1998 or earlier, no matter whether interludes of economic recovery temporarily manifest themselves.

As a result of this slow but inevitable collapse, the center of the new world economic order will move to those nations that have the least world debt–loaded economy as either lenders or borrowers—to those nations that do have long-term economic planning as contrasted with those that have only short-term forms of it. There is little predictive doubt that this new center will gravitate largely toward Asia (as discussed in chapter 25).

20

GLOBAL INTERVENTION IMPACTS OF THE MILLENNIAL TRANSITION

All economic and financial matters have high visibility and charisma. Many believe that if those matters can be cured in some positive sense, then all other matters can be resolved accordingly. But most positive or negative conditions of economic and financial matters are epiphenomena of more basic concerns, which can be identified as patterns of human behavior that are more than anything else the causes of economic and financial conditions.

The epiphenomena may have high visibility, but the future-seer has to "see" through that visibility to the causative behavioral factors hidden beneath. Patterns of behavior originate from *inner* mind-dynamic activities, but their results are experienced in *outer* (physical) ways. The future-seer is obliged to consider them in this dual aspect.

Human behavior ranges along a complex behavioral scale, but generally from genius, through average, then to stupid. It is, however, difficult to see where a particular action or foresight belongs on that scale until its outcome is experienced.

From the future-seeing point of view this situation is very important since all three general behavioral patterns produce change-routes both positive and negative leading into the future. If you want to flex your future-seeing muscles, you can begin to make lists of what (or sometimes who) you perceive falls into these three categories. You will of course need to rise above your own reality-anchors, penetrate through patterns of expectation, and escape encumbering telepathic osmosis syndromes. All three categories are prediction-rich if your intellect is prepared to deal with them. Your intuitus-intellecting and indwelling Nostradamus Factor will come to your aid in making predictions based on what you perceive.

You might begin your list, for example, with local behavioral situations around you, at home, in the office, or in society. But you might also in the same way consider the Third World's $10 trillion debt economy or, as given for 1990, the $3,233.3 billion debt economy of the United States. It is impossible to believe that these staggering debt economies are the product of genius. But whether of genius or stupidity, they *are* producing change-routes into the future, and you might attempt to spot what or who is producing them, as well as try to predict their outcomes.

THE INTERVENTION IMPACT OF POPULATION ON EARTH'S CARRYING CAPACITY

Intervention impacts consist of a category of causes that originate outside human control of them. People would not permit these events to occur if they had either control over them or the foresight to prevent them. Some intervention impacts, such as a significant and beneficial discovery of some kind (the discovery of vaccines, or of the New World by Columbus), can produce future-positive change-routes. But we generally consider such events to be a "development," not an "intervention."

Two general types of intervention impacts exist:

1. those that originate from outside us, such as "acts of God" or significant natural phenomena (such as hurricanes, volcanoes, or a comet striking earth); and,
2. those that originate from humans themselves. People begin events that sometimes get out of control. World War II is an example of this, as was the advent of nuclear bombs.

Intervention impacts have aftermaths and change everything, and it is hard, sometimes impossible, to put things back as they were before. People have to adjust to intervention impacts and their effects. These impacts intervene in human affairs and cause them to be change-routed in ways humans would not choose. In the simplest cases, humans can merely move out of the way of intervention impacts or pretend they do not exist for as long as possible. The change-route aftermaths of some intervention impacts are very hard to "conquer."

Recovery from intervention impacts is dependent on the scope of the impact. Since we have been successful in conquering intervention impacts that are less than global, we tend to pride ourselves on our intervention impact–overcoming arts and methods. For example, we can recover from hurricanes, tornadoes, volcanic eruptions, and so forth, and soon things are back to normal.

The central problem inherent in suffering from most intervention impacts is that they take us by surprise. Often our lack of experience of these events paralyzes us if and when given intervention impacts assume gigantic proportions, perceived or real, at the individual, social, or global levels.

Global intervention impacts, such as catastrophic worldwide ecological disruptions, however, have no precedent in the past and elude human capacities to ameliorate them quickly. Back-to-normal recovery from such disruptions is clearly in doubt. And it is very likely that such catastrophes will change how people can best survive amid the disaster-effects outside human control. Their predictable effects will kill, maim, destroy, set issues and matters into irrecoverable decline, and force humans to take extraordinary steps for which no past precedent has existed.

It is beyond any reasonable doubt that the millennial transition will undergo at least one global intervention impact. It will not be an act of God or of nature. It will be of our own making.

Our population growths have exceeded earth's human carrying capacity. The first inhabitants of the twenty-first century must inherit the epiphenomenal problems that result from this overpopulation. These problems will increasingly characterize the millennial transition.

All economic matters of the transition are related both directly and indirectly to this intervention impact. But its basis resides in human behavior patterns—which, as we have seen, range from genius, through average, to stupid.

Predicting the future course of earth's overpopulation megaproblem is, unfortunately, all too easy. The clear facts of this particular problem are more visible than any other future-negative situation. And they are easily available, principally through the work of the Population Crisis Committee, which has headquarters in Washington, D.C., and affiliates worldwide.

To understand the facts, though, it is necessary to distinguish between mind-sets who think in terms of numbers of people and mind-sets who can think in terms of earth's carrying capacity. These two mind-sets can produce different patterns of behavior and expectations.

Numerical population counts can be juggled and arranged to suit particular mind-set beliefs. For various humanitarian reasons we can consider that increases of populations are natural and rightful. Every foetus resulting from an impregnated human egg has its right to life. But considerations of earth's carrying capacity are a different matter, for that carrying capacity has much to do with *what kind of right to life everyone will have in the future.*

This distinction is seldom made. But it is a very important one to future-seers—*if* they propose to see into the real future rather than into mind-set telepathic osmosis.

Understanding the limits of *earth's carrying capacity* introduces a new vista of ecological change-routes into the future. If earth *did not* have a carrying capacity, or if it had an inexhaustible one, then there could be no overpopulation problem.

But everything we know of has a carrying capacity. A train can be loaded with only so many passengers before the overload begins to fall off. An economic megastructure can carry only so much of a debt load before it begins to falter and fail. Only so many vegetables can be planted in a garden, and when too many are planted the whole harvest is stunted. Only so many sardines will fit in a can. These are all illustrative of the law of diminishing returns.

It is difficult for us to think that earth's human population can be affected by the law of diminishing returns. Yet new human lives equate to investing in the future and a positive yield is expected from them. *More* human lives are good for expanding economic yields, since population increases equal more consumers. One of the acclaimed goals of scientific progress is to preserve more lives, while the perceived need to preserve more lives justifies investment increases in science.

But, using the sardine can analogy, earth's carrying capacity will hold only so many sardines. The law of diminishing returns *activates* when attempts are made to insert more sardines into earth's carrying capacity than are feasible. When this is done, the change-routes typical of the *unfeasible* start up.

The carrying capacity of earth is hotly debated, principally by those who theoretically believe that technological advances will discover ways and means of "correcting" the effects of human overloads on earth's carrying capacity. If such technological interventions would or could be the case, then the assumed dimensions of the carrying capacity are extendable.

But *what is* earth's carrying capacity? At the time of Christ's birth, world population is estimated to have been about 250 million. Between Christ's birth and the year 1800, earth's population only increased to about 1 billion. Population nearly doubled during the next one hundred years to about 1.8 billion, and ecological destruction associated with densely packed urban centers began giving rise to special problems. The planet's ecological carrying-capacity systems, however, were still pollution-free.

We are relatively certain that world population was 2.5 billion in 1950. But the *1989 Demographic Yearbook* of the United Nations places the sum of world population somewhere in the vicinity of 5 billion as of 1991. Population had nearly doubled during the hundred years between 1800 and 1900. But in only *thirty-nine years* between 1950 and 1989 it had doubled again.

I have not been able to discover any authoritative documentation that hazards an estimate of the earth's actual carrying capacity. But it was during the early 1950s that various planetary ecological problems began to be visible—problems that have taken on megamagnitudes since then. It is feasible to assume both that the appearance of planetary ecological pollution and destruction appears when earth's carrying capacity is actually bypassed and that the planet's ideal carrying capacity then appears to be somewhat less than 2.5 billion but certainly far less than our present 5 billion.

In the figure on page 215, the dotted line represents the earth's ecological carrying capacity, and the solid line represents earth's human population. If humans were to live on earth without threatening its ecological carrying capacity, then the two lines should never be allowed to intersect. As population exceeds the carrying capacity, the latter is less able to give ideal life-support to the former. At a certain point in the future, the awesome increase in population will render ecological life-support impossible.

Conservative estimates are currently predicting that human population will exceed 10 billion by 2010 and reach 15–25 billion somewhere between 2020 and 2040. I predict that the 10 billion feasibility figure will actually be reached somewhere just after the year 2000, although it might take ten years of difficult census-taking to confirm it. By 2010, the virtual population of earth, having increased exponentially rather than arithmetically, may well range between 15 and 20 billion—which is to say, some 75 percent or more beyond earth's actual carrying capacity, which I have estimated in the preceding.

It is feasible, then, to predict that the change-routes during the millennial transition include those leading to *significant* increases in ecological breakdowns. These breakdowns will be inherited by the first inhabitants of the twenty-first century, and they will have to live within them.

The earth of the immediate future may romantically be considered a socioeconomic "global village," but it will be a very polluted one by 2010. And the inhabitants of this future village are going to be very angry with those of the twentieth century who unconscionably pursued their affairs as if earth's carrying capacity did not exist.

The progress of ecological destruction, of course, is not news. But the future-negative message implicit in the news is often marginalized in curious telepathic-osmosis ways. Patterns of expectation generally hold that ecological problems can be "cured" on the assumption that "someone" will discover how to do so. The direct relationship between exponentially increasing population and ecological breakdown impacts is hardly ever mentioned—this relationship being of great interest to aspiring future-seers.

As an example of the relationship we can consider the case of

EARTH'S ECOLOGICAL CARRYING CAPACITY VS. WORLD POPULATION GROWTH: A.D. 1 TO 2060

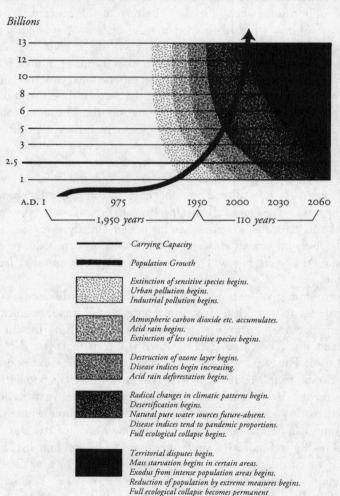

Billions

Carrying Capacity

Population Growth

Extinction of sensitive species begins.
Urban pollution begins.
Industrial pollution begins.

Atmospheric carbon dioxide etc. accumulates.
Acid rain begins.
Extinction of less sensitive species begins.

Destruction of ozone layer begins.
Disease indices begin increasing.
Acid rain deforestation begins.

Radical changes in climatic patterns begin.
Desertification begins.
Natural pure water sources future-absent.
Disease indices tend to pandemic proportions.
Full ecological collapse begins.

Territorial disputes begin.
Mass starvation begins in certain areas.
Exodus from intense population areas begins.
Reduction of population by extreme measures begins.
Full ecological collapse becomes permanent
        for the next 500,000 years.

Mexico City. The population of Mexico City was approximately 7 million in 1965. It is slightly more than 20 million in 1991 (for comparison, the 1991 population of the whole of Canada was 27 million). Mexico City population overload is expected to increase to 32 million somewhere just after the turn of the century.

Mexico City, though, has no natural oceanic disposal for its garbage or human excrement. As of this writing its civic engineers are beleaguered with what to do with 350,000 tons of human feces daily. This is a megaproblem of no mean proportions, which is being resolved so far by mechanically piling the feces in open, standing mountains on the peripheries of the metropolis. The dominolike implications of this should be made clear, since they give future-negative shape to the whole overpopulation picture.

The sales of feces-moving equipment, of course, allow for profits to be taken by those who manufacture it. But the open or even subterranean storage of such amounts of feces automatically ensures that its noxious residues will flow into the area's water-table systems. When this happens, if it has not happened already, Mexico City will have to import all its water—which will in turn make profits for water mongers but will in no way resolve the original feces problem.

Open storage of feces in such amounts leads to diseases. As it decomposes its particles become airborne. It is already medically proven that one can get hepatitis merely by breathing the air in Mexico City on hot, humid days, which will contribute to a decline in tourism. The Mexican capital is verging on ecological extinction. Mass exodus from Mexico City will increase as the city's population heads for the 30 million mark by 2008—only sixteen years hence.

Mexico City may represent a future-negative example whose implications can be avoided merely by avoiding Mexico City. But the global bodily and industrial waste products of 5 billion humans have already taxed the imagination as to what to do and how to dispose of them. Consider, for example, that as of 1989 Tokyo-Yokohama had 28 million people; New York and Sao Paulo, Brazil, had 17 million each; Los Angeles had 11.5 million, London had 11.25 million; and Paris had 10 million. These urban populations will increase by 50 to 100 percent by 2010 or slightly thereafter and will verge on ecological collapse.

Industrial wastes created by manufacturing consumer products for 5 billion people will double by 2010 in order to make consumer products for 10 billion. The current levels of industrial wastes are already an enormous problem resulting in the extinction of species, intolerable increases of carbon dioxide in the atmosphere, and depletion of many resources absolutely necessary to the quality of future life on earth.

Earth's carrying capacity, its overpopulation, its economic systems, and the quality of life of the first inhabitants of the twenty-first century are intimately interrelated.

WERE WE FOREWARNED? If the future always foreshadows itself, then forewarnings of this mega-ominous scenario should have started showing up some time ago. In 1798, the English sociologist Thomas Malthus (1766–1834) published his first *Essay on Population*, contending that poverty and distress are unavoidable since population increases by geometric ratio and the means of subsistence by arithmetic ratio. Uncontrolled geometric-ratio increases of population would overwhelm the means of subsistence. His "distress" is what we today refer to as ecological destruction.

Malthus first accepted only war, famine, and disease as checks on population overgrowth. But he later concluded that moral restraints imposing limits on population overgrowth would probably be the only permanent recourse in the future for keeping populations in accord with what is now being called earth's carrying capacity.

The *Malthusian Doctrine* (as it was called) regarding the potential dangers of overpopulation has been consistently and bitterly contested since Malthus's time, largely by economic, philosophical, and religious mind-sets that naturally have seen population growth as equating to larger consumer markets. Enormous economic systems and commensurate profits have been accumulated in modern times simply because population *has* increased since 1798. And these systems and profits have played a great role in defeating the institution of moral population-control restraints.

Malthusian doctrine *was* foreshadowing and forewarning of things to come, of what was about to happen if population balances were not seen to. But this doctrine ran counter to patterns of expectation and defied their appended telepathic osmosis. These, in turn, blinded real future-seeing. And this future-seeing is being marginalized even today.

CAN THE POPULATION BE STABILIZED? Stabilizing population growths is seen as a solution to overcoming ecological and economic unbalancing effects. But there is a large difference between merely stabilizing population growth per se, and stabilizing it *in relation to* earth's ecological and resource carrying capacity—which has already been exceeded. Birth control is seen as a way to stabilize population growth in excess of population deaths. But if it is true that earth's carrying capacity has already been exceeded, then stabilizing the population at, say, 10 billion becomes irrelevant as a corrective measure regarding the carrying capacity.

Even if population control were the answer, the two things it would take to achieve population stabilization at the *20 billion mark* by the year 2040 is worldwide cooperation at birth control and *the amount of time necessary to effect it.* As of the beginning of the millennial transition, the affairs of humans on earth have neither— and only about sixteen to twenty years remain before a near-complete ecological collapse.

The millennial transition *must* then experience several kinds of negative change-routes into the future, caused by accelerated population growth. Some of these are global warming, deforestation, water pollution, desertification, species extinction, resource depletion, ozone loss, increase of disease indexes, and breakdown of urban centers—and, as well, the ultimate loss of public faith in megasystems that themselves will probably fail because of their inertia-indecision to undertake population-control intervention as far back as the 1950s, or even the 1800s.

Before you read more, you may wish to flex your own future-seeing muscles regarding this matter. To help correct your own reality-anchors, the Population Crisis Committees in Washington, D.C., and other cities offer very graphic information packages that recast the Malthusian message in up-to-date terms. Look in your telephone book for their number. Compare the implications of this information with the mind-sets around you and with prevailing patterns of expectations. Consider the change-route law of diminishing returns. Then make your own predictions.

During the millennial transition, then, the historical relationship of humans to earth's sustaining environment (its carrying capacity) will be broken by ecological intervention impacts. Earth's carrying capacity will increasingly collapse, and the collapse will take its coalescing, negative-change ravages on the former.

In short, the first generations of the twenty-first century will largely inherit an ecologically wrecked earth. And it will have been the generations of the twentieth who wrecked it the most. These twentieth-century inhabitants will be viewed *as Enemies of the Future*, more interested in short-term consumerism than in the long-term salvation of the earth for their descendants.

Earth's ecological carrying capacity is a megasystem made up of thousands or millions of subsystems that must function harmoniously and in balance in order to remain future-positive. Earth's human population is also a megasystem. But the overall health and well-being of the human megasystem is completely dependent on the harmony and balance of the ecological megasystem. In other words, the human megasystem is subservient to the greater ecological megasystem.

The ashes-making change-routes already coalescing are now largely unalterable, save by measures so extraordinary that they are beyond human control.

I have no hesitation in predicting, first, that personal mind-sets that cannot willingly and constructively acknowledge the critical-mass dimensions of earth's overpopulation crisis will be increasingly harshly dealt with by the successors of the twentieth century; and second, that the issues involved *must* come to a head during the millennial transition.

21

THE FRAGILE FUTURE

Never before has the future been so fragile in the global sense. The world's debt economy is past the point of feasible reversal. The only way to keep that economy from collapsing is to continue increasing its already ominous debt overload—this "solution" being nothing more than the paper version of rubber bands, scotch tape, and glue. Population overgrowth, with its concomitant future-negative ecological implications, is in the process of wrecking earth's carrying capacity—probably permanently so.

Increases in acid rain, ozone depletion, and carbon dioxide content of the atmosphere *will* change the quality of life on earth because they *must* change it (for a brief description of these ominous outer phenomena, see *Life Magazine* for April 1992). We can still skirt around these issues at the beginning of the transition because they are building gradually. But by 2010, the accumulations of these buildups will have had their future-negative effects. And these gradual buildups will have had their economic and social repercussions.

So, the peoples of 2010 will not enjoy the quality of life of the twentieth century simply because that quality will no longer be attainable.

The predictive questions before any future-seer, then, concern which of these ominous, ashes-making phenomena will accelerate the most, and what the effects of the acceleration will be.

The "Great Winds" of the Millennial Transition

The history of cycles analysis clearly reveals that seasonal and weather patterns do go through major cyclic variations. In keeping with these cyclic variations, it is presumed by cycle analysts that we are approaching a cycle of major worldwide drought that, if it comes about, will seriously alter the locations and patterns of food production—and will do so at a time when human overpopulations can least sustain or adjust to such changes.

This will be complicated by the capitalist factor in which the supply of food is controlled by profits. As these changes progress, then, consumer costs of purchasing *food* will escalate. As *this* change-route escalates, the welfare-oriented mandates of nations will become overburdened and eventually be beyond the ability of a tax-paying economy to sustain.

Natural climatic variations are, of course, beyond human control. But uncontrolled overpopulation of the planet originates from humans themselves, and the overpollution that results exacerbates natural climatic variation. Climactic shifts due to this factor are already in process. These shifts will destabilize the earth's delicately balanced economies—and ultimately give emergency grounds for extremely radical profuturist restructuring, which will redefine the contexts of "the Economy" and humanitarianism.

When free-market structures cannot (read: "refuse to") accommodate the needs of increasingly starving populations, those structures will fail and fall. This will become visible when phrases like the "food revolution" begin to become functioning *ideas*—ideas that will encode new worldviews and belief systems and *result* in dramatic and ahistorical activities—"ahistorical" because the problems will, for the first time in history, be *global*.

A number of books and a vast amount of other literature have appeared that predict several kinds of future-negative outcomes of what is still fondly being referred to as the ecological "problem." A *problem* implies a matter for which solutions can be found. Some have begun referring to the ecological "crisis." A *crisis* refers to a turning point for better or worse, and the use of this term gives the impression that choices for the better still remain an option.

Those completely familiar with the facts of ecological destruction fully realize that certain ecological catastrophes are now unavoidable and that their future-negative effects *must change* the way the future unfolds. I predict that certain environmental changes will be one of the accelerated causes that decrease American and European power in the world.

One category of intervention-impact phenomena arising from future-negative ecological processes has not been predictively assessed anywhere else, to my knowledge. It concerns what I will dub the "Great Winds." I predict that natural and nonnatural ecological situations will combine to produce an increase in both the frequency and volume-power of winds—hot, dry, moisture-consuming winds in summer months; cold, wet, moisture-producing winds in winter months. This prediction-set is based on the following feasibility considerations:

1. A forthcoming global drought cycle of some magnitude during the next twenty years can tentatively be predicted as the result of cycles analysis. Natural weather patterns have to change for drought to occur.

2. Artificial, human-caused destruction of the ozone layer and increases of atmospheric carbon dioxide will also increase. Destruction of the ozone layer will give rise to higher indexes of diseases and possible genetic mutations. Increases in atmospheric carbon dioxide result in planetary warming, called the *greenhouse effect*.

3. Global warming will increase temperature variations. But it also has an aspect that is not being fully considered. The greenhouse effect will bring about increases of planetary geo-electromagnetic imbalances—of the kind associated with storms. As the atmospheric carbon dioxide count increases, then not only planetary warming will increase but also the number, intensity, and volume of storms.

It is scientifically understood that planets (Venus, for example) that have higher densities of more electromagnetically active gases (such as carbon dioxide) also undergo "hothouse" effects and more volatile atmospheres, characterized by violent winds and electronic storms. The dynamic wind relationship between hot and cold weather patterns will surely intensify if the earth's atmosphere becomes increasingly carbon dioxide–loaded.

Such would lead to wider and more intense variations in earth's usual weather patterns, and when these become dramatic enough it would be expected that their increased imbalances would negatively affect food production, which, in turn, would have great economic repercussions in the supply and demand for food—and which, again in turn, is already very delicate because of earth's increasing population overload versus its carrying capacity.

Even small redistributions of weather patterns will have severe implications if they are long-term enough. Small geo-electromagnetic redistributions will surely alter the usual pathways of the prevailing westerly winds. And with this alteration, radical fluctuations in earth's hot summer and cold winter weather pattern would ensue. I predict that these radical fluctuations will take place as the earth's delicate geo-electromagnetic patterns are altered by excessive buildups of industrial and urban-caused carbon dioxide.

The result will be the Great Wind storms of the millennial transition.

The omnipresence of powerful winds changes tidal patterns (as in hurricane or superstorm tidal floods) and pulls at natural physical structures. Increases in the number and nature of tornadoes can be expected, dust bowls will form, kilotons of earth-matter will dust areas not accustomed to such, and cold wet rains will flood areas unaccustomed to an increased volume of water.

This particular intervention impact will gradually form, as it already apparently is, and I presume it will be referred to by some such jargon as the "Epoch of the Winds." It will astonish weather experts and will be interpreted by millennial doomsayers as one of the "signs" of the Millennial Calamity and God's Wrath.

Even if wind increase is not very dramatic, minimal shifts in the earth's wind patterns could carry great economic implications. But I will predict the emergence of great winds during the millennial transition and the appearance of superstorms that will be reflected in increased magnitudes of tornadoes, typhoons, hurricanes, and electric storms.

The future-seeing feasibility is also very great that increased volcanic activity will emerge if the earth's geo-electromagnetic activity is increased (for example, the activation of the Cascade chain of volcanoes along America's West Coast). These eruptions would result in instant atmospheric sulfur dioxide increases. Also, since the human biophysic organism is very sensitive even to subtle geo-electromagnetic changes, human psychology may begin to experience strange psychic disruptions.

The Winds, and their radically increased storm potentials, will adversely affect food-production rates of the United States and Europe. These two great economic powers are especially vulnerable to variations of the prevailing westerly wind patterns as they build up over the Pacific and Atlantic oceans. But the Far East, and especially China, are more protected from radical changes in the westerlies because the Winds tend to deplete their wrath over the trans-Siberian and westernmost parts of the Asian continent before they reach the great fertile landmass of China.

India and Asian countries susceptible to monsoon activity can expect deadly increases in such activity, but monsoons do not as a rule penetrate deep into the China landmass. As will be seen ahead, China is largely self-sustaining anyway, and its link to the larger world free-market economy is an economic artifact that is not absolutely necessary to its actual survival. The economies of the United States and Europe, however, are inseparably linked to the world free-market economy, which, in turn, is linked to precise weather patterns characteristic of the past.

When this relationship even minimally negatively changes, extraordinary dominolike, systemic stresses will occur in the United States and Europe, reducing their competitive economic powers worldwide.

The increases of carbon dioxide pollution will make the Americas and Europe more vulnerable to radical weather patterns. These weather-pattern changes will in turn reduce their functional economic capacities in relation to the balance of powers prevailing at the beginning of the 1990s. This is the ultimate price to be paid by industrial emissions of carbon dioxide and the exorbitant increase of automotive vehicles powered by carbon fuels.

GLOBAL INCREASES IN DISEASE

The delicate atmospheric balance of oxygen and carbon dioxide is well understood. It is also understood that oxygen is lethal to many harmful anaerobic microorganisms. If the air we breathe contains increases in carbon dioxide and the balances of oxygen and carbon dioxide in our bodies change even a little, then harmful anaerobic microorganisms might flourish. This is a potential factor not being considered even by advocates of the greenhouse effect.

The ozone layer around the earth prevents many harmful solar radiations from penetrating into the atmosphere beneath it. Such radiation would also be conducive to the proliferation of many harmful microorganisms as well as to the kind of cell overgrowth associated with many forms of cancer. It is no news that the protective ozone layer is becoming depleted, but the reason is not very well understood. But increases in atmospheric carbon dioxide, sulfur dioxide, and other pollutants are obviously associated with the depletion.

During the year that I conducted the American Prophecy Project, I published in its April 1990 newsletter an astrological analysis of the cyclic recurrence of disease epochs, indicating that a new one had commenced during the late 1970s. The astrological correlates of this new disease cycle will extend into the millennial transition.

Under natural circumstances, its virulent peak might begin to abate about 1998. But we can now see that the future-negative change-routes of unnatural ozone depletion and atmospheric carbon dioxide increases will coalesce with the astrological correlates.

These combined future-negative change-routes will also coalesce with those of increasing overpopulation. The more densely packed a given population is, the easier it is for harmful microorganisms to find new hosts. More densely packed populations experience sanitation difficulties, as we have seen in the case of Mexico City. The overall conditions, then, are favorable to disease outbreaks, such as the cholera epidemic currently afflicting Latin America.

The twentieth-century inhabitants of the developed nations prided themselves on "conquering" and "eradicating" diseases, by either medically curing them or preventing their occurrence by vaccination and improved sanitation. But eradicating diseases often meant only containing them by erecting barriers that prevented certain diseases from being translated from infected regions into those less affected. These barriers went nominally under the term *quarantines*—to isolate from normal association or intercourse.

Today, quarantines are considered to interfere with the freedom of movement and the right to association or intercourse without social or governmental controls. Thus, quarantines are held to be inhumanitarian and an infringement of human rights and do not generally exist anymore.

The result has been the worldwide transmission of diseases, and the only control of them is their treatment when they do occur. Among other diseases, for example, certain antibiotic-resistant forms of syphilis and tuberculosis are being transmitted to every nation on earth, as the April 3, 1992, article shown below reveals.

Many kinds of destructive pleomorphic (shape-changing) organisms are appearing in areas whose medical doctors are not even trained to look for them. Not least among these is the strange immunosuppressive disease AIDS. The actual cause of AIDS is not

'MELTDOWN'

Federal officials warned yesterday that tuberculosis has reached "the meltdown stage" in New York City.

In New York City — which accounts for more than one in six cases in the country — a study found 70 percent of turberculosis cases resistant to at least one anti-TB drug.

understood, as is clearly indicated in Jad Adams's penetrating book *AIDS: The HIV Myth* (1989). But what is becoming increasingly understood is that the HIV virus probably is not the cause or at least the sole cause of AIDS, as has been loudly claimed.

Aside from health and mortality issues associated with disease epochs, these epochs have direct ashes-making relationships to medical facilities and their capabilities, to health insurance capacities, to economic balances, to welfare programs, and, not least, to human behavior. If disease indexes are to increase for the reasons given above, this one increase alone is an intervention impact sufficient to alter the change-routes of the millennial transition. If the increase of carbon dioxide is favorable to dangerous microbiotic growth then any medical recourse is not enough to prevent or contain that growth.

During the intensely materialistic period of the Modern Age, scientific interest in plagues and epidemics was focused exclusively on discovering their biological causes and methods of medical intervention. Indeed, today we completely assume that diseases and plagues occur *only because of* biological causes. Scientific investigation into the biological causes of diseases was, of course, well and good, but it left two questions unanswered: why do plagues and epidemics come into existence in the first place? And, why, after having arisen, do they "spend themselves out" rather than just go on and kill everyone?

A good case in point was the Black Death plague that began roughly about 1346, from which an estimated one-half to three-quarters of the population in Europe and the Middle East died—destroying the economic superstructure of the medieval world. Conceivably, this plague could have continued infecting humans until they all were dead. However, the plague pandemic "spent itself" around 1351 and disappeared. The biological causes of this plague and others like it are well known. But it did not cease because of medical intervention. There was none at the time. But it did die out, and why it did so is one of the greatest medical mysteries of all time.

Not long ago, *Smithsonian* magazine (February 1990) published an article describing this plague. The author noted, in an offhand way, that some astrologers of the time had predicted the plague, saying that it would come because of the future-negative conjunction (coming together at the same degree of the zodiac) of the planets Saturn, Mars, and Jupiter on March 20, 1345. The mention of this astrological aspect awakened my interest in the possibility of repeating major disease cycles that might correlate with predictable Saturn-Mars-Jupiter aspects.

The following great plagues and epidemics *were preceded* by strong future-negative aspects of Saturn-Mars-Jupiter, with the planet Neptune (which the earlier astrologers were not aware of, since it was only discovered in 1846) frequently involved:

> the great plague of A.D. 542, during the reign of the Emperor Justinian, which best estimates guess killed one-half the Middle Eastern population;
>
> the Black Death of 1348 (mentioned in the preceding);
>
> the plague of 1525, which similarly decimated Europe during the early years of Nostradamus (who first became famous for curing some people infected with it);
>
> the worldwide cholera epdemic beginning in 1881;
>
> the influenza epidemic of 1918, which claimed 25 million lives in the United States and Europe before it suddenly abated;
>
> the polio epidemic around 1952, which claimed twenty-three thousand lives and would have claimed more were it not for the discovery of the Salk vaccine;
>
> the cholerea epidemic in Africa in 1970, with a 50 percent death rate;
>
> the beginning of the present AIDS pandemic, beginning roughly around 1979; and
>
> the cholera epidemic of Latin America, which began early in 1990 and is currently spreading.

The periods listed here also saw general but less dramatic rises in many other diseases that also abated naturally—presumably, as astrological lore would have it, when the future-negative effects of the Saturn-Mars-Jupiter aspect weakened and abated.

Whatever one may think of astrology, correlations between the planetary configurations and the often calamitous rise in diseases do exist.

In this sense, it is interesting to note that some astrologers have referred to planetary aspects as *contaminants* of either destruction or well-being. We normally think of "infect" in a negative sense, but we can be infected by joy as well as misery. Scientific studies have established that subtle changes in geo-electromagnetism affect biological nervous systems either positively or negatively and that many subtle geo-electromagnetic changes correlate with planetary aspects.

Increases in diseases of the kind that result in epidemics and pandemics correlate with planetary aspects—and so the astrologers of 1345 were correct in predicting a coming plague.

The point of this roundabout discussion has to do with epidemic change-routes of the millennial transition. The 1989–90 onset of the millennial transition took place during one of the longest conjunctions of Saturn and Neptune in centuries. This long conjunction was also complemented by many Jupiter and Mars future-negative aspects, and these will continue to repeat at intervals for some years to come.

If the robustness and virulence of diseases result from some kind of geo-electromagnetic variability favorable to the explosion of diseases, then, from the astrological viewpoint *and* from the increase of atmospheric pollution, we can expect increases in disease indexes for some time to come.

The predictive question for the millennial transition, then, is whether disease indexes will continue to rise and, if they do, how they will affect change-routes into the future. The "stage" of the millennial transition is certainly set for disease disasters. What will be the results? The unconscionable destruction of the ozone layer, for example, could escalate the incidence of cancer into the statistical stratosphere and ultimately have such an extreme result as the confinement of human activity to the night side of the planet or the development of underground cities.

Diseases were not conquered or contained during the twentieth century, and the illusion that they were has led to social irresponsibility concerning them—including the failure of even developed nations to protect themselves from their transmission routes. The recontainment of diseases, then, is one more problem that the first inhabitants of the next century will inherit.

Thus, there are feasible grounds for predicting that increasingly future-negative change-routes resulting from the increase of atmospheric pollution will unfold during the millennial transition. Ominous climactic changes *and* increases in diseases will result. Both these future-negative phenomena bear direct relationships to local and global economic matters, which are already in a precarious state, and to the challenge to earth's carrying capacity by geometrically increasing population overgrowth.

Human mind-set activities of the past have "achieved" their self-created ashes.

The many future-negative forms of these ashes will manifest themselves during the next twenty years.

And we must now turn predictive attention to what will arise out of those ashes.

All the factors discussed so far represent outer feasibility phenomena that the aspiring future-seer is obliged to consider. None of these phenomena can be separated from one another. They are all interactive.

But you need not take my word for them. If you are inclined to do so, erect a "map" of them. I have consulted many special sources, but my own map has really been constructed merely by clipping newspapers and categorizing the clippings by topic. If these same newspapers are read only on a daily basis, they present a disjointed view of what is about to happen. But when you organize the clippings according to topic, over time, you will be able to see how what is about to happen is progressing.

My niece helps me to organize and maintain my clipping files. She is young and intelligent, but she was completely unaware of the shocking change-routes into the future that *forewarn* of what is to come. These change-routes are *published* in our daily media, and all it takes to discover their feasibility routes is to clip and categorize. Your own organized clippings will "adjust" your reality-anchors. My niece can now make predictions based on the organized clippings. So can you, if you take the time. And you need not even be an astrologer or psychic to do so.

MAKING THE PHOENIX

22

THE SURVIVORS OF THE TWENTIETH CENTURY

The overall predictive picture I have painted in the last few chapters is very gloomy. But it is entirely feasible. And its assured coalescing future-negative change-routes *must* manifest themselves in a variety of forms during the millennial transition. There are only two outstanding questions:

1. what will be the *feasible intensities* of those forms?
2. and what will be the *human behavior-responses* to the intensities?

The crux of this gloomy scenario is that although it has been brought into existence by ongoing mind-sets of the past, solutions to it *do not* exist either in those mind-sets or in past precedents. The solutions, if they are to come about, will be found in the future—and then only by those who can escape the baleful mind-set influences of the ashes-making past. The solutions, then, will be ahistorical ones, and their discovery will detach the phoenixlike future from the asheslike past.

Prevailing patterns of expectations here at the beginning of the transition do not account for the situation this way. Rather, it is expected that existing mind-sets can adopt new realities that will eventually ameliorate the gloomy scenario. But this involves deep systemic restructuring that, if human nature is considered, will not be undertaken until the law of diminishing returns manifests itself in confirmed catastrophes. It is then too late to avoid the catastrophes, since they will be upon us.

We are aware of impending catastrophes. But it is characteristic of prevailing mind-sets to believe they can be cured before they become full-blown. Thus, as many have already observed, too little is being done too late.

Look at it this way: you are alive, say in 1998 or 2000. Economic and ecological breakdowns have occurred, the sources of which are the ruinous mind-sets that "created" them.

Your future is ahead of you. You realize that the well-being of your future, and that of your children and the planet itself, is directly in the future-making path of a convoy of sixteen-wheeler trucks being driven by the ruinous mind-sets "programmed" in past "realities."

The "cargo" of the trucks consists of the future-negative change-routes of those mind-sets in the Now of 1998 or 2000 and the about-to-happen future of 2010. There is no longer any time to reprogram those mind-sets before the convoy totals *your* future.

Will you let the mind-set convoy, with its future-ruinous cargo, pass intact into your future? Or will you shoot the mind-sets dead before they haul their ruinous cargo into your future?

The future magnitude and intensity of increasing economic and ecological collapses that clearly *will* take place during the millennial transition will predetermine the awakening of the phoenix of the future *and its first radical expressions.*

In its first expressions it will be a very angry phoenix. This angry expression is *not* being included in present patterns of expectations. For example, new world orderists predict an increase in the economic division between haves and have-nots. Will the have-nots

stand idly by during the next twenty years while the division increases? If the division does increase, must workers' security lifelines
into their future increasingly be in jeopardy? Will workers meekly
consent to this? Can the world's debt economy continue to increase
without general economic deterioration in the quality of life? And
will not the masses begin to resent the causes of that deterioration?

Since increasing ecological dangers are directly tied to profit-
making by the already wealthy few, will the "rights" of that few to
create those dangers go unquestioned or unresisted as the dangers
amass and assume serious manifestations? Can deteriorating ecological conditions be *survived* through the time it might take to
figure out how to resolve them—survived not just with expressions
of mere concern but with pronounced expressions of anger?

When in 1998 or 2000 you and your children must increasingly
try to survive, or perhaps die from, toxic food, water, air, a depleted
ozone layer, and increases of carbon dioxide and sulfur dioxide, will
you not begin to determine that there is a difference between what
went on in the past and what must go on in your future?

The well-being of that future cannot be constructed upon the
very many intolerable diminishing returns already in existence at
the transition's beginning. At some point the patching up or cam-
ouflaging of those diminishing returns must fail. These failures will
not take place in 2050 or 3000. Many of them are *already* past the
point of no return, and their future-negative change-routes will
increase in intensity between the beginning of the transition (our
Now) and 2010.

So, existence, during millennial transition, of the communalizing
angry phoenix of the future *is very feasible.*

And that communalizing anger will be exacerbated by one particular factor: the mind-sets of the past, whose ruinous activities
have brought about the present deteriorating state of affairs, naturally believe their orientations and ongoing activities will be conveyed into the future. Hence, it is unlikely that those mind-sets
will willingly abdicate what they see as their right to exist in the
future.

Where is the point at which those ruinous mind-sets must be
forced by angry profuturists to desist and go out of existence? If

survival is to be possible in the future, the terrible legacy of past mind-sets must be interdicted—regardless of the costs to those mind-sets. The angry-phoenix idea that a sharp dividing line between profuturists and propastists (as it were) *must* occur is very feasible.

And this mind-dynamic idea is timed and predetermined by forthcoming astrological correlations that have held true in the past. These same astrological correlations also portend the renaissance that will very shortly commence and abruptly serve to liberate the phoenix of the future from the ashes of the past. So it is worth our future-seeing time to sidetrack into a little astrology to understand the correlations and the reasons why certain predictions can be drawn from them.

THE "PLUTO" GENERATIONS

In astronomical terms, Pluto is the small, outermost, slowest-moving planet, orbiting the sun in 248-year cycles. But its astrological significance is that its orbit also passes successively through the twelve signs of the zodiac—from Aries through Pisces. Pluto on average "occupies" one of these succesive signs for twenty years and then moves to the next sign. But since its orbit is slower when it is farthest from the sun and faster when it is nearest, Pluto occupies Taurus for about twenty-two years and Scorpio for about twelve years.

A great many people are born in each period during which Pluto inhabits one sign of the zodiac. These people are collectively referred to as a "Pluto generation." Thus, in astrological terms, there exists a Pluto-in-Aries generation, a Pluto-in-Libra generation, a Pluto-in-Scorpio generation, and so forth.

Pluto entered Libra in 1971, Scorpio in 1983. It will pass into Sagittarius in 1995. These three Pluto generations will be the youngest and therefore the most literal inheritors of the twenty-first century. Because of population increases since 1971, they will also numerically constitute the biggest Pluto generations in history. What the future will become is in their hands.

In astrological terms, Pluto represents the "sociological urge,"

and so the individuals composing each Pluto generation share relatively similar sociological realities, viewpoints, and worldviews.

Formal astrological definitions of each of the Pluto generations
hold that they constitute an organized group that acts as an instrument to amputate parasitic growth on the body politic in order to
reconstruct society and their future along more altruistic lines. These
"altruistic lines" are peculiar to each Pluto generation, but each
generation forms worldviews that are calculated to bear fruit through
the succeeding generations. Each Pluto generation, collectively, is
capable of manifesting total disregard for formerly constituted authority or vested rights—except when these, according to them,
may be administered for the good of all.

Each century, of course, sees the communal existence of several
Pluto generations and, in the absence of circumstances to the contrary, these generational mixes tend to flow somewhat smoothly
from the oldest to the youngest. But in the end the youngest of
them inherit the future. If a sense of righteous indignation is aroused
within a given Pluto generation by social miscalculations of the
earlier Pluto generations, it will not only disregard the authority
and vested interests of the miscalculating generations but also attack
and attempt to destroy their particular mind-sets.

As an example, the Pluto-in-Taurus generation tends to be stubborn and confrontational, even among themselves. The last Pluto-
in-Taurus generation was born between 1852 and 1882. The
majority of these matured just after the turn of the century, and the
youngest of them were sixty-three years of age in 1945. The years
between 1900 and 1945 were among the most confrontational and
bloodiest in human history, giving rise to the two World Wars.

These Pluto-in-Taurus epochs can be traced back to the birth of
Christ, and each of them corresponds with increases in wars and
conflicts. And in each case, Pluto generations subsequent to the
Pluto-in-Taurus generation took it as their dramatic duty to cause
society to back away from that generation's self-constituted rights
and vested interests in war and bloodshed.

If we trace earlier Pluto-in-Libra and Pluto-in-Scorpio generations, it is easy enough to recognize them. With respect to the
earlier Pluto generations, they have always manifested sociological

phenomena ranging from protests (in the case of the Libra generation) to social violence (in the case of the Scorpio generation). Both these Pluto generations have always been extremely profuture in their mind-sets, and so there is no astrological reason to assume that the present Libra-Scorpio crop will be any different.

The oldest of the Pluto-in-Libra generation will be twenty-nine as of 2000, and the oldest of the Pluto-in-Scorpio generation will be seventeen. They will be thirty-nine and twenty-seven, respectively, in 2010. They will constitute the two largest Pluto generations in history (with the exception of their successive Pluto-in-Sagittarius generation), and obviously they will consider the future *theirs* to make.

These three young Pluto generations will be the first to experience the future-negative change-route effects of the millennial transition. *They* will be the ones to live among those effects. They will be the ones to suffer the most from them. And they will be the ones who will be compelled by absolute necessity to figure out what to do about them.

In essence, if there is to be phoenix mind-set rebirth from the ashes being created by the mind-sets of the past, these three generations are the ones to accomplish it. Since each Pluto generation is capable of disregarding or attacking old constituted authority and vested interests (and since the Libra and Scorpio generations tend to do so anyway), it is astrologically feasible to predict that they will have set to work doing so by 2000.

Just look at what these three generations are about to inherit: elements of ecological-planetary destruction, elements of failing socioeconomic systems, elements of "positive" patterns of expectation that are not grounded in reality, elements of telepathic osmosis of the head-in-the-sand complexity. Would you want to inherit this mess?

The only question, then, is when will these young Pluto generations become righteously indignant enough that their adrenaline starts pumping, their anger at their inherited future-negative lot aroused? All it will take to *arouse this anger fully* will be further ecological and economic deterioration—at which point they will begin attacking old authority and vested interests fully with the intent of destroying them for better or worse.

Astrological correlations for this phoenix-anger-arousal indicate that it will begin to awaken between 1994 and 1998 and be in full feather by 2000. The old mind-sets, lacking in astrological expertise, currently have no idea that this anger directed at their failing authority and vested interests is possible. The angry phoenix is not being incorporated into any conventional forecasting I know of. But competent astrologers are, of course, expecting it.

Shortly after 1994 and certainly by 1998, many "profuture" radicals will appear and gain increasing power. They will

1. increasingly attempt to seize economic, ideological, and political powers on behalf of ensuring a more positive future;
2. militantly work literally to destroy historical practices and mind-sets out of which have arisen future-negative effects they must increasingly live among; and
3. unforgivingly begin to encode radically new profuture philosophies and practices designed *not* to perpetuate ruinous historical policies, attitudes, and worldviews but to replace those with new and unique methods for which there is no historical precedent at all.

The essential and fundamental computation upon which these new, radical activities will be based is: if the ruinous policies of the twentieth century are allowed to be forwarded intact into the twenty-first century, then the planet is surely doomed. I predict that these profuture radicals and their increasing number of sympathizers will staunchly place themselves between *their future* and the ruinous practices of the past—and do so in ways that resemble the blockading of the military-industrial establishment by the "hippies" of the 1960s.

The new world order expectations of the 1980s and 1990s, based as they are on ecologically ruinous twentieth-century economic philosophies and practices, are fated to meet headlong with these new profuture activities. And I predict that by 1998, if not earlier, the "war to save the future from the past" will be evident. The confrontation will ultimately be won by the profuturists—and for at least four reasons:

1. The destructive effects of ecological destruction will increase rather than decrease as events of the millennial transition unfold. The increasing visibility of these destructive effects will underscore the absolute need to tackle their causes rather than treat them as correctable symptoms. Public sentiment will gravitate toward the profuturists as the quality of everyone's life begins to decline.

2. The free-enterprise new world order is basically a move to colonize earth by big businesses on their own behalf, a colonization that will increase the economic gulfs between the haves and have-nots. As the attempted colonization progresses in the face of increasing ecological disorder, coupled with the also obvious growing gulfs between the haves and have-nots, any justifications for the colonization will be hard to maintain.

3. The growing gulfs between the haves and have-nots may be interpreted in one way as gulfs between the developed and the Third-World nations (or Third-World situations). But the gulf will also come to include the increasingly apparent distinction between the haves as "guilty" shareholders of megabusiness enterprises and the have-nots, who are their workers or labor forces. The latter are expendable as the colonializing shareholders divert work and labor to the cheapest Third-World labor markets possible in order to increase the size of their profit-making.

   This change-route pattern is already prominently visible as regards, for example, the United States, where workers are finding themselves increasingly unemployed as labor is diverted to cheaper labor markets in other countries. It is easy enough to predict that, if the economic colonization of the world actually means that workers *are* increasingly expendable, worker unrest and rebellion will threaten the justifications of new world orderists.

Massive worker strikes (which strategically affect consumerism) are the only way workers have of bringing self-
preserving pressure to bear on shareholders. And as these
unfold (from 1994 onward), the concerns of the workers
will be perceived as somewhat analogous to those of the
profuturists. The justifers of the new world order, then, will
be doubly assailed.

4. Finally, the most significant card in the profuturist deck is
the fact that the ostensible new world order is almost exclusively the product not of the young, who are about to
become the first inhabitants of the twenty-first century, but
of their influential elders committed to the socioeconomic
(read: "business") visions and practices of the twentieth
century. The reality-anchors of this older generation are
rooted in the past, which is already being seen as ruinous.
Most of them will be dead by 2005, or at least by 2010—
and with them their anchored visions and practices, and
with the death of these so too the death of their envisioned
new world order based exclusively in economic colonization
of the earth.

The increasing numbers of profuturists will not, because they
cannot, opt to forward these past ruinous visions and practices into
their future once the influential elders become future-absent in body
and mind. In fact, in order to assume their unique politic identity,
the profuturists as a necessity will have to distinguish and identify
themselves as *opponents* to *all* past ruinous mind-sets and their practices. And the most economical way to achieve this will be to
deconstruct or jettison the philosophies and practices of the past
altogether. Doing so will provide them not only with their profuture
activist cause and its unique future-oriented vision, but increasingly
attract political foundations to that cause and vision.

All causes, if they are to succeed by gaining influence among the
masses, require an anthem or a rallying cry that appeals to an identity
the masses can share—an anthem that, in this case, will emotionally
separate the profuturists from the ruinous past, yet that gives them

special identity with regard to it. By virtue of being forced to live in deteriorating economic-ecological circumstances, the profuturists will surely identify themselves as *victims* surviving the twentieth century.

In dumping ruinous twentieth-century mind-sets, the profuturists are almost certain to see themselves as *survivors* of what they have dumped or from what they must escape—as survivors in much the same psychological way that victims of rape are survivors of their traumas, adults have survived child abuse, Jews consider themselves to be survivors of the Nazi holocaust, and blacks who consider themselves to be the survivors of slavery.

Having to launch their future in the face of the many difficulties they are to inherit from the past, the Survivors of the Twentieth Century will have the never-again attitude typical (and desirable) of survivors of all kinds. From the profuturist point of view, never again will the earth be allowed to descend into stagnation and ruination *because* of misguided and unforesightful human activities.

And here is the change-route fireball of pending conviction that, although it has not completely awakened as of the early 1990s, will flare into intense activity by the year 2000.

If any part of what has been discussed and predicted in the preceding proves to be true as the millennial transition proceeds, then it is easy enough to foresee that many of the change-routes directing the pathways of the transition and prefiguring the future will lead into a future that is largely unanticipated today.

But that increasing economic and ecological breakdowns will take place is 90 percent certain. Such historically unprecedented breakdowns will clearly detach the future from the past simply because no functions on earth will stay the same, nor will any person on it be able to live the way his or her historical predecessors did. And if the inheritors of the past cannot live the way their predecessors did, then they cannot preserve their predecessors' values, beliefs, attitudes, visions, or reality-anchors—or any of the future "realities" derived from them.

A new human must emerge in practically every sense of the term *new*, and this new human must assist in its own birth without the midwifery of the past.

In other words, the times of the past are *over*. A completely new time is about to happen, and for better or worse, the future belongs little to the past but to that new time and its self-birthing new human—to whom, by the way, I extend my heartfelt salutations. For the onset of this new time is to be terrible in the first instance— but later sublime, if the Survivors of the Twentieth Century can prove their survivorship: by surviving.

If you want to flex your future-seeing capacities regarding all this, begin paying special attention to the activities of "ecological extremists." These are the ones who burn down fur-coat warehouses, topple electromagnetic-polluting power lines and grids, spike trees to defeat loggers, and liberate animals from research laboratories. I am not suggesting that they are right or wrong in their "angry" commitment. But they constitute a profuturist phenomenon based on activism the future of which, from the future-seer's point of view, needs to be considered without consulting your reality-anchors to judge it in advance.

Will there be more or fewer of these prototypical-profuturists during the millennial transition? Make your predictions based on their perceived feasibility. Wonder when the profuturists will begin to lock horns with the convoy of sixteen-wheelers with their future-ruinous cargo. Keep predictive notes of what your intuitus-intellect coughs up.

23

ENERGISM: THE RENAISSANCE-PREGNANT PHOENIX

The first activist expressions of the indignation of profuturist anarchists, terrorists, and extremists may cloud certain issues during the millennial transition.

But clearly the sociological urge to amputate parasitic growths on the economic-ecological body politic cannot be left to those who are reluctant to amputate—and who will be perceived as playing to vested interests by their lack of willingness to do so. Profuture anarchism will serve to clarify vested-interest issues in the long run, and the mind-set dust arising from their activism will have cleared by 2008.

But meanwhile, the mainstream structure of past mind-sets is in the process of collapsing on another phoenixlike front. This front is renaissance-pregnant with *energism*. We need to describe this in order to grasp what the millennial renaissance will be and how its future-positive change-routes will abrogate what is left of present mainstream reality-anchors.

THE PHILOSOPHICAL DEATH OF MODERN MATERIALISM

"The ashes of materialism" is more than a figurative phrase. The pursuit of materialistic goals during the twentieth century has produced physical results that are future-negative in the form of economic and ecological difficulties. These future-negative results are the "ashes" of the twentieth century, out of which some new uniting philosophy must arise if human existence is to continue in some future-positive form.

The modern philosophy of materialism, gaining social power around 1847, produced mind-sets whose mind-dynamic reality-anchors were firmly rooted in the doctrinal mistakes of the philosophy. Materialism's mind-dynamic anchors collectively flowered into what was called the *Progressive* Modern Age, whose particular vision dominated twentieth-century mainstreams in the areas of science, culture, economics, education, psychology, art, politics, war-making, diplomacy, sociology, and world planning for the future. Since the philosophy itself was founded on certain future-negative mistakes whose change-routes had to manifest themselves negatively at some future point, it was to be predicted that breakdowns in all these areas would eventually take place.

It is important to note that the greatest advocate of progressive materialism formed as the self-contained Soviet Union mind-set and was walled from the rest of the world by the Iron Curtain. The Soviet Union's collapse in 1989 confirmed that pure progressive materialism had been impractical and future-negative to begin with. This collapse stands as the clearest signal possible that all of materialism's mind-sets and their works worldwide are fated for similar kinds of ashes-making collapses.

In order to begin predicting the phoenixlike forms that will arise out of these ashes, the aspiring future-seer is obliged to understand why materialism's mind-sets were ashes-making in the first place. This involves some bitter realizations of rather large magnitude—realizations that have change-route implications for all the mainstream areas enumerated above.

Central to the philosophy of materialism was how "highest values and objectives" were to be perceived. Many early materialist manifestos proclaimed that these existed *only* in the pursuit of increase of material well-being. Thus, as materialism became more entrenched as a culture-forming philosophy, its most devoted adherents were obliged to teach that human life began with its physical birth and ended with its physical death. The highest values and objectives, therefore, had to be achieved during physical life *and* achieved in material terms. Living for the material present, then, fulfilled the highest necessity of living.

In other words, get and enjoy it while you can, for there is nothing for you after your death. In this way, human experience became limited to only what could be experienced in physical ways during the life span—after which there was *nothing*. Among other important human aspects, since future-seeing was not possible from the material Now, this valuable human power was jettisoned. The age of materialism became noted for its lack of foreseeing anything at all.

The realization, based exclusively in materialist philosophy, that human life was headed toward an ultimate nothing gave rise to two submaterialist mind-sets whose impacts on culture were unquestionably future-negative. Indeed, the future-negativity inherent in these submind-sets (nihilism and existentialism) was claimed by their adherents *to be a virtue*.

Twentieth-century *nihilism* held that *all* values and beliefs are unfounded and that existence is senseless and useless; that objectives and moral truths do not exist; and, as one of its most extreme doctrines, that conditions in social organization are so bad as to make destruction desirable for its own sake independent of any constructive program or possibility—a point, I predict, that will not be missed by certain profuture activists to come.

Existentialism is chiefly a philosophy whose definition, as admitted by existentialists themselves, is hard to define. Basic to the existentialist premise, though, is the idea that the universe does not make sense and that there are no rational patterns discernible in it, an idea that caused some to label existentialists as "disappointed rationalists." Existential doctrine, if it may be called that, taught that human existence is not exhaustively describable or understandable in idealistic or scientific terms and that the analysis of the meaning of human existence is therefore not possible save as that existence is experienced between birth and death, usually by the kinds of anxiety, guilt, dread, anguish, and isolation arising from existing in a universe that does not make sense.

Together with materialism, nihilism and existentialism in a variety of forms were the foundations upon which modern mind-sets formed, and together the three philosophies, none of which is future-positive–oriented, *infected* (exact word) human consciousness of the twentieth century.

As the philosopher Sidney Hook pointed out in his book *Pragmatism and the Tragic Sense of Life* (1974), which assessed the impacts of twentieth-century philosophies, the culturally fashionable materialistic, nihilistic, and existentialist meditation on death rather than on life could not contain "much wisdom, and that we cannot count merely upon the passage of time alone to diminish our stupidities and cruelties."

The very influential existential extremist Jean-Paul Sartre held that "if we must die then our life has no meaning." And by extension one could express the future-negative construct that if life has no meaning then we need not be responsible for it in the Now or in the future. And in this way, the fashionable mainstream philosophies of the twentieth century became overburdened with the tragic sense of life that has pervaded not only many social institutions, but our arts, sciences, education processes, and even our "entertainments." And this sense has yielded, as well, the mind-set basis for megadisasters.

Clearly, a renaissance cannot occur if these future-negative philosophies are to be perpetuated unchallenged into the future. I predict, then, that the centralizing nucleus of the renaissance will effect something of a radical about-face with regard to these matters. Something along the lines of, Yes we do die, but does that mean we should abandon all life likewise and take it down with us?

It is reasonable to assume that materialism will be future-absent and that the survivors of the twentieth century will have founded a new conceptual, future-positive image or definition of the human. Without this new conceptualized image, they would have no alternative but to perpetuate historical mind-sets—which the survivors will be *unable* to do because such mind-sets will be as unworkable in the future as they have already proven to be. This means that most of the philosophical mind-sets of the twentieth century anchored in materialism, nihilism, and existentialism will be future-absent.

I predict that the forthcoming profuturists will decide *not* to continue these future-negative mind-sets into *their* future. In short, *fatalism* will be out because it has to be if those in the future are to have a future.

It is relatively safe to predict that the mind-sets of the survivors will at least have to become centered around specific human attributes notoriously absent in twentieth-century mind-sets: vitalism, human powers, and wisdom, which became obscured within the fatalistic constructs of materialism, etc. These latter constructs, as of the beginning of the millennial transition, are still largely dominant in our arts, literature, and social programs, albeit in updated, altered forms.

The point of the preceding excursion through these particular twentieth-century ashes-making mind-sets has been to isolate what the inhabitants of the twentieth century *did not develop* but that the inhabitants of the next century must relocate and hastily develop if they are to survive. Sidney Hook put his finger on this matter when he noted that the cultural meditation (fixation would be a better word) on death rather than life could not contain much wisdom, nor inspire it either.

It should be clearly stated that if death is conceived as the ultimate human end, then there is no real need to fertilize and nurture wisdom. Human powers pale before the ominous and ultimate specter of death, and vitalism (enduring life force) is but an illusion. Indeed, if wisdom had been abundantly present and under increasing development in dominant twentieth-century mind-sets, then the great ecological and economic calamities would neither have come about nor even be pending. The detachment of the future from the past would not be necessary.

Wisdom cannot be present where human powers are absent, and there is no reason to develop human powers if life itself is conceived of as an ultimate nothing in a universe that does not make sense. One lives for the moment, for the fulfillment of material desires and physical appetites, and for the exploitation of matter from which money is derived so that the physical desires and appetites can be satisfied.

THE MILLENNIAL TIME OF REWISDOMING

But now come the great questions regarding wisdom: what does it consist of and how is it attained? This is a matter of some importance to any future-seer.

During the nineteenth century, *wisdom* was defined as accumulated philosophic and scientific learning, which in turn was the definition of knowledge. The term *wisdom* was still used in my youth, but somewhere in the 1950s it became culturally unfashionable to continue using it *at all.* And, as the facts stand today, we have accumulated a great deal of scientific knowledge, most noted for its absence of wisdom if the ominous situations that have come about are taken into account.

The traditional meaning of *wisdom*, abandoned in modern times, held that it was *the relationship or application of knowledge to life.* This is an echo of *intellectus,* as has been discussed in part one.

Surely the application of knowledge to life is a different matter from merely accumulating it for no practical life-making purposes save to exploit the immediacy of the material universe for the short-term material goals of the past and our present.

The application of knowledge to life requires a definition of *life* so that it can be understood what that knowledge is being applied to. The materialist definition of life held that it was the *state* of a material complex or individual characterized by the capacity to perform certain functional activities including metabolism, growth, and reproduction. Materialism's "wisdom" then centered on discovering what knowledge could be applied to the material complex of functions that defined, for materialists, what life was.

But was materialism's wisdom correct regarding its *basic* definition of life? If it was, and if it is to be correct regarding the future, then the meditation-on-death syndrome of the twentieth century will continue to project its ominous and life-demoralizing change-routes into that future.

Here it must be remembered that philosophical materialism, although present in ancient times as an optional philosophy, never achieved wholesale culture-making dominance until 1870–1920. In fact, the philosophy of *vitalism* tended to occupy this strategic slot in human affairs from time immemorial. And when materialism did win the day, it did so only by merely "showing" that vitalism was "unscientific"—which is to say, the adherents of materialism used the tool, evolved by their *own* philosophy, to confirm the righteousness of its own doctrines, to discredit phenomena that fell outside those doctrines.

This selfsame process is otherwise known as politicizing in accord with doctrinaire agendas.

Vitalism's major definition of life held that it is *the quality* that distinguishes a vital and functional being from a dead body or purely chemical matter. Vitalism *was* primarily a pre–twentieth-century metaphysical doctrine that was also held by its advocates to be scientific until scientific materialism "proved" that it was not. Vitalism bit the dust in about 1915, and by about 1925 it was laid in its historical grave by adherents of scientific materialism.

The least scientifically fashionable definition of vitalism (as given in the 1967 *Encyclopedia of Philosophy*, edited by Paul Edwards) is that there exists "a presence in living systems of a substantial entity that imparts to the system powers possessed by no inanimate body." The physical body itself is composed only of inanimate substances. These separately or altogether cannot and do not become *animate* in the absence of the "presence."

It is this presence that vitalists referred to as life and that, in a psychic sense, animates the otherwise inanimate chemicals of the biophysic life-unit.

It is this presence that philosophers and religionists historically referred to as "the soul." And it was the soul that was anathema to scientific materialists, nihilists, and existentialists alike. Materialists dumped the soul and vitalism because they extended the definition of life beyond the physical limits of the body and its life span. And if we carefully examine the outcomes of this dumping, we can see something quite important with regard to the future by considering the question of whether the material body itself is capable, as it were, of generating wisdom. The average life span of the physical body is about sixty years, and only forty-three years in some nations.

How much wisdom can be accumulated and applied during such a relatively short period? Part of the answer involves the concept, essential to vitalism, that wisdom resides in the psychic aspects of the animating presence, not in the inanimate aspects of the bioorganism. The physical corpus, made up only of inanimate matter, does not an *animate* organism make.

We can well wonder, if our Now-prevailing wisdomless mind-sets *are* perpetuated into the future, whether those who inherit the future will deal with its emergencies any better than the wisdomless mind-sets are doing today. Clearly not. And clearly, too, those inheriting the future will be obliged to restore wisdom to their educational agendas—and in restrospect classify the wisdomless twentieth century as the Dark Age of Wisdom.

But the restoration of wisdom (which foreshadows any renaissance) also implies the knowledgeable restoration of *the presence*—that is, the restoration of vitalism—for wisdom is not to be found within the material body.

With regard to the topic of human powers, it should be somewhat clear that if human powers had vigorously existed during the twentieth century, then humans should have been able to thwart the emergence of the dismal situations now being forced forward into the hands and minds of its Survivors. Human powers are needed to keep human affairs under control and driven in wisdomlike directions and, as well, to foresee the outcomes of human-made situations.

The powers exclusive to the physical body are limited, often narrowed to push-and-shove contexts. The human body by itself cannot cause things to happen at a distance from it, and so its powers are only one-dimensional. Also, the interactions between physical bodies alone are very limited, and we clearly cannot define our humanness and humanity by virtue of our physicality alone.

But we do define our humanness *and* interactions by the mind-dynamic ways in which we *think*, and it is the ways we think that transcend our physical inanimate limitations. Clearly the ways we think (via our anchored mind-sets) are as limited and ineffective as they remain uninspired by the absence of wisdom and the interacting powers it generates. Vitalism, human powers, and wisdom are interrelated and interdependent, and they collectively produce the conditions of what we call *life*. All paths to wisdom and human powers lead directly to the central issue of vitalism—to the "presence" that imparts to the chemical-organic system powers not otherwise possessed by that system.

Perceiving the presence or absence of wisdom is extremely important to future-seeing in that its absence automatically leads into future-negative change-routes whereas its presence leads into future-positive ones. You can demonstrate this to yourself. Select a situation and study it with regard to its wisdom quotient. This consists basically of merely determining if wisdom is present or absent in it. Once you can "see" the wisdom quotient, images *will* begin to form regarding where the situation is headed—and many of its change-routes into the future will become apparent. If you *diagram* these step by step, your NostraFac will activate and add more images.

In my predictive opinion, it is not possible for the Survivors of the Twentieth Century to survive *unless* they redefine *why* they should survive. If physical bodies are to live within deteriorating physical environments of an ecologically destroyed planet, what would be the reasons for continuing attempts to survive? The survivors will be able to revisualize the reasons only by revisualizing themselves as "the presence."

And thus vitalism, albeit probably under different names, will be restored, and new visions regarding the potentials of wisdom and human powers will commence.

From this overall situation, the following feasible predictions can be derived:

From 1994 onward, mind-sets and institutions that act to prevent this revisioning will begin to be vigorously assailed by profuture philosophers.

As twentieth-century Survivors bring their plight more and more into *their* clearer focus, this assailing will take on militant and terroristic proportions.

At some point, probably around 2008, the Survivors will become heartless with regard to *eliminating* the remaining mind-sets and institutions, which work to prevent the new realizations the survivors will need.

Around this time, a phrase that in our present terms means "universal psychic reconstruction" will serve as yet another motto for the Survivors, who will vigorously seek to detach from the past and encode new future-positive mind-sets, sciences, cultures, and philosophies.

Terms meaning "reenchantment," "reempowerment," "revitalizing," and so on, will replace our contemporary catch phrases *political correctness, deconstruction, revising the system,* and so on. (Such terms have already come into existence.)

It is possible to predict all this because the Survivors of the Twentieth Century will have to become reempowered and rewisdomlike if they are to survive. Survivors of any kind are usually desperate. Desperation makes survivors heartless. They will probably make mistakes, to be sure, but any mistakes they might make will pale in comparison to those that have already been made by the inhabitants of the twentieth century.

I will also predict that 1998 will be the year in which the future becomes irrevocably detached from the past. The completeness of the failure of most twentieth-century systems, mind-sets, and affiliated institutions will be clearly visible by then. The *reasons* they will have failed may not be exactly clear, but those reasons will no longer be of any importance or interest to the Survivors. Their future-positive reasons will be of their own making, and they will have no need of the past.

Twentieth-century system failures will result in great senses of betrayal and great, unifying anger. It is out of this great anger that the centralizing, reempowering highest values and objectives of the third millennium will arise. These values will not remotely resemble those of the twentieth century. We cannot recognize them today because we scarcely recognize vitalism, human powers, and wisdom—and so few of us are able to realize what reempowerment and rewisdoming actually mean. But the Survivors will, of absolute necessity, need to relearn what these concepts mean if they can hope to script *their* times in future-positive ways.

This rewisdoming is already being foreshadowed—as it should be if it is true that the future *always* foreshadows itself.

Have you, as an ostensible future-seer, ever pursued wisdom or tried to discover what it is? It is perhaps the final piece in the future-seeing mosaic.

Your wisdom is the only wisdom you will ever have. And your wisdom resides in the relationships of things that you can perceive, if and when you do not judge those perceptions by appealing only to your reality-anchors. These may be negative or positive relationships, but in either case the relationships will reveal what is about to happen because of them. Relationships portray their own change-routes into the future.

Your perceptions of relationships will constitute whatever quantity and quality of wisdom you have. Remember, as was discussed in part one, relationships carry meaning, meaning carries change-routes, and perception of change-routes will make you a future-seer.

Select a few topics. Consider, for example, the meaning of your present love affair to your future, or your present job or occupation, or your tolerance of throwaway plastic grocery bags, or the national debt if you want. Study them not for their appearances or for what others say they are. Study them instead for the meanings *you* can perceive in them and for those meanings in relation to other meanings. Time will loop when you perceive the correct meanings and their future change-routes. See where the wisdom change-routes go forth and toward what they lead.

If your perception is blocked in this regard, examine the block until it goes away. You cannot foresee what your mind-dynamic reality-anchors do not want to foresee. Reread the laws of future-seeing and the passages on mind-dynamic defense mechanisms. Work until the block gives way. Meaning and wisdom will then reinstate themselves.

Gather information from all sources possible. But do not consult the media for wisdom.

24

THE GREAT AWAKENING OF THE
MILLENNIAL TRANSITION

Many truly dark and ominous future-negative change-routes exist, and their destructive outcomes are at least partially inevitable. Thus, it is difficult to think that a future-positive "renaissance" can awaken amid them. But several change-routes are leading into one. Were this not so I don't think I would have had the courage to write this book.

If the aspiring future-seer gains enough of a long-term scope then it becomes clear, first, that the future always foreshadows itself; second, that history approximately repeats itself; and third, that human events correlate with the repeating cyclical activity of the planets. Many "about-to-happen" phenomena can remain invisible for a long time if these three workhorse concepts are not applied to future-seeing efforts. The forthcoming renaissance is still largely invisible today, but its emergence can confidently be predicted not only because it is already being foreshadowed but because of repeating cyclical activity of the planets.

RENAISSANCE

The French term *renaissance* means rebirth. What history refers to as the great European Renaissance of the fifteenth century was not called a *renaissance* until the mid-seventeenth century. The people of that renaissance did not use the term *rebirth* except as it applied to the rebirth of literature. They thought in terms of awakening, restoration, or recovery. The use of these terms clearly implies that the people of *the* Renaissance realized there was *something* to be awakened and recovered from and that certain lost culture-making factors needed to be restored. But more importantly, the people of the Renaissance generally aligned themselves with what they called "the New Knowledge."

The "something" with which the New Knowledge contrasted was the old knowledge of the Middle (or Dark) Ages—during which mainstream social consciousness in Europe was dominated and guarded by antiscientific doctrines emanating from the powerful Holy Catholic Church at Rome. Since all doctrines, if applied to the extreme, induce reality-anchor somnolence in human mind-dynamic systems, it is difficult to perpetuate new energyinformation through them. The result can be cultural ossification from which mind-dynamic systems need to be awakened if progress is to resume.

From the future-seer's point of view, such awakenings take place when it is recognized that cultural ossification is future-negative and needs to be recovered from by restoring future-positive change-routes. The awakening serves to detach the future-negative change-routes of the past from its own new future-positive ones.

Historians generally believe that it is the emergence of new, vital information that stimulates renaissancelike activity. Mind-sets based in the past then have to *stop*, and new ones based on the new information have to *start*. But another, more subtle, factor must also be considered from the future-seer's point of view.

Complete mind-set—ossifed systems (closed-circuit mind-sets) automatically imply that those systems could not continue what is presumed to be *the major* human evolutionary mandate. This is sometimes expressed as the perfection of human consciousness or the growth and development of it. The human mission into the future is always seen in the light of this evolutionary mandate. Without it, we would have long ago stabilized our evolution, much as we have the "consciousness" of the shark, termite, or cockroach species that have not changed in millions of years.

Awakenings from the somnolent stupor of doctrinaire, closed-circuit, ossifying mind-sets are therefore obligatory if humanity is collectively to continue its evolutionary mission into its *own* future.

THE FUNCTION OF NEW KNOWLEDGE

Intellectually discovering and adapting to new information and knowledge are parts of this awakening, missionlike process. But at a more deeply structured level it is unfeasible to assume that this mission would have commenced at all unless these future-oriented processes were not built into our mind-dynamic systems in the first place.

After all, humans are biologically and mind-dynamically constructed to survive into the future—an effort that would surely fail in the absence of *natural* triggers that will dissolve ossified mind-sets. The effect of these active mechanisms is to awaken consciousness when that consciousness "descends" into counterevolutionary ossifications of its own making.

From the future-seer's point of view, then, the evolutionary human mission will be composed of periods of awakenings and ossifications. It is the introduction of doctrinaire "certainties" into stabilizing mind-sets that brings about their counterevolutionary ossification, the escape from which requires awakening. In the larger picture, then, the alternating order of awakening and ossification is an "eternal" chain (as it is often described).

If the aspiring future-seer can see the sense in all this, it becomes grist for his or her future-seeing mill. For preseeing cyclic periods of ossification and awakening will clearly establish what kind of change-routes will precede or predict them. Foreseeing the cyclic rise and fall of mind-set doctrines is one of the major keys to competent future-seeing, since the arising of doctrines predicts their eventual ossifiction, and their fall predicts new-knowledge awakenings.

THE ASTROLOGICAL FEASIBILITY OF A GREAT AWAKENING

Phenomena that repeat at more-or-less regular intervals are called *cyclic*. When we know what the intervals are we can predict when the phenomena will occur again. Specific relationships of the distant planets repeat themselves at predictable intervals. Cycles analysts can show that specific terrestrial phenomena—for example, repeating cycles of war or peace, of social confusion or certainty, of growth or decline, as regards not only food production but philosophies, arts, cultural shifts, and pessimism or optimism—repeat themselves at fairly regular intervals and have done so for thousands of years.

Both historians and cycles analysts can show that specific kinds of phenomena are either *present* or *absent* throughout long periods of history. What is likely to be present or absent in the future is important to the future-seer, who, of course, should begin thinking in those terms. The study of outer information in the form of cycles analysis is meaningful, for inclining and declining cycles portend what will be future-present or future-absent. Cycles are sometimes interrupted by unexpected phenomena. But they hold true on average. Cycles must be graphed or diagrammed (image-built), not merely considered "in the head." If they are diagrammed, then NostraFac (psychic) components will produce various predictive images.

The astrologer can show that the presence or absence of phenomena correlate with the cyclical positions of the planets. In this sense, then, historians, cycles analysts, and astrologers meet each other coming and going. But historians cannot predict very well. The predictive edge goes to cycles analysts and astrologers, and the science of cycles analysts tends to correspond to the craft of astrologers.

The question of whether an astrological feasibility exists for change-routes in the human scene is clearly answered by astrologers who correlate such changes with the positions of the planets, exactly as cycles analysts have begun to do.

For example, Neptune orbits around the sun in 164 years. It thus successively "resides" in each of the twelve signs of the zodiac for periods (or epochs) of approximately 13.6 years. During each of these periods, historically repeating phenomena appear that are specific enough "to the sign" to differentiate them from Neptune's residing in the other eleven zodiacal signs.

The general "effects" that Neptune "causes" in each of the twelve zodiacal signs has been very competently packaged for the lay reader by the astrosociological historian Stan Barker, in his breakthrough book *The Signs of the Times: The Neptune Factor and America's Destiny* (1984). Neptune "entered" the zodiacal sign of Capricorn in 1984, where it will reside for thirteen years and will then enter the sign of Aquarius in 1998. The astrological meaning of Capricorn holds that it is the sign of conservatism; of the renewal of interest in and return to historical values and traditions; of preoccupation with the economy; of the growth of business and a commensurate growth of government to counter it; of enhancement of foreign relations; and of the escalation of interest in the welfare of the poor and the disenfranchised.

Capricorn also imparts illusions of permanency and stability—with the further illusion that the future can be "handled" by all of the foregoing working in concert in New World Order kinds of ways. From the astrologer's point of view, then, it is no surprise that illusory ideas of the present New World Order schemes have become manifest while Naptune is in Capricorn.

Mr. Barker refers to the Neptune-in-Capricorn "wave" as the "Big Dad" epoch that generally repeats itself once every 164 years. In the United States, the last Capricorn wave (1820–34) centered on the Big Dad presidencies of John Quincy Adams and Andrew Jackson and the implementation of the Monroe Doctrine regarding New World Order foreign affairs. All the Capricorn phenomena given above also became manifest. The present Capricorn wave has focused on the Big Dad presidencies of Ronald Reagan and George Bush, and all the other Capricorn phenomena have manifested themselves too, as we well know.

The zodiacal sign following Capricorn is Aquarius. As well as carrying other attributes, Aquarius is the sign of social agitation, unrest, anarchism, revolution, and demands for reform of Capricornian policies that have become intolerable. The last Neptune-in-Aquarius wave of 1835–48 manifested these phenomena. The Communist Manifesto, long in the progress of conception, was published in 1848 as a summation of what was needed to correct Capricornian Big Dadism—and from the future-seer's point of view the meaning of this document extended far into the future. The next Neptune-in-Aquarius wave will begin in 1998 and last until 2011.

Now, it is almost unthinkable that such a complex sociological phenomenon as an awakening or a renaissance is cyclical and also correlates with specific planetary arrangements. But if this can be shown to be the case, then we can predict that the forthcoming renaissance will indeed occur.

As we have seen earlier, Pluto circumnavigates the zodiac every 248 years, residing in each of its signs from 13 to 22 years. History shows that a future-positive renaissance or awakening occurred each time Pluto passed through Libra, Scorpio, and Sagittarius. Each of these awakenings was preceded by social unrest (Pluto in Libra) and the rejection of old knowledge (Pluto in Scorpio). The great awakenings occurred because of the demands for new knowledge (Pluto in Sagittarius).

The European Renaissance (roughly 1490–1550) can be directly correlated with Pluto passing through Libra, Scorpio, and Sagittarius. Approximately 208 years later Pluto again entered Libra, and the same awakening sequence was repeated in what was actually called the Great Awakening in both the United States and Europe. An awakening of similar magnitude has taken place approximately every 209 years, and these can be traced back to the time of Christ. In fact, Jesus was born as Pluto was entering Libra, and his new knowledge took hold when Pluto was in Sagittarius.

Pluto is in the late part of Scorpio as I write, and all around are the gloomy scenarios of old ossifying orders and mind-sets breaking down, dramatized as they are by death-oriented cultural phenomena. Just inside these gloomy scenarios, however, are the demands for newly awakening knowledge, which will redirect the times to come in future-positive ways. Pluto will pass out of Scorpio in late 1995 and once again enter Sagittarius, the sign of abundant new knowledge—the sign of great awakenings and renaissance.

If this particular astological cycle holds true, as I am obliged by my learning to predict it will, then the millennial renaissance is just ahead. It may not be called a renaissance, but it will be an awakening.

FORESHADOWING OF THE MILLENNIAL AWAKENING

Those who have kept up with postmodern developments will recognize that the seminal forms of this new knowledge are already extant—and that old, ossifying mind-sets must ultimately retire because of them.

New knowledge can be defined in two ways—first, as what is discovered was neither known or was misunderstood before; and second, as what breaks down old, ossified mind-sets and releases from them the positive opportunities inherent in the future, which literally belong to the future and not to the past. In either case, dramatic social and cultural changes must and will result.

Since some forms of new knowledge take place all the time, and since some old mind-sets tend slowly to adjust to them, we typically see new-knowledge inputs as constituting gradual change. However, gradual new-knowledge changes are never described as a rebirth or an awakening. Awakenings are associated with extreme social dissatisfaction with old orders, with the development of momentous emergency situations whose solutions do not exist in the mind-sets of the old orders, and with discoveries so devoid of historical precedent that they simply cannot be absorbed by old-order mind-sets.

When old mind-sets will no longer suffice, new ones must be "born" on a major scale—and it is this large-scale magnitude that is referred to as a rebirth, renaissance, or new-knowledge awakening.

The social precursors to the Great Millennial Awakening are many. I refer the reader to the bibliography, for example, where I have offered a selection of new-knowledge books under the rubrics of "Quantum-Holographic Reality," "Quantum Space-Time," "Bio-Electromagnetism," "Astrology—Astro-Cycles," and "Extraterrestrial."

The sum of all this new knowledge indicates strategic *must-changes* that will give shape to the future for which no past precedents exist. Consider, for example, that we are increasingly hearing of such new concepts as quantum energy and healing, bio-electromagnetism, bioenergy, virtual reality, energism, the holographic mind and the holographic universe, past-life recall, multidimensionalism, future-life "memory," time-bending, and biofeedback techiques to discover and increase subtle human powers.

None of these concepts existed as terms within old-knowledge contexts centered on materialism, for they could not.

THE NEW-KNOWLEDGE HUMAN AS AN "ENERGY-BEING"

If we look for *one* new-knowledge aspect that will destroy old mind-sets and their traditional institutions and give birth to new ones and new institutions, then we must turn some predictive attention to new discoveries that will not only encode new realities but must also act as destroyers of dominant old realities. Since the major dominant reality of the nineteenth and twentieth centuries was that of materialism, and since the pursuit of materialistic goals has ultimately brought about so much destruction, we can turn our predictive attention to what will destroy materialism. A bit of history is necessary to prepare us to do so.

Materialism essentially held that chemical matter was the only reality and, therefore, that the "highest values and objectives" were in the scientific, economic, and cultural pursuits of material well-being. But what if material reality were *not the only reality?* If other realities exist, then the predictive question becomes twofold:

1. If organic-chemical life is *not* made up of only matter as the primary substance of the universe, then what *is* it made up of? You will remember that materialism's manifestos placed the material world as primary and thoughts about this world as secondary—as epiphenomena of chemical interactions.

2. If it is considered that matter may not be the primary foundations of existence, then matter is secondary to something else—something else that needs the new terms *virtual reality, quantum energy, holographic, multidimensional, bioelectromagnetism,* and so on, to help describe it.

The idea that there might be something "beneath" matter is not new—and, in fact, was an accepted idea before modern materialism arose to its culture-shaping power. In 1870, a young physicist, William Kingdon Clifford, had suggested to the Cambridge Philosophical Society that a particle of matter might really be nothing more than a kind of hill in the geometry of space.

Shortly after that, in 1873, another gifted physicist, James Clerk Maxwell, hinted that although the electromagnetic field seemed continuous, the study of its singularities and instabilities might tend to remove the mind-set prejudice of the material continuity of things. Roughly speaking, Maxwell began speaking of discontinuous virtual thoughtlike reality around which or because of which matter formed. And in a dramatic moment he offered the warning that it might turn out that the cosmos could be the product of one big nonmaterial "thought."

Subsequently, the physicist Niels Bohr soon proved that light and energy could be both wave and particle—the particle generally being considered material, the wave not. When Einstein produced a wave of continuity of sorts with his theory of general relativity, he not only ended the dichotomy of time and space but eventually proved that matter and energy share the same equation.

Later, during the 1930s, the Nobel laureate Werner Heisenberg demonstrated that the objective world in space-time (the world of matter) no longer existed at the subatomic level. And he further noted that mathematical symbols of theoretical physics referred merely to possibilities and probabilities, not even to facts—as had earlier been suggested by Clifford.

The point here is that once it was seen that "something" existed subatomically beneath "matter," the materialist's world dematerialized.

In short, as of the late 1930s, *energy* was now seen to be primary, matter (particles) secondary, with energy and thought (information) practically synonymous. Energy "makes" patterns, and from these patterns matter assumes form because the patterns somehow solidify "atoms" into their particular shapes and functions. In this sense then, energy must exist before matter can.

More recently, geneticists are well aware that our genetic DNA-RNA physical basis is made up of specific energy patterns that "cause" their respective physical manifestations. Our genes are pre-packaged energyinformation "thought-units" and are in effect a kind of "blueprint" upon which, and because of which, the physical body manifests itself the way it does.

To summarize, then, humans (like all other life forms) are made up of "fundamental waves" that can conveniently, if not completely correctly, be called electromagnetic energy in some special *bio-electromagnetic form*—which is to say, we are *electronic patterned beings* before we are physical bodies. This is tantamount to saying that we are infoenergy-thoughts before we are physical, since thoughts themselves are electronic in nature.

The cutting edge of science has reached the point at which it is now certain that energy is the "fundamental essence" and, further, that it is indestructible. If it is true that we are energy beings, then we are indestructible, at least so far as our energy "forms" are concerned. This clearly represents "new knowledge."

And its future-positive nature has been foreshadowed in a number of books: Harold Saxton Burr, a neuroanatomist of the Yale University School of Medicine, published the seminal book *Blueprint for Immortality: The Electric Patterns of Life* (1972). The Soviet scientist A. P. Dubrov, a member of the Soviet Academy of Sciences, published *The Geomagnetic Field and Life* (1978), a geophysical expansion of Burr's electric-patterns evidence. Robert O. Becker and Gary Selden published *The Body Electric: Electromagnetism and the Foundations of Life* (1985), and the British biochemist Rupert Sheldrake published his book *A New Science of Life: The Hypothesis of Formative Causation* (1981), which some ossified materialist mindsets said should be burned. "Formative causation" is otherwise known as morphogenesis or morphic resonance, which, roughly speaking, refers to the genesis of living organisms in energy-thought-pattern—making kinds of ways. In other words, our vital *origins* are to be found not in the material universe but in what is beneath it. If we are anything at all, we are in the first instance energy-electronic beings.

Beneath the realities of electromagnetism and bio-electromagnetism may lie *quantum reality*, *virtual reality*, and the *holographic universe*, which open the door to multidimensionality, in which matter, energy, space, and time exist only as artifacts of "thought." Since thoughts do not make for a complete or valid cosmology (the metaphysics of the universe as an orderly system), the new cosmology of the great millennial awakening will have to include what was never included in any cosmology before—quantum and virtual multidimensional reality, which either interact with each other or singularly produce the holographic universe.

At this point, the roots of the coming awakening may be hard to grasp. I think we can see the difficulties that any aspiring future-seer will have in penetrating future developments that will be very alien to their reality-anchors as they are currently constructed. But, for one thing, if all the preceding is only *somewhat* true, then it is entirely possible that the highest achievement of science and technology so far—computer technology—may become obsolete in the future.

We can hardly imagine the future without this technology and, in fact, fully expect it to flood much improved and enlarged into the change-routes of that future. But if the new holographic theories of the universe are true and human mind-dynamic systems can merge with that universe, then computers will become more like kindergarten toys than the top-of-the-line technology they represent now.

The best description so far of holographism directed at the lay reader is found in the late Michael Talbot's book *The Holographic Universe* (1991). Those who have not studied this important book are probably familiar with photographic holograms, which are three-dimensional images projected into space with the aid of a laser. Briefly, our physical bodies are holographic projections of our minds, which, in turn, may be holographic projections of the universal mind. If you wish to dig into the details of holographism, the two most important scientific architects of the holographic nature of the universe are the physicist David Bohm (of the University of London), a former protégé of Einstein, and the Stanford neurophysiologist Karl Pribram, one of the world's most respected quantum physicists and foremost leader with regard to our understanding of the mind.

From the point of view that true knowledge-wisdom is what can be applied to future-positive life, the importance of holographic theory is that it accounts for such diverse phnomena as, among others, "psychic" acquisition of information out of the cosmos, electromagnetic participation with all that is, telepathy, near-death and out-of-body experiences, the unsolved riddles of body/mind, miraculous healing, accelerated transformations of all kinds, astrology, future-seeing, and the human-experienced feelings of *cosmic unity*—in other words, phenomena that may as well be called "energyinformation thinking," which is not limited by the artifacts of matter, energy, space, or time.

If energyinformation "thinks" at all, as it now appears to do, it therefore possesses "intelligence." And because energyinformation is universal, the entire cosmos must be pervaded by intelligent energyinformation-thinking, and the method or structure of energyinformation thinking is via holographic projection throughout the cosmos. This, of course, approaches the traditional understanding of "God," which, as the traditions say, has "thought" the cosmos and everything in it into existence.

And here, then, is the profound basis for the nature of the millennial awakening whose change-routes will begin to concretize the future, as they already have.

When humankind redefines itself in such a strategic manner, it can detach its new future from the future-negative change-routes emanating from the past.

I do not think the advocates of the old mind-sets will abdicate to the new without protest and interference. But their times are over.

The profuturists are coming, Pluto will enter the new-knowledge sign of Sagittarius in 1995, and necessity will do the rest.

PART THREE

THE ULTIMATE PIECE OF THE FUTURE-SEEING MOSAIC

Intuitus knows and shows the way.

25

THE GENERAL SHAPE OF THE FUTURE

The ultimate "piece" of the future-seeing mosaic concerns what *needs* to be foreseen. Natural or developed psychics sometimes correctly predict unexpected events, and our NostraFacs generally alert us to specific forthcoming events. But foreseeing unexpected events *in* the future is not the same as predicting and forecasting the *general shape* of the future. The general shape is more the territory of futurologists, cycles analysts, and astrologers who, with or without psychic inputs, utilize past precedents, trends, and feasibility studies.

Both specific events and the general shape of the future need to be foreseen. Foreseeing the larger general shape stimulates many specific foresights; and since in the long term the general shape will affect many more people than short-term specific events will, foreseeing its larger important outlines would seem to have priority over the latter.

In this case, the question of what most shapes the future becomes significant. If the different "whats" can be identified, then the types of change-routes discussed earlier can be applied to them—bearing in mind that completely unconceived and unexpected occurrences can considerably change the perceived "whats."

Determining what will shape the future becomes the necessity and the prerogative of individual future-seers who may not always see eye to eye on these matters. From my own point of view, though, it seems that mind-set changes give more shape to the human future than anything else.

MIND-SET CHANGES RESHAPE THE FUTURE

Mind-sets and mind-set changes are central to human-engineered forms of future-negative *fate* and of future-positive *destiny*, of future-negative and future-positive change-routes. They are also the most dangerous and volatile of all human phenomena because they all are enveloped in telepathic osmosis and have *their* particular expectations as to what the future should and should not be. Mind-sets are also based in value norm anchor-points and possess defensive mechanisms. Thus, they change because of many complex reasons. But since all mind-sets are always transitory ones in some way in that they *will change because they do change,* any future-seer who can perceive why and how they are changing can also perceive what needs to be predicted.

DEEP-CORE SOCIAL REALITIES

There are, however, millions of different kinds of mind-sets both minor and major. Obviously, changes in major mind-sets are more future-shaping than those in minor ones, and the future-seer needs to discriminate in some way among them. For my own use, I've determined that five important kinds of mind-sets are *always* in existence and that change-routes emanating from these will always give some kind of predictable shape to the future. These five mind-sets establish ongoing (if changing) deep-core socializing realities, and have to do with:

1. social control of violence, sexuality, and biological reproduction;
2. national and cultural unities and the power struggles between them;
3. the distribution (in some form) of wealth;

4. how the future is to be seen and engineered;
5. basic religious, philosophical, social, and scientific concep-
   tions of what the human is, which includes concepts of
   human origin.

These five deep-core socializing mind-sets cannot always be separated from one another, and their change-routes will affect many
other kinds of mind-sets. And, obviously, other important core
mind-sets exist whose own change-routes will affect these five.
Hundreds of predictions can be mounted upon the change-routes
of these five and others that will interact with them.

But using the millennial transition epoch as a predictive basis, I
have been able to locate at least eleven major mind-set change-
routes (described beginning below through page 300) that with some
confidence can be foreseen as giving general shape to the mind-set
future as it will be by 2010 or 2015. The future *meanings* of these
major change-routes will have an impact on other kinds of mind-
sets on which the aspiring future-seer might wish to work.

MIND-SET CHANGE-ROUTES REGARDING
SOCIAL CONTROL OF VIOLENCE, SEXUALITY,
AND BIOLOGICAL REPRODUCTION

CORE CHANGE-ROUTES REGARDING THE MILITARY SYNDROME

Core-belief regarding the absolute necessity of military violence is
very old and has in fact sometimes been justifiable. Military mind-
set edifices, therefore, have been enormous throughout our history,
and war has played a predominant future-shaping role in it. Military
edifices, though, are expensive. And so the largest economic systems
on earth have always been military ones in which people are expendable but economic support is not.

The combined total cost of the world's *annual* military expenditures, as published in 1991 by the World Game Institute in Phil-

adelphia, is $1 trillion—and possibly twice that if covert military expenditures could be included.

In the past, the violence of war was perceived as the way to prevent future-negative social consequences if war was not waged. The existence of a greater future-negative new "enemy" was not foreseen or even considered as possible—with the result that no war-consciousness mind-sets formed, either to combat it or to *foresee* the wisdom of devoting money to finance the combat.

This new "enemy" has arrived in the form of the ominous ecological disasters facing not only us today but the people of the future to come. It consists of extremely dangerous future-negative consequences that will affect everyone no matter their mind-set differences: global warming, acid rain, population stabilizing, and more.

The annual costs of working to correct these ominous ecological and sociological problems and eradicate some of them from the future have been estimated by the World Game Institute as *slightly less than one-fourth* of the world's total annual military expenditures. For about $240 billion annually, the world could retire the debits of developing nations; have safe, clean water and renewable energy; provide shelter for everyone; eliminate starvation; provide universal health care; stabilize population; prevent soil erosion and oceanic depletion; prevent acid rain and deforestation; and so forth. All this could be accomplished for less than one-fourth the world's annual military expenditures. (For five dollars, the World Game Institute [3508 Market Street, Philadelphia, Pa., 19014 (215) 387-0220] will send you a booklet entitled *Doing the Right Thing,* which contains explanations and a telling chart of annual military versus ecologically corrective costs.)

In the figure on page 271, I've provided an analogous chart reflecting the costs of the future-seeing priorities alluded to in this book.

The ominous ecological scene, however, comprises not only geophysical components but also the mind-sets whose future-ignorant activities brought it into existence in the first place. The future-seer predicting mind-set changes will quickly realize that merely pouring money over the geophysical problems will hardly correct

APPROXIMATE YEARLY COSTS OF SAVING THE GLOBAL FUTURE COMPARED TO THE WORLD'S ANNUAL MILITARY EXPENDITURES

Disclosed annual world military expenditures is estimated by several watch-dog organizations to be a whopping $1 trillion, as shown in the pyramid below. By comparison, annual costs of global ecology programs absolutely essential, and other programs desirable to the future would amount to approximately 26% of the world's annual military expenditures.

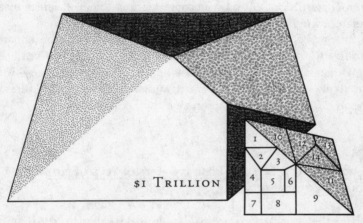

$1 TRILLION

ABSOLUTELY ESSENTIAL TO THE FUTURE	(TOTAL: $127 BILLION)
1. *Population stabilization:*	10 BILLION
2. *Prevent global warming:*	10 BILLION
3. *Stop and reverse deforestation:*	10 BILLION
4. *Prevent acid rain:*	9 BILLION
5. *Prevent soil erosion:*	10 BILLION
6. *Stop ozone depletion:*	5 BILLION
7. *Stop destruction of species:*	8 BILLION
8. *Stop pollution of oceans:*	15 BILLION
9. *Preserve / provide everyone fresh, clean water:*	50 BILLION

DESIRABLE TO THE FUTURE	(TOTAL: $135 BILLION)
10. *Retire developing nation's debt:*	30 BILLION
11. *Provide safe, clean, renewable energy:*	50 BILLION
12. *Provide world-universal health care:*	15 BILLION
13. *Eliminate starvation world-wide:*	19 BILLION
14. *Provide shelter for everyone in the world:*	21 BILLION

them in the long term unless the mind-sets behind them are changed or eradicated. It is easy enough to predict that those future-ignorant mind-sets will not "go" without protest and will in fact take active measures to maintain themselves.

The ominous ecological scene is not yet conceived as a war since the solutions are still envisaged as both pouring money (which has not yet been made available) over them and persuasion of anti-ecological mind-sets to "change" their ways and understanding. There is little point in pouring the money if mind-set change does not take place simultaneously. Since an in-depth study of mind-sets shows that most of them will not volunteer to change their deep-core beliefs, the realities of the Great Ecological Wars of the millennial transition will soon become matters that will affect many different kinds of mind-sets.

Increases of pro- and antiecological violence can be anticipated during the millennial transition, first as skirmishes (up until approximately 1998) and thereafter as organized *military* warfare—with the likely outcome that the entire annual military expenditures of the *world* may be needed to finance the Ecological Wars.

ENVISIONING A FUTURE-POSITIVE ANTIDOTE TO EPIDEMIC SOCIAL VIOLENCE

Given that populations are to double in less than thirty years, if mind-sets prone to creating violent environments are maintained into the future, then the future will have twice the violence of today. Violence may be seen, in the fascist sense, as one way to cure the overpopulation problem—and I predict that many groups will try to implement this solution. But on the whole, the people of the twenty-first century will realize that violence per se must be resolved on behalf of their profuture.

In their book *Reincarnation: A New Horizon in Science, Religion, and Society* (1984), Sylvia Cranston and Carey Williams compared the crime (violence) rates found within the core-beliefs of Judeo-Christian, Muslim, Hindu, and Buddhist societies.

Core belief	Violence rate
Judeo-Christian	1 out of 274 people
Muslim	1 out of 856 people

| Hindu | 1 out of 1,361 people |
| Buddhist | 1 out of 3,787 people |

Rates of violence, then, can be directly associated with the core-belief mind-sets of socializing systems that apparently account for different violence-environments. The enormous difference between the Judeo-Christian and the Buddhist violence rates is surely significant at the core-belief level. Further, no Buddhist society has ever launched a war, although some have been attacked and forced to defend themselves.

The core-values of mind-sets that "produce" violence are surely to come into the gun-sights of profuturists as the millennial transition progresses. Profuture Buddhist-like philosophies will emerge (as they already are)—perhaps without all the trappings of formal Buddhism but in ways geared to diminish violence ratios. And this clearly prefigures the emergence of a new "religion." The term *militant Buddhism* may seem contradictory at first, but it will begin to make sense to profuturists—especially after 1998, when Buddhist-like values will begin to redefine the parameters of basic education and rewisdoming.

CORE-BELIEF CHANGE-ROUTES OF SEXUAL MORALITY

I am reluctant to discuss this particular mind-set issue because it is extremely complex and volatile in all its aspects. But a large part of the future cannot be predicted unless attempts are made to tackle this socially sensitive issue. So, simply put: the most straightforward aspect of this issue is that humans interact sexually throughout their lives—there is no way around this; and past mind-sets have not sought to understand the broader physical and psychic meanings of this activity.

Instead, they have sought to impose separatist moralistic controls and legislative containment procedures regarding it—in spite of the historically demonstrated fact that these are largely ineffective and themselves introduce bitter resentment and violence, perpetuate socially demeaning ignorance, and result in large-scale social mind-set problems that sometimes have little to do with sexual activity itself.

As to the befuddling complexity of this issue, as of 1992 sexuality has become inextricably linked with disease-transmission routes, the family unit, abortion and right-to-life issues, matters of sexual choice, genetic manipulation, religious moralism seeking abject control over civic legislation, cultlike ideas of supremacy and inferiority, increasingly extensive sexual-cult undergrounds, extensive and expensive law-enforcement procedures—and, notwithstanding, dramatic escalations in sexual violence and crime. All this has happened in the face of the fact that humans have been sexual from day one—yet as of 1992 have resolved nothing and have managed to sustain sexuality above all others as the most tortuous issue. The deliberate and even enforced ignorance of sexual matters is appalling.

At least three specific change-routes into the future are evident, and each of these will have had core mind-set–change intervention impacts on sexuality by 2010. Each of these will require the jettisoning of past inadequate mind-sets.

THE AIDS PANDEMIC. It is accepted that sexual ignorance, maintained by socioreligious moralism, is partly responsible for the agonizing spread of sexually transmitted AIDS. Since a majority of humans interact sexually in spite of mind-set sexual moralism, "abstaining" is not a solution. "Safe sex," however, requires sex education from the ground up, a measure that is thwarted by socioreligious moralism. Although these issues are under moralistic debate, AIDS continues to infect principally through unsafe sexual activities.

Dependable statistics regarding AIDS are hard to come by, as I discovered in researching this book. I have determined that the reasons for this are principally on behalf of 1) minimalizing and marginalizing the actual AIDS scene so as to maintain moralistic attitudes that oppose even minimal safe-sex education; 2) the fears of many nations having to do with reductions in tourism; and 3) cover-ups regarding early failures and completely irresponsible activities of official disease-control facilities.

In his 1991 book *The Slow Plague,* Peter Gould published a series of demographic charts (reproduced in several major media magazines) of the spread of AIDS in the United States. In 1980, confirmed AIDS cases were reported in only about .5 percent of the United States, but confirmed cases were reported by 1990 in over 60 percent.

I have put together all available (as of late 1992) AIDS statistics from the World Health Organization, the Centers for Disease Control and Prevention in the United States, and a number of other responsible sources. According to these combined statistics, in 1991 in the United States a total of 11 million undetected AIDS carriers is completely feasible—meaning that by 2000 there may be 100 million–plus, *one-third to one-half of our population* (given as 248,709,873 in the 1990 census). *

This ominous statistic could have been avoided in large part by safe-sex education. As it is, though, moralistic avoidance of safe-sex education has bequeathed to the future a pandemic of immeasurable importance, the nature of which is sure to have a violent impact on the moralistic institutions directly responsible for it. Other contributing factors must certainly be considered—but even if a cure were found during the millennial transition, its delivery to the entire population would require ten years or more.

Here is a vivid precursor to social, medical, and humanitarian breakdown and anarchy. There can be little doubt that AIDS-free

*The following increased statistics on population and AIDS were published as this book was going into print. On December 19, 1992 the Federal Census Bureau published figures reflecting an increase in the United States population from 248.7 million in 1990 to 256.6 million in 1992—an increase of 7.2 million in just two and a half years—largely due to legal and illegal immigration. If this growth rate continues, the United States will have a population of more than 301 million by 2010—another 43.2 million, somewhat equal to the combined total populations of Texas, California, Colorado, New Mexico, Arizona, Utah, and Idaho. In January 1993, the World Health Organization (WHO) conservatively reported more than 600,000 cases of AIDS, indicating that the real total was likely four times or more as high. WHO also said that about 13 million people had become infected with HIV. The United States reported 242,146 cases, more than one-third the world's known total.

populations will seek not only to educate themselves sexually but to isolate themselves from the infectious AIDS framework as well. *Their* core mind-sets will be hardly anything like those seeking yet to prevail today. But it will be their mind-sets that will survive and encode the future.

GAYLIFE-STYLES. The traditional core-belief, sociocultural definition of homosexuality as a "mental-moral aberration" rests only on religious or pseudo-scientific assumptions that have sought to colonize legislation on their behalf. These mind-set attitudes *do not* rely on research, but on doctrine. If, however, biological grounds can be discovered (as they are in process of being) that homosexuality is "genetic," then any opposition to it must surface as the heterosexual fascism it was all along.

There are at least 10 million male gays in the United States today as officially counted, although twice that many or more may actually exist. Female gays probably number as many. These, then, make up a 20 million–strong socioeconomic-cultural voting bloc with *real* claims to representation.

What is not being considered in this regard is that gay life-styles are at least one antidote to the enormous problems of population control and reduction. As the overpopulation problem increases in magnitude, by 2000 it will be accepted that increased and socially supported gay life-styles are one solution to it. Gays do not biologically reproduce in any great numbers, and so sterilization need not be forced upon them as may ultimately be the case with heterosexuals by 2010.

Thus, the assumed-as-righteous heterosexual core belief has to give way because it *must*. A great deal of religious, psychological, and scientific dogma will have to be rescripted—and this will be yet another nail in the coffin of past core beliefs. Since the gay liberation movement began in 1969, gays have increasingly demonstrated their militant willingness to demarcate their own future-positive "front." If and when the "genetic" reasons for the "aberration" are determined, clearly gays' militancy will increase—and thus the hetero-homo wars that began in 1967 will increase in intensity until about 2008, at which time the "population control" value of homosexuality will be realized.

MAPPING THE GENOME. All living organisms possess a pool of genes that are genetically transmitted to their children. Each gene itself possesses "markers" that result in specific traits in the genetic individual. The mixture of the marker possibilities is enormous but ultimately limited to the extent of the gene pool. The whole of the gene-marker pool is called the *genome*.

The technology exists for separating the markers from their genes and splicing them in different arrangements, thus producing a genetically engineered individual. What is missing so far is the mapping of all the marker-mixes of the genome. But when the mapping is complete, it will be possible to take genetic materials of *different* individuals and resplice all the markers. Disease markers can be eradicated, power markers can be introduced, and the deliberately engineered human will become not only feasible but actual.

Gone will be the days when the human came into existence because of random copulation. The impact this may have on the future is stratospheric. Sex need not necessarily be engaged in for the purposes of creating children and will in large part be confined to sensual fulfillment. Society will immediately separate into perfect, genetically engineered and randomly created humans. And future-making power will gravitate into the hands and minds of the genetically perfect—because it *must*.

Is this real? Ask yourself: if your children could be genetically perfect . . . ?

The Japanese are hard at work mapping the human genome and are about ten years ahead of the United States in this regard. They may have the genome mapped by 2002, and, if so, by 2010 the first genetically engineered humans could be eight years old.

Estimate the future-shaping dimensions of this one—and estimate as well the impact of these dimensions on old sexual core-belief systems.

MIND-SET CHANGE-ROUTES IN NATIONAL AND CULTURAL UNITIES AND THE POWER STRUGGLES BETWEEN THEM

THE FLICKERING WORLD POWER OF THE UNITED STATES

The 1980 Report of the President's Commission for a National Agenda for the Eighties forewarned of "an increasing inability on the part of Americans to form effective coalitions for the general good." The authors of this report were not predictive astrologers, of course, but even so they had inadvertently spotted one of the principal phenomena resulting from the passage of Pluto through Libra, which began in 1971. This particular phenomenon would become meaner when Pluto entered Scorpio in 1983.

By 1984, Theodore C. Sorensen, who had served as special counsel to President Kennedy, noted in his book *A Different Kind of Presidency: A Proposal for Breaking the Political Deadlock* (1984) that the 1980 report's forewarning was "a masterpiece of understatement." As of 1992, it has proven to be a masterpiece of future-seeing.

In fact, the inability to form effective coalitions for the general good represents a problem and a flaw in the democratic processes when those processes are interpreted as mandating proportional equal representation for all who demand it. For astrological clarification, equality and proportional representation is a "Libra" characteristic that became socio-astrologically "sensitized" when Pluto entered Libra in 1971.

Proportional representation can turn future-negative because no checking mechanisms have been found to avoid the inevitable political deadlocks it inspires. The democratic system then begins to fail.

From the future-seer's view, democratic processes resulting in political deadlock are subject to inertia and thus to the future-negative change-route law of diminishing returns. The sum of all this can be expressed as the inability to form *effective* coalitions for the common good since this inability is "achieved" when proportional representation induces political gridlock. As Sorensen expressed in his book, proportional representation, if not yet an official policy, is de facto in the United States and has resulted in political gridlock.

Tens of thousands of gridlocking components have clogged the political processes: political action committees, lobbyists, trade associations, ideological entities, industry and labor groups, single-issue organizations, and so on, accompanied by armies of investigative reporters and self-appointed intellectual sleuths—all out to discredit, demean, and defeat not only one another but any administration or official standing in the way of achieving their local politicized goals.

This is democracy by competition—not democracy of and for the commonweal, or of and for the common*wealth* either.

This particular issue is significant to the aspiring future-seer. For the deadening *inertia,* inherent and kept in place by the gridlock, has already set in motion future-negative change-routes that Americans *must* experience—simply because it will take time to unlock it.

There can be little doubt that the twentieth century has been the American century—in much the same way that the nineteenth century was the British century and the seventeenth century was the Spanish century. Like the Spanish and British during their respective centuries, the United States was able to extend various types of military, economic, scientific, and moral-cultural hegemony throughout the world, thus achieving its superpower status.

During the twentieth century, though, the status of America as the world's largest creditor shifted to a point where it is now the world's largest debtor. As the economic historian Paul Kennedy points out in his book *The Rise and Fall of the Great Powers,* when the Spanish monarchy (ca. 1650) found itself burdened under massive debts and inefficient industries, compromised by special interests at home, and dependent on foreign manufacturers, the Spanish were no longer Numero Uno in the world. And history clearly shows that economic power is actually identical to world power, and where the former goes, the latter soon follows.

Americans can still feel themselves to have military superpower status. But many economists point out that the military glitter associated with the Gulf War diverted attention from far deeper American difficulties that, in their unresolved state, are in process of shifting the balance of world powers away from the United States.

The tell-tale signs of a momentous world-power shift are evident in this regard, signs that indicate that the United States cannot maintain its premier world posture without undertaking wholesale restructuring. The predictive problem here is that wholesale economic restructuring requires considerable time to be achieved, assuming that internal politicized special interests permit it to be undertaken in the first place.

Compared to other countries, on a per capita basis and as a two hundred–year–old *democracy*, we have become the most household-violent nation in the world and the most corrupt; we have the highest divorce and crime rates; we waste the most resources and spend the most money to do so; we consume 46 percent of the world's natural resources used annually; and we have the biggest and most expensive public education system, but it produces the lowest-quality education.

Per capita, we have the most lawyers but the most injudicious judicial systems; the largest and most numerous prison systems; the biggest and most inefficient psychological industries; the highest rates of inner-city ruin and farm abandonment; and the highest rate of health problems but the most expensive health-care system ($800 billion in 1991—which will cost $1,250 billion by 1997).

Our wealthy have the highest rates of profit-making, but our workers have the least secure lifelines into the future. We have the biggest, most expensive, and most inefficient welfare system—which is also the most demeaning and threatening to its users. We have the highest rates of dissension regarding what constitutes moral values as well as the highest rates of dissension at the top of our higher education systems, where unity should coalesce.

We have the highest rates of avoiding central structural and restructural issues. We are also the most consistent perpetuator of the world's debt economy and the most willing to pour credit money into its bottomless "needs." *And*, ironically, we have the highest

patterns of expectation (surrounded by nearly impenetrable telepathic osmosis), of perpetuating our flagship status in the world of
the future, of which we perceive ourselves to be the chief guardians.

I invite all aspiring future-seers to study these matters and make
predictions of their own. You can flex your future-seeing muscles
by having a go at this one. Ask you future-seeing self, What is the
change-route nature of all this? You hardly need me to lead the
way.

I will contribute the following, though:

> We had better hope that the inability to form effective
> coalitions for the common good *does* "belong" to the Pluto-
> in-Scorpio sociological manifestations and that this situa-
> tion will ease when Pluto enters Sagittarius in 1995.
>
> Even assuming an about-face can be effected by sufficient
> popular commitment to permit it, what length of time into
> the future will be required for such restructuring?
>
> If this restructuring will be future-absent even as of 2000,
> then history confirms that fascism awaits those who cannot
> or will not work toward forming effective coalitions for the
> general good.
>
> And, indeed, if you have been paying close attention to
> developments, covert fascist organizations in the United
> States are preparing themselves for their "day" as America's
> future. Fascism "resolves" the self-perpetuating confusions
> of proportional representation and the inability to form ef-
> fective coalitions if and when that inability is misinterpreted
> as desirable. The present failure of communal American
> consciousness to perceive this potential will, I predict, result
> during the millennial transition in increases of civil, racist,
> fascist, and cultural conflicts and the economic and ideo-
> logical sectorizing of the nation. Grim words, indeed.

THE COMING NEW WORLD SUPERPOWER

In reality, the Japanese have only played the American capitalist game and have done it better. Japan has done nothing American capitalists would not have done for themselves had they the wits and foresight to do so.

The principles of any successful econofuture are, first, the availability of resources (material and intellectual) and their long-term quality control into the future; and second, the willingness of the labor forces to work hard for the specific long-term goal of maintaining their *own* security lifelines into the future. When either of these "fails," the other does too.

All short-term policies of the past will soon fail in the face of the longer-term necessities of the oncoming future. Since most Western nations are engaged principally in short-term patterns of expectations, the hold over the longer-term future will gravitate toward those nations that *can* set up long-term quality planning.

In other words, the control of the future will gravitate toward Asia, at least between now and 2010.

The People's Republic of China contains one-fifth of the world's total population, while other Asian nations probably account for another fifth or more. The most economically vital nation in the world is Japan, one of the smallest with regard to its landmass.

If you were Asian, you might ask yourself this: would you adopt, for your future, the Japanese long-term planning model or the American/Western short-term one? The results of both models are now very much in evidence.

Several past predictions have indicated that during the twenty-first century Asians will "rule the world." And because of the contexts of what has been discussed above I must now align my own predictions with those previous ones.

But there are to other reasons to predict Asian ascendence. Western ideologies and methodologies have served as the focal point for emergent progress for some time now. And the past great militant missionary attempts of the Christian churches have led the West somewhat into the idea that the whole world might be ideologically colonized by all kinds of Western practices.

The predictive question is, Why should they be colonized? There is, after all, an Asian way of life far older than anything Western. And this way of life is possessed by as much as one-half the world's population. I say one-half because we forget something that we should not: we consider Russia a Western country because of its past close alignments with Europe and the West. But Western historians conveniently forget that most of the peoples inhabiting Russian Asia are *Asians* in their genetic stock and in affinity.

It is unthinkable that Asia would permanently permit itself to be exploited solely on behalf of Western short-term profit-making. In the future, then, arises the interesting specter of an empowered Asia versus an increasingly unempowered West. Asia might be glad to get Western bubble-gum, soft drinks, and fast food, but will it adopt values and methodologies that have served in the long run to bring a considerable amount of ecological, cultural, and economic wreckage to the West?

I predict that Asia (including Russian Asia) as a whole will opt to investigate other options. And in this way I arrive at the feasible prediction that an Asian economic bloc will emerge, which will define its own cultural and methodological values. The potential emergence of this Asian bloc already worries many Western economists. As was expressed in, among other sources, the *New York Times* ("The Asia Test for Mr. Bush," October 9, 1991), in order to guard against Western dominance in geoeconomics "some Asians are flirting with establishing their own trade bloc."

I first identified the future emergence of this bloc in November 1989 and published periodic updates of it during the course of the one-year experimental future-seeing project described in chapter 14. At the very least, this huge economic bloc will absorb all the nations of Asia, including Russia and India, and also Australia.

It may also include most of the Middle East, and it most certainly will encompass Mexico and perhaps other Latin American countries. There is a surprising affinity between the Mexicans and the Japanese, as I witnessed for myself when I visited both countries. As of this writing, it is common knowledge that many children of Mexican officials are sent to Japan to learn the Japanese language and Japanese educational and business methods.

I have termed the Asian economic bloc a *bloc* to differentiate its nature from that of, for example, the European Economic Community, which is in part struggling (and faltering) to place Europe within the economic contexts of the ostensible new world free-market order. If there is to be a New *World* Order, it must come to include Asia as part of the world community *and* comity. I predict that organized Asia will not consent to this comity so long as Western capitalism sees Asia only as a source of profit-taking and a consumer market for Western capitalist products. Aligned Asian nations will block attempts to enjoin and cannibalize Asia on behalf of Western designs, and in this sense it will be a bloc.

China, whether communist or not, possesses one attribute that will be consistent with the 2008 Pluto-into-Capricorn sociological phenomena: China has always had a precise hierarchical consciousness. The Chinese *expect* leadership from the top down. Whatever turmoil in which China is embroiled, none of it should be confused with our American struggles to achieve divisive proportional leadership representation. As soon as the Chinese turmoil is over, the hierarchical structure immediately reaggregates.

So, where will China "go"? The horoscope of the People's Republic of China indicates that that particular form of government in China is close to its formal and acknowledged end, possibly even occurring before this book reaches print, or soon thereafter. But in actuality, the end of the communist regime has already taken place, and what remains of it is a kind of pageantry, albeit one with residual power. We in the West tend to think that at some point the Chinese must align themselves with the West for *their* own benefit. But to think thus is to misunderstand China. The Chinese actually need not "go" anywhere.

Because of its enormous landmass and increasingly highly educated populations, China is the only nation that can afford to sit and wait out what is happening in the short-term rest of the world and feel itself secure in doing so because of its impenetrability. And the Chinese *know* this. It is we, the Westerners, who do not acknowledge this. In the end, then, those who want to deal with China must go to it and settle for what China is prepared to offer.

Thus, the eventual formation of the Asian economic bloc will give character to the future in ways that capitalistic Westerners embroiled in their systemic-capitalism failures will not be able to recognize.

The power of China can stand clearly revealed if we consider that while the other two superpowers (the United States and the former Soviet Union) are disarming and demilitarizing themselves, hardly anyone has dared to *suggest* that the *other* remaining superpower, China, do the same. The final power-point of China (in the predictive context of this book) is that it is the only nation on earth that at this moment is, or can be, completely self-sustaining. Its internal economic systems, whatever they may be, are not very deeply extended into systemic capitalism networks.

I will predict that the natal outlines of the Asian economic bloc (already visible to some) will generally be quite visible by 1998 and possibly as early as 1994. At that point, China's communist framework will have disappeared. But nonetheless, China will not "go" into Western ways and will avoid adopting systemic capitalism, whose flaws will be completely visible by 1998 and surely overwhelmingly so by 2008. Many of these flaws are cogently described in *Capitalist Fools* by Nicholas von Hoffman (1992).

MIND-SET CHANGE-ROUTES REGARDING THE DISTRIBUTION IN SOME FORM OF WEALTH

When the radical profuturism movement emerges, it will have the double duty of encoding a new future *as well as recovering from the ashes of the past.* Someone, somewhere, has to begin the Great Recovery somehow. *Economic* signals of this recovery are very important, and I have isolated two of them as follows:

WORKER AS OWNER

Ostensible new world free-market orderists may aspire to their vision of a planet ruled by economic competition and opportunism. The obvious contradiction is built into this vision. But in any event, it is difficult to see how *stable* economic conditions can ensue from the free-market practice of using labor as a throwaway commodity to be employed when it is useful and discarded when not.

Economic competitiveness requires determining the cheapest labor markets and diverting work to them. Labor, then, can be diverted, for example, from the United States, where it is expensive, to Indonesia, where it is cheaper. But this leaves many American workers high and dry with salary cuts or the increasing likelihood of unemployment and disruption of their security lifelines into the future—regarding salaries keeping up with inflation, pensions, health-care benefits, and so on. The unemployed then become a burden to the taxpayers, whose taxes must escalate to allow them to continue sustaining the burden but who likewise may encounter their own labor expendability.

This growing crisis is already being foreshadowed. It will become endemic between 1994 and 1998. The source of the crisis is to be found in the difference between the owner-employer and the worker-employee. The worker owns nothing save his labor, which is increasingly expendable as owners divert labor to more competitive labor sources.

Described more precisely, the Western free-market capitalist system is formed around the concept of investor ownership, which is determined by the number of shares any given investor holds. The biggest shareholder takes the largest amount of the profits, and the shareholder also enjoys the one share–one vote prerogative. Shares can be traded on the open market, and anyone can buy them. Anyone accumulating the largest number of shares also gains a transactional-economic-control voting majority of any given capitalist enterprise—whether he or she works within it or not. The worker has no role in this process save to provide labor.

The pervasive owner-worker paradox centers on how workers are to achieve their security lifelines for their entire lives. This includes not only preparing workers for a working slot but also their overall education in general, their health care, and their post–working age security, among other things.

Most of the developed nations have tried to resolve these issues by assigning these nonwage-working areas to the public trust in the form of public education, social security, and certain health-care plans. But even assuming that labor is vitally employed, these solutions encounter the law of diminishing returns, as has been discussed.

The only stable economic structure that acknowledges the rights of workers to perpetual security lifelines is one in which the workers become owners of it and legitimately share in its profits. Otherwise, as the economic theorist Kenneth Lux points out in his book *Adam Smith's Mistake: How a Moral Philosopher Invented Economics and Ended Morality* (1990), to have an owner-group (the stockholders) determining the fate of another group (the workers) is tantamount to having citizens of one country make decisions for those of another. In capitalist nations, many companies are owned by foreign stockholders, and the fate of those companies' workers is determined by those stockholders, who are naturally interested in profits, not in the security lifelines of the workers.

The idea that workers should own shares in the companies they work for is not new, of course. But the worker who buys, for example, ten shares has only ten votes if they are voting shares, and no voting voice at all if they are only dividend shares. The shareholder who has 51 percent of all voting shares controls not only the objectives of the company but the fates of the workers as well.

During the 1950s, all this was given startling illumination by one Father Arizmendi, in the town of Mondragon, Spain. The question he undertook to solve was how the security lifelines of workers could be systematically and perpetually guaranteed. He introduced a worker-owner system in which each worker actually became an investor in his or her company. This system is described at length in Mr. Lux's book. Briefly, a worker can become an owner in a company through contributing funds to an *individual capital account (ICA)*. Each worker-owner has a record (ICA account) with the company of his or her capital contribution to the company. All the company's capital assets are covered by these accounts, so that the worker-owners (now called "members") constitute the total capital holdings of the firm.

The firm can seek outside capital, but only through loans or bonds, not by selling shares of stock in the company. Only those who actually work in the company can have capital accounts. Furthermore—and this is the most critical point—voting participation in the company's policies and direction occur on a one person—one vote basis regardless of the number of shares in a member's capital account. This is the full principle of democracy in the context of work and stands in high contrast to the stock-ownership principle of voting, which is based on the number of shares.

In the Mondragon cooperative, labor employs capital, rather than vice versa. The difference here is strategic. The worker-members elect their own board of directors from among themselves. Thus, in one stroke of internal economic democracy, outside control of companies vanishes and the worker's place as an economical commodity ends. The pyramidal paternalism of capitalism is abolished, as is the indifference of the wage labor system. The fraternalism of human community comes into being, and wages as advances on profits are shared among all ICA holders.

As Lux indicates in his book (which every person concerned with the economic future will want to read), a few of these ICA companies have failed. But in the longer run, most have succeeded. The successes represent the only kind of general economy that can guarantee advances against profits for *the life* of the ICA holder. Such profits can also be diverted into sustaining the health, education, and welfare of all ICA holders and their families. And, in fact, in Spain ICA companies have formed *their own* wholly owned banks, hospitals, schools, and universities, which provide perpetual security lifelines to all ICA account holders and their families.

By using this system the enormous economic pitfalls of stratified capitalism and socialism are transcended. An ICA account company is lifted out of government interventions and the dangers of transactional and debt economies and is impervious to economic takeovers by outsiders. An ICA account company is probably subject to the effects of various growth and decline cycles, but good management can find ways to transcend these.

As a result of this Spanish economic model, investing in the wealth of the few has been converted to economic investing in the well-being of the many. And this new kind of economic security lifeline approach can exist so long as only workers in a company can have capital accounts in it, and only one vote regardless of the number of shares in their capital account. The workers have become their own owners, and their fates or destinies are also now in their own hands—not in those of someone else who has little or no real interest in their long-term security lifeline fates.

The emergence of the ICA system in Spain (which is already being duplicated in Italy, France, and Brazil) is not good news to aggressive capitalist investors who wish to take over profitable enterprises by buying up shares in them. And it is quite likely that capitalists may wage some kind of war to defeat this new system. But in many ways it is akin to the Japanese company system that subsidizes security lifelines of their workers and considers investments in their long-term lifelong well-being to be *a duty*.

The ICA system not only is profuture so far as worker-owners are concerned but also is a profuture method to escape the horrible and unresolvable complexities of its contrasting system. I predict that by 2010 the ICA system will constitute the growing nucleus of the true new world economic order, which is extendable into the indefinite future.

MANAGEMENT BY STATISTICAL QUALITY CONTROL

Japan's unexpected emergence as the world's economic giant has set into motion not only economic envy, astonishment, and Japan-bashing but specific long-term change-routes into the future. Even if these have their ups and downs, they still have importance regarding what the state of the earth's affairs will be by 2010 and during the interval of the millennial transition.

To get a future-seeing grip on this, certain facts need to be stated:

1. In 1945, Japan was a ruined and conquered nation governed by the United States.
2. America aided in Japan's recovery and encouraged it to adapt to the competitive capitalist free-market system.
3. By 1975, Japan had become a competitive capitalist free-market nation.

4. By 1983, and fully within the due process of competitive free-marketeerism, it had economically outflanked not only all other free-market nations but the United States as well.

5. By 1989, Japan-bashing had commenced and, for reasons that are neither explainable nor credible, many felt that Japan should somehow have volunteered to gear *its* economic growth so that it remained second to that of the United States.

6. Geographically, the great, economically threatening Japan is about 12 percent *smaller* than California!

Take a good look at these six facts—and see if they do not make for a lot of silly telepathic osmosis on our parts. The future-seer must ask what the Japanese did to accelerate their economic growth—for only by determining this can he or she foresee the related change-routes into the future.

As it turns out, other than relying on their historical commitment to *work*, the Japanese did only two things.

The first is described in Akio Morita's and Shintaro Ishihara's book *The Japan That Can Say "No"* (1990), in which the authors pointed out something that makes Americans very uncomfortable. The Japanese had no future in 1945, and so they had to organize and *plan* for one by establishing effective coalitions for the future common good. Morita and Ishihara irritated Americans by demonstrating that Americans lack effective coalitions for the common good, and so they cannot plan much past the objective of tomorrow—and certainly not for ten or twenty years hence. This was called America-bashing, even though the truth of it had already been retroactively acknowledged by observant Americans themselves.

The other "secret" of Japan's success is described by Mary Walton, a staff writer for the *Philadelphia Inquirer Magazine*, in her book *The Deming Management Method* (1986). This book reveals that W. Edwards Deming was the "genius who revitalized Japanese industry" because the Japanese adopted his management method on the largest scale possible.

Dr. Deming was an American working at the Department of

Agriculture in 1927. He developed the management by statistical control method, the original brainchild of one Walter A. Shewhart, a statistician at Bell Telephone Laboratories in New York. Dr. Deming's method was ignored in the United States. The Japanese invited him to Japan in the early 1950s, and Japanese businesses took his theories to heart.

To understand the Deming-Shewhart method, we first have to understand the major method utilized by American businesses that have emphasized short-term profits. The most popular way to achieve short-term profits was by utilizing the management by objective (MBO) method, formulated during the 1920s by an influential industrial engineer named Frederick Winslow Taylor.

Briefly put, Taylor's method was known as the "assembly-line" system, in which production (and jobs) were broken down into simple, separate steps to be performed over and over again without deviation by different workers. This method first establishes a short-term "objective" to be attained (always seen as profits) and uses only performance evaluations related to acquisition of the objective as a way of measuring success. The evaluations encourage short-term performance at the expense of long-term planning. All else (such as workers unnecessary to the short-term objective) is seen as expendable within the scope of this focused goal.

The evaluations discourage risk-taking, engender fear of failure with relation to deviating from the preconceived objective, undermine teamwork, and pit people against one another for the short-lived reward of being part of the short-term objective reached. The management-by-objective method also requires cadres of managers to keep the objective in sight, which results in the top-heavy American corporate structure. Short-term profit-taking is one of the hallmarks of the open free-market system and clearly the hallmark of American business history since the 1920s.

Within the guidelines of the management-by-objective method, *quality control* came to mean only the end-of-the-line inspection coupled with the short-term objective. Dr. Deming's statistical quality control method distributes quality control throughout all aspects of manufacturing or business in the light of longer-term rather than shorter-term objectives. The method begins not with short-term "targets" but with long-term planning and the institution of policies with regard to it. The process then proceeds by long-term quality control of administration, education, information enhancement, analysis of general and special problems, the certainty and perpetuation of worker participation, highest-possible quality standardization, quality assurance, effects, and future-plans.

None of these factors are isolated from one another for any short-term purposes. And statistical methods of envisioning and controlling each and all sectors of the *future-seeing plan* are pursued not only until saturated quality can be perpetuated but until the quality of the future can be foreseen.

Basically, the Japanese plan for the future and assure a positive one by perpetual quality control not only of their products but of their perpetual way of life. Within the contexts of the free market, once a quality product can be produced, it becomes more desirable to consumers, and more of it is can be produced more cheaply. Long-term profits are then assured—as are worker security lifelines.

As an aspiring future-seer, you may want to read Mary Walton's profound book about W. Edwards Deming and the Deming statistical quality control method. If you do, you can obtain a clearer understanding of ways to change the coalescing of so many future-negative change-routes that are currently in progress.

In my predictive opinion, the future belongs to those who can undertake long-term plans, not to short-term profit-taking. The long-term plans *must* reveal in advance the *quality* difference between future-positive and future-negative change-routes, as they did for the Japanese.

I predict that the worker-as-owner concept and statistical quality control will constitute the major economic overviews of those who survive the economic failures and breakdowns of the millennial transition. To save humanity itself, however, two more factors will be implemented.

MIND-SET CHANGE-ROUTES REGARDING HOW THE FUTURE IS TO BE ENGINEERED

Although all the predictions offered in this chapter have to do with engineering the shape of the future, the following two are strategically important.

PROFUTURIST VOLUNTEERISM

A future-negative idea of most Western nations is that nothing can be done unless someone pays for it.

Ecological problems are mounting to the degree that merely paying for their correction is swiftly becoming unfeasible. The solution to all this is being foreshadowed in the form of civic volunteerism. Earth's ecosystems must be preserved even without paying for doing so, and prototype volunteer groups have formed in local areas not only to determine ecologically corrective procedures but also to contribute their labor and resources free of charge.

This volunteer concept will, for the general good, become one of the central rallying cries of the forthcoming profuturist activists, and it will be militant by the year 2002. By the year 2010, government, correction, and protection against further ecological damage will have been undertaken by military draft when it proves that volunteerism has been lackadaisical, superficial, or unrealistically ambitious.

If you think this is unlikely, remember that the population of the world in about 2010 will be approaching the ten billion mark. By then, ecological dangers will have tripled in intensity since 1987. Consider how those in 2010 will respond. The sociological patterns of Pluto in Scorpio cannot conceive of ecological preservation by drafting efforts to correct it. But I predict that the Pluto-in-Sagittarius profuturists will put all this into a priority perspective and that the Pluto-in-Capricorn changes will contribute the needed hierarchical militant authoritarianism.

If you, as an individual, corporation, industry, or government, want to live on the earth in 2010, you will have to *contribute* your working share free of charge to its cleansing and housekeeping. Merely pouring out tax dollars in futile humanitarian gestures alone will not do it.

THE COMING ANTIDRUG WARS

The Report of the European Parliament published in December 1991 presented trends and statistics indicating that the multibillion-dollar-a-year drug trade not only has achieved the potential to undermine society itself by increasing drug usage and addiction and associated escalation of crime rates but that its cartels have accumulated enough financial and political power to challenge nation-states.

This is the diplomatic way of saying that the drug cartels *are* challenging nation-states and that the efforts of the latter to resist the challenge have begun to fail. Several officials of the Drug Enforcement Agency (DEA) and Interpol have stated that the drug problem is out of control and that the combined efforts of all international agencies are losing the battle.

The future-negative meaning of this is quite clear to the future-seer: if in the future competitive free-marketeers do not achieve economic rule of the earth, drug-cartel overlords will. The drug cartels are in process of achieving the power to shape the future to their own benefit and ultimately to become a quasi-secret, highly nomadic, economic governmental network with awesome power over established governments.

The full meaning of the European Parliament's adequate forewarning cannot saturate the Pluto-in-Scorpio sociological sensitivities that are fixated on the charm of human nature's basest manifestations—the thrill of addictions. So effective coalitions for the common good are yet missing in this regard since they cannot be formed by Pluto-in-Scorpio sociological orientations.

Fix your future-seeing "eye" on this one and see what your intuitus-intellectus reveals.

Somewhere along the change-routes into the future, the takeover of sociopolitical-economic systems by drug overlords or their paid front-people must be interdicted. This interdiction is being sporadically foreshadowed by people heroically trying to take back their neighborhoods from dealers. But since heroism is anathema to Pluto-Scorpio sociological configurations, social support for the greater antidrug-cartel impulses must await Pluto's passage into Sagittarius late in 1995.

At that time the prediction-rich question will become, How will the citizens of the world respond to the virtual takeover of their societies by drug lords once the true magnitude of the situation is realized? It is very feasible to predict that the situation will begin to be seen as a war and not as a mere social problem—a war in which every concerned citizen will accept a role, even outside the law.

Extraordinary antidrug-traffic vigilante violence can be expected. The role of the drug users will be redefined. They will no longer be viewed as victims of society who opt for drug usage because society has made them unhappy—with the added conviction that society must reclaim them. Instead, they will be viewed as the source of economic power for the drug lords. Since it will be this economic power that must be destroyed, the *source* of it must be destroyed— and probably not merely by threats of stiff legal prosecutions and long-term prison sentences for which the taxpayers must pay. The present motto "Drugs Equal Death" will take on new meaning with regard to users.

When it is acknowledged that a state of embattled war actually does exist, concerned citizens will form and launch what will amount to mercenary attacks on users, traffickers, and biological and chemical sources of drugs. These radical attempts will be seen as heroic measures to save society. Their occasional successes will be interpreted as meaningful in future-positive ways. This in turn will cause support for official military intervention within the Pluto-in-Sagittarius sociological milieu now prepared to form coalitions for the common good. In fact, leaders and governments may fall if they demonstrate reluctance to interdict the socioeconomic drug processes by active measures.

Drug syndicate responses—establishment of increased terrorist networks, access to biological and nuclear warfare potential—will complicate the world picture. The price to be paid for lack of earlier, aggressive drug-eradication of dealers and users alike will be fully apparent by 2002. And those of 2010 will have a truly hot potato on their hands if they wish to be anything but vassals to the drug lords of the world.

MIND-SET CHANGE-ROUTES REGARDING WHAT THE HUMAN IS

THE DISCOVERY OF BIOPSYCHIC-ELECTRONIC REALITIES

Anyone who studies how mind-sets are architecturalized can clearly understand that core-reality belief-making is the agony and ecstasy of the human condition. Since so many core-beliefs will have become altered by 2010, this issue cannot remain a marginalized one during the millennial transition.

The dominant mainstream core-belief of the twentieth century was *materialism*. The fatal mistake materialists made was to consider that human beings were composed exclusively of matter whereas energy was outside of them. Since scientists of the dark Modern Age believed that our chemical processes were unique to each physical body and not directly sharable with others, our chemical processes represented a "closed" system that could not interact directly with other closed systems.

From this point of view, psychic phenomena were "impossible," since no direct neurochemical links between physical bodies existed. In other words, humans *could not* "pick up" or "tune in" to one another's images or thoughts because there were no direct psychophysical linkages that could account for doing so. Thus, whatever a human thought or visualized was solely the result of his or her own closed neurochemical system.

However, the fact that people *did* tune into and pick up on one another's thoughts was obvious. This activity was referred to as *telepathy*, the direct sending and receiving of information across the spaces between two human closed psychochemical-physical systems. Indeed, people sometimes could literally feel pain that others were experiencing even though they were separated by vast distances and completely out of the range of one another's physical closed-system perceptions.

But materialism was doomed the moment the extent of the electromagnetic spectrum was discovered—and surely when radio was invented. Radio waves and frequencies could be sent across a space to receivers. It is now known that closed-system neurochemical processes take place *because* of a bioelectromagnetic "blueprint," which itself is *not* a closed system. Rather, it is an open one, because the facts of electromagnetism *link* all that is electromagnetic.

The essential nature of the blueprint is therefore one of "thinking" energyinformation, which is bioelectromagnetic. If energyinformation thinks at all, it is therefore intelligent. Since energyinformation is universal, the entire cosmos must be pervaded by energy-thoughts that "electronically" interlink. And if all energyinformation is interlinked, then it is accessible to humans, who only need to discover how to link into it cognitively.

Here is the core basis for a radical, but real, biopsychic-electronic mind-set formation that is stupendously different from all past mindsets. Surely it can be foreseen that the "psychic" sciences (albeit under other names) are going to be enhanced in the future as the details of biopsychic energyinformation are understood. And with this enhancement a different kind of human will be emerging as of 2010—*the electronic superhuman* human whose operative advantages will be valuable in future-positive kinds of ways. *In fact, I predict that this electronic superhuman will be artificially engineered shortly after the human genome is mapped* (probably by 2008).

THE EXTRATERRESTRIAL INTERVENTION IMPACT

Superimages of what we think we are provide not only deep core beliefs but also the most enduring aspects of historical continuity. The central issue of these superimages revolves around two great questions: where did we come from, and how did we originate? The existence of these superimages is a very important source for future-seeing predictions if and when it becomes feasible that new, earth-shaking changes are in store.

There is considerable deep-core investment on earth in the notion that the intelligent human is unique in the universe. This concept provides us with our basic image of ourselves and the sense of our important place in the cosmos. If it were proven in any way that the human is not the *only* intelligent "beast" in the universe, the entire historical and hereditary lore of intelligence originating on earth must undergo severe adjustment.

The first verifiable shred of evidence of extraterrestrial superintelligence will clearly constitute an intevention impact of most serious and alarming dimensions. *But, I predict, it will also unite the entirety of humans on earth,* since the implications will transcend all ideological-cultural barriers that generally divide us.

All ancient cultures on earth uniformly held that humans were created by "gods." The Bible specifically refers to the Hebrew *Elohim* (gods) as those who created us in *their image.* Advancing anthropological scholarship (see the bibliography) has established that an ancient space-race, the *Anunnaki* (the *Elohim* in Hebrew) visited the earth several times.

The Sumerian texts have an advantage that the biblical texts do not in that they were compiled some three thousand years earlier. The Sumerian texts correctly describe the planets of our solar system, including Uranus, Neptune, and Pluto, which were not rediscovered until modern times. All the astronomical aspects of the Sumerian texts have proved to be correct. The correct ancient knowledge is a feat of some mystery—but it leads to the high possibility that *all* the Sumerian texts *are* accurate.

According to these, the *Anunnaki* or *Elohim* (literally "those who from heaven to earth came") were space travelers from a twelfth planet who came to earth and bioengineered humans. And during their frequent sojourns to earth thereafter they imparted the correct astronomical nature of the solar system to their creations.

The orbit of this twelfth planet (*Nibiru* in Sumerian) is angular to the orbits of our other planets. But it periodically comes close to the sun, which brings it into the vicinity of the rest of the solar system's planets. Prior to the rediscovery of the three outer planets during modern times, it was held that the Sumerian texts and the cosmology detailed were "mythic." But since it is now known that the ancient texts gave correct astronomical details of the now-known planets, including their correct size, distance from one another, and surface conditions, *many astronomers today are hunting for the twelfth planet.*

Evidence coming from researchers at Ruhr University in Germany indicates that a disruptive gravitational pull does exist as regards the known outer planets. Only another Planet X could account for this gravitational pull. It is estimated to be about five times the size of the earth, making it almost twenty-four thousand miles in diameter and the third-largest planet in the solar system—as the Sumerian texts stated in 3000 B.C. Planet X is also assumed to have an angular orbit. Scientists are using an orbiting infrared astronomy satellite (IRAS) to find this planet, which they believe is currently approaching the sun from the constellation of Cassiopeia or Libra.

When the existence of this planet is confirmed, as it will be by 2000 or earlier, its discovery will also confirm the accuracy of the Sumerian texts—which state that when the planet gets near enough to earth its inhabitants *always* make a visit. The Sumerian texts also say that the *Anannuki* or *Elohim* also use Mars as a stopoff point to get to the earth. If you have been keeping up with Martian developments, you will realize there is a great debate taking place concerning "buildings" on that planet's surface.

NASA photographs of these structures are available in Richard C. Hoagland's book *The Monuments of Mars* (1987). The first photographs were taken during the 1970s by NASA's Viking spacecrafts, especially in the Cydonia region of the Red Planet—but were somewhat "ignored" until the middle 1980s. Even a cursory glance at the photographs reveals why they were ignored: they have *significant* implications for all core-realities on earth.

The moment *any* shred of extraterrestrial evidence is confirmed, whether it involves UFOs, Planet X, or the confirmation of buildings on Mars, the *entirety of deep core beliefs* on earth will have mind-set quakes of no mean dimensions. Our core-conceptions of ourselves as God's creation or evolution's supreme achievement will collapse in heaps of historical rubble.

I predict that when Pluto enters Sagittarius (the zodiacal sign of the "great out-there") late in 1995, the following will occur:

1. interest in outer space will increase;
2. the existence of Planet X will be confirmed;
3. by 2000 the existence of buildings on Mars will be confirmed; and
4. by 2002 humans will know they are not alone in the galaxy and never have been.

At that point every "reality"-anchor we have held since approximately 500 B.C. will have to alter; future history will detach from most mind-sets of the past, and a whole new ball of wax will have to start rolling.

Epilogue

THE PIECES OF THE FUTURE-SEEING MOSAIC

Although many more pieces of the future-seeing mosaic may exist, those discussed in this book are fundamental. In my opinion, none are more important than others, and all of them must function together. They are:

increasing image-building skills;
erecting and expanding a precise future-seeing vocabulary;
expanding psychic perceptions by any and all means possible;
cultivating inner sensitivity to future-seeing impressions;
communally and socially accepting the indwelling Nostradamus Factor and its capabilities;
accepting that other and "higher" forms of consciousness exist;
linking the waking intellect with the Nostradamus Factor;
diagramming the relationships of the NostraFac with the intellect;
diagramming intellect mind-dynamic processes;
deadapting from antifuture-seeing attitudes;
diagramming and sketching forewarning dreams;
diagramming and sketching forewarning visions and daydreams;
locating "reality" blocks to future-seeing;
demythologizing future-seeing;

escaping social and environmental resistance to future-seeing processes;

understanding future-seeing as right action;

understanding future-seeing as prosurvival;

sharing and comparing communal future-seeing inputs;

recording communal future-seeing experiences;

studying past successful future-seers;

diagramming our multiple minds;

erecting maps of our consciousness spectra;

studying the specialized functions of the left and right hemispheres of our brains;

diagramming forms of intuitus-intellectus;

understanding anchor-points, their limits, and their defense mechanisms;

diagramming value norm anchor-points;

diagramming time-looping;

studying and diagramming each of the laws of future-seeing;

observing and diagramming telepathic osmosis and patterns of expectations;

understanding that knowledge limits or knowledge failure distorts accurate future-seeing;

studying predictions that have failed and why;

undertaking feasibility studies of all kinds;

exploring astrology and astro-cycles;

diagramming all discernible change-routes into the future;

studying the future as the about-to-happen rather than as the times to come;

identifying, mapping, and diagramming future-negative phenomena and their change-routes into the future;

identifying, mapping, and diagramming future-positive phenomena and their change-routes into the future;

understanding the law of diminishing returns and how it applies to what is about to happen;

identifying intervention impacts and their positive or negative change-routes into the future via feasibility studies and psychic inputs;

identifying and diagramming cycles;

searching for what will be future-present or future-absent;

determining the priorities of what needs to be foreseen;

tracking current affairs and events continuously;

and having the courage to predict or forecast the future as it
will be—not as you or others dream it or would like it to
be.

I salute all future-seers past, present, and to come. And I salute,
too, those who will be alive in the year 2010, for it will be they
who can judge the predictions in this book (many of which I hope
are in error). And I wish them well, for whatever earth's and our
human future will be, it is theirs to design and engineer. Let them
learn how to have done so better.

BIBLIOGRAPHY

The following bibliography, by no means exhaustive, is offered to direct interested readers to meaningful sources that extend the feasibility of topics discussed in this book. Highly recommended sources are preceded by an asterisk.

SEEING INTO THE FUTURE

*Day, Harvey. *Seeing into the Future*. London: Thorsons Publishers, 1966.
*Dublin, Max. *Futurehype: The Tyranny of Prophecy*. New York: Dutton, 1991.
*Forman, Henry James. *The Story of Prophecy*. New York: Tudor Publishing, 1940.
*Glass, Justine. *They Foresaw the Future*. New York: G. P. Putnam's Sons, 1969.
*Greenhouse, Herbert B. *Premonitions: A Leap into the Future*. New York: Bernard Geis Associates, 1971.
*Lemesurier, Peter. *The Armageddon Script: Prophecy in Action*. Wiltshire, England: Element Books, 1981.
*Ryback, Davis. *Dreams That Come True*. New York: Doubleday, 1988.

QUANTUM-HOLOGRAPHIC REALITY

*Chopra, Deepak. *Quantum Healing*. New York: Bantam Books, 1990.
*Dienstfrey, Harris. *Where the Mind Meets the Body*. New York: Harper-Collins, 1991.
*Grof, Stanislav. *The Holotropic Mind*. San Francisco: Harper, 1990.
*Talbot, Michael. *The Holographic Universe*. New York: HarperCollins, 1991.
*Zukav, Gary. *The Dancing Wu Li Masters: An Overview of the New Physics*. New York: William Morrow, 1979.

POPULATION

Cities: Life in the World's 100 Largest Metropolitan Areas (chart). Population Crisis Committee, 1990.
Poor, Powerless, and Pregnant (chart). Population Crisis Committee, 1990.
Why Population Matters. National Audubon Society and the Population Crisis Committee, 1991.

ECOLOGY

*Dowling, Claudia Glenn. "This Precious Planet." *Life* (April 1992).
*El-Sayed, Sayed Z. "Fragile Life under the Ozone Hole." *Natural History* (October 1988).

*Gore, Al. *Earth in the Balance: Ecology and the Human Spirit.* New York: Houghton Mifflin, 1992.

*Gribbin, John. *Forecasts, Famines, and Freezes: Climate and Man's Future.* New York: Walker, 1976.

*———. *Future Weather.* New York: Delacorte, 1983.

*Washington, Warren M. "Where's the Heat?" *Natural History* (March 1990).

THE SOCIOECONOMIC FUTURE

*Adams, Jad. *AIDS: The HIV Myth.* New York: St. Martin's Press, 1989.

*Anderson, Walter Truett. *Reality Isn't What It Used to Be.* San Francisco: Harper & Row, 1990.

*Attali, Jacques. *Millennium.* New York: Random House, 1991.

*Bloom, Allan. *The Closing of the American Mind.* New York: Simon & Schuster, 1987.

*Calleo, David P. *The Bankrupting of America: How the Federal Budget Is Impoverishing the Nation.* New York: William Morrow, 1992.

*Cetron, Marvin, and Owen Davies. *Crystal Globe.* New York: St. Martin's Press, 1991.

*Choate, Pat. *Agents of Influence.* New York: Alfred A. Knopf, 1990.

*Coleman, Kenneth. *The Misdirection Conspiracy: Or, Who Really Killed the American Dream?* Buena Park, Calif.: Seraphim Press, 1982.

*Davidson, James Dale, and Sir William Rees-Mogg. *Blood in the Streets: Investment Profits in a World Gone Mad.* New York: Summit Books, 1987.

Dines, James. *The Invisible Crash.* New York: Random House, 1975.

*Lux, Kenneth. *Adam Smith's Mistake.* Boston: Shambhala, 1990.

*Mitroff, Ian I., and Warren Bennis. *The Unreality Industry: The Deliberate Manufacturing of Falsehood and What It Is Doing to Our Lives.* New York: Carol Publishing Group, 1989.

*Osterberg, Rolf. *Corporate Renaissance: Business as an Adventure in Human Development.* Mill Valley, Calif.: Nataraj Publishing, 1993.

*Silk, Leonard, and David Vogel. *Ethics and Profits: The Crisis of Confidence in American Business.* New York: Simon & Schuster, 1976.

*Sorensen, Theodore C. *A Different Kind of Presidency.* New York: Harper & Row, 1984.

*von Hoffman, Nicholas. *Capitalist Fools.* New York: Doubleday, 1992.

*Walton, Mary. *The Deming Management Method.* New York: Putnam Publishing Group, 1986.

*Yatri. *Unknown Man: The Mysterious Birth of a New Species.* New York: Simon & Schuster, 1988.

QUANTUM SPACE-TIME

DeWitt, Bryce S., and Neill Graham. *The Many-Worlds Interpretation of Quantum Mechanics.* Princeton: Princeton University Press, 1973.

*Hawking, Stephen W. *A Brief History of Time.* New York: Bantam, 1988.

Hoyle, Fred. *The Intelligent Universe.* New York: Holt, Rinehart & Winston, 1983.

Sheldrake, Rupert. *A New Science of Life.* Los Angeles: J. P. Tarcher, 1981.

*Toben, Bob, and Fred Alan Wolf. *Space-Time and Beyond.* New York: Bantam, 1983.

*Wolf, Fred Alan. *Parallel Universes.* New York: Simon & Schuster, 1988.

*———. *Star Wave: Mind, Consciousness, and Quantum Physics.* New York: Macmillan Publishing, 1984.

*———. *Taking the Quantum Leap: The New Physics for Nonscientists.* San Francisco: Harper & Row, 1981.

BIO-ELECTROMAGNETISM

*Becker, Robert O., and Gary Selden. *The Body Electric: Electromagnetism and the Foundation of Life.* New York: William Morrow, 1985.

*Becker, Robert. *Cross Currents: The Perils of Electropollution—The Promise of Electromedicine.* Los Angeles: Jeremy P. Tarcher, 1990.

*Burr, Harold Saxton. *Blueprint for Immortality: The Electric Patterns of Life.* Essex, England: Nevil Spearman, 1972.

Popp, Fritz-Albert, and Gunther Becker, eds. *Electromagnetic Bio-Information.* Munich: Urban & Schwarzenberg, 1979.

Presman, A. S. *Electromagnetic Fields and Life.* New York: Plenum Press, 1970.

ASTROLOGY—ASTRO-CYCLES

*Barker, Stan. *The Signs of the Times: The Neptune Factor and America's Destiny.* St. Paul, Minn.: Llewellyn Publications, 1984.

Burt, Kathleen. *Archetypes of the Zodiac.* St. Paul, Minn.: Llewellyn Publications, 1988.

*Dewey, Edward R. *Cycles—Selected Writings.* Irving, Calif.: Foundation for the Study of Cycles, 1968.

*Gauquelin, Françoise. *The Psychology of the Planets.* San Diego: Astro Computing Services, 1982.

*Gauquelin, Michel. *The Cosmic Clocks: From Astrology to Modern Science.* San Diego: Astro Computing Services, 1982.

*———. *Cosmic Influences on Human Behavior.* New York: Aurora Press, 1985.

*———. *Written in the Stars: The Proven Link between Astrology and Destiny.* Wellingborough, England: The Aquarian Press, 1988.

*Greene, Liz. *The Astrology of Fate.* York Beach, Me.: Samuel Weiser, 1984.

*————. *The Outer Planets and Their Cycles: The Astrology of the Collective.* Reno: CRCS Publications, 1983.

*Lundsted, Betty. *Planetary Cycles: Astrological Indicators of Crisis and Change.* York Beach, Me.: Samuel Weiser, 1986.

*Mayo, Jeff. *The Planets and Human Behavior.* Reno: CRCS Publications, 1985.

*Playfair, Guy Lyon, and Scott Hill. *The Cycles of Heaven: Cosmic Forces and What They Are Doing to You.* London: Souvenir Press, 1978.

*Townley, John. *Astrological Cycles and the Life Crisis Periods.* York Beach, Me.: Samuel Weiser, 1984.

*West, John Anthony. *The Case for Astrology.* London: Penguin Books, 1991.

*Williams, David. *Simplified Astronomy for Astrologers.* Tempe, Ariz.: American Federation of Astrologers, 1969.

EXTRATERRESTRIAL

*Harrington, Robert S. "The Location of Planet X." *Astronomical Journal* (October 1988).

*Hoagland, Richard C. *The Monuments of Mars.* Berkeley, Calif.: North Atlantic Books, 1987.

*Sitchen, Zecharia. *The 12th Planet.* Santa Fe: Bear, 1976.

*————. *Genesis Revisited: Is Modern Science Catching Up with Ancient Knowledge?* Santa Fe: Bear, 1991.

ADDITIONAL SOURCES

Alexander, John B., Richard Groller, and Janet Morris. *The Warrior's Edge.* New York: William Morrow, 1990.

Anderson, Wing. *Prophetic Years: 1947–1953.* Los Angeles: Kosmon Press, 1946.

————. *Seven Years That Changed the World: 1941–1948.* Los Angeles: Kosmon Press, 1940.

Arieti, Silvano. *The Intrapsychic Self.* New York: Basic Books, 1976.

Baker, David. *The Shape of Wars to Come.* New York: Stein and Day, 1982.

Bear, Sun, and Wind Wabun. *Black Dawn–Bright Day.* New York: Fireside, 1992.

*Blakemore, Colin, and Susan Greenfield. *Mindwaves: Thoughts on Intelligence, Identity, and Consciousness.* New York: Basil Blackwell, 1987.

Bohm, David, and F. David Peat. *Science, Order, and Creativity.* New York: Bantam Books, 1987.

*Bolles, Edmund Blair. *A Second Way of Knowing: The Riddle of Human Perception.* New York: Prentice Hall, 1991.

*Boorstin, Daniel J. *Hidden History*. New York: Harper & Row, 1987.

*Bragdon, Claude. *Four-Dimensional Vistas*. New York: Alfred A. Knopf, 1925.

Brennan, Richard P. *Levitating Trains and Kamikaze Genes: Technological Literacy for the 1990s*. New York: HarperCollins, 1990.

Broughton, Richard S. *Parapsychology: The Controversial Science*. New York: Ballantine Books, 1991.

Campbell, Joseph, ed. *Man and Transformation*. New York: Pantheon Books, 1964.

*Capra, Fritjof. *Uncommon Wisdom*. New York: Simon & Schuster, 1988.

Clarke, I. F. *The Pattern of Expectation 1640–2001*. New York: Basic Books, 1979.

———. *Voices Prophesying War 1763–1984*. New York: Oxford University Press, 1966.

Cole, K. C. *Sympathetic Vibrations: Reflections on Physics as a Way of Life*. New York: William Morrow, 1985.

Cournos, John. *A Book of Prophecy*. New York: Charles Scribner's Sons, 1942.

Cousins, Norman. *The Pathology of Power*. New York: W. W. Norton, 1987.

Coxhead, Nona. *MindPower: The Emerging Pattern of Current Research*. London: Heinemann, 1976.

Crane, Diana. *Invisible Colleges: Diffusion of Knowledge in Scientific Communities*. Chicago: University of Chicago Press, 1972.

Cranston, Sylvia, and Carey Williams. *Reincarnation: A New Horizon in Science, Religion, and Society*. New York: Crown, 1984.

De Becker, Raymond. *The Understanding of Dreams*. London: George Allen and Unwin, 1968.

De Nicolas, Antonio T. *Habits of Mind*. New York: Paragon House, 1989.

Dixon, N. F. *Preconscious Processing*. New York: John Wiley & Sons, 1981.

———. *Subliminal Perception*. London: McGraw-Hill, 1971.

Dubrov, A. P., and V. N. Pushkin. *Parapsychology and Contemporary Science*. New York: Consultants Bureau, 1982.

Dunne, J. W. *"Intrusions"?* London: Faber & Faber, 1955.

*———. *The Serial Universe*. London: Faber & Faber, 1952.

Eco, Umberto. *Travels in Hyperreality*. New York: Harcort Brace Jovanovich, 1986.

Edelman, Gerald M., and Vernon B. Mountcastle. *The Mindful Brain: Cortical Organization and the Group-Selective Theory of Higher Brain Function*. Cambridge: MIT Press, 1978.

*Edwards, Betty. *Drawing on the Artist Within*. New York: Simon & Schuster, 1986.

*———. *Drawing on the Right Side of the Brain*. Los Angeles: J. P. Tarcher, 1979.

*Epstein, Gerald. *Healing Visualizations: Creating Health through Imagery.* New York: Bantam, 1989.

*————. *Waking Dream Therapy: Dream Process as Imagination.* New York: Human Sciences Press, 1981.

Feldman, David Henry. *Nature's Gambit: Child Prodigies and the Development of Human Potential.* New York: Basic Books, 1986.

*Feyerabend, Paul. *Against Method.* London: Verso, 1988.

*Fincher, Jack. *Human Intelligence.* New York: G. P. Putnam's Sons, 1976.

Fisher, Joe, and Peter Commins. *Predictions.* New York: Van Nostrand Reinhold, 1980.

Fontenrose, Joseph. *The Delphic Oracle.* Berkeley and Los Angeles: University of California Press, 1978.

Francis, Chuck. *Beyond the Subconscious: The Ultimate Mind Game.* Cincinnati: Imagination Store, 1988.

Garan, D. G. *Our Sciences Rules by Human Prejudice: Humanly Necessary Causal Blindness Persisting Even in Sciences.* New York: Philosophical Library, 1987.

Gardner, Howard. *Frames of Mind.* New York: Basic Books, 1983.

Gauquelin, Michel. *Birth-Times: A Scientific Investigation of the Secrets of Astrology.* New York: Farrar, Straus & Giroux, 1983.

————. *Dreams and Illusions of Astrology.* Buffalo: Prometheus Books, 1979.

*Gawain, Shakti. *Creative Visualization.* New York: Bantam Books, 1985.

Gennett, Hal Zina. *The Lenses of Perception.* Berkeley: Celestial Arts, 1987.

Gleeson, Patrick, *America Changing . . .* Columbus, Ohio: Charles E. Merrill, 1968.

Glenn, Jerome Clayton. *Future-Mind: Artificial Intelligence and Merging the Mystical and the Technological in the Twenty-first Century.* Washington, D.C.: Acropolis Books, 1989.

Goodavage, Joseph F. *Astrology: The Space-Age Science.* West Nyack, N.Y.: Parker Publishing, 1966.

Green, Elmer, and Alyce Green. *Beyond Biofeedback.* New York: Delacorte Press, 1977.

Growth of the World's Urban and Rural Populations 1920–2000. Department of Economic and Social Affairs. Population Studies no. 44. New York: United Nations, 1969.

Hall, Peter. *London 2000.* New York: Frederick A. Praeger, 1969.

Hampden-Turner, Charles. *Maps of the Mind.* New York: Macmillan, 1981.

Harding, M. Esther. *Psychic Energy: Its Source and Goal.* New York: Pantheon Books, 1947.

Hathaway, Edith. *Navigating by the Stars: Astrology and the Art of Decision-Making.* St. Paul, Minn.: Llewellyn Publications, 1991.

Hayles, N. Katherine. *The Cosmic Web.* Ithaca: Cornell University Press, 1984.

Head, Joseph, and S. L. Cranston. *Reincarnation: The Phoenix Fire Mystery.* New York: Crown, 1977.

Heidegger, Martin. *Being and Time.* New York: Harper & Row, 1962.

Hewish, A., ed. *Seeing beyond the Visible.* New York: American Elsevier, 1970.

Hillman, James. *Re-Visioning Psychology.* New York: Harper & Row, 1975.

Hogue, John. *Nostradamus and the Millennium.* Garden City, N.Y.: Doubleday, 1987.

Hunt, Diana, and Pam Hait. *The Tao of Time.* New York: Fireside, 1990.

*Inglis, Brian. *Trance: A Natural History of Altered States of Mind.* London: Collins Publishing Group, 1989.

*Jaynes, Julian. *The Origin of Consciousness and the Breakdown of the Bicameral Mind.* Boston: Houghton Mifflin, 1976.

Johnson, Paul. *Intellectuals.* New York: Harper & Row, 1988.

*Kimball, Roger. *Tenured Radicals: How Politics Has Corrupted Our Higher Education.* New York: Harper & Row, 1990.

Kuhn, Thomas S. *The Structure of Scientific Revolutions.* Chicago: University of Chicago Press, 1962.

Lebedoff, David. *The New Elite: The Death of Democracy.* New York: Franklin Watts, 1981.

*Lehman, David. *Signs of the Times.* New York: Poseidon Press, 1991.

*Lemesurier, Peter. *Beyond All Belief: Science, Religion, and Reality.* Wiltshire, England: Element Books, 1983.

Lewinsohn, Richard. *Science, Prophecy and Prediction.* New York: Harper & Brothers, 1961.

Lichter, S. Robert, Stanley Rothman, and Linda S. Lichter. *The Media Elite: America's New Powerbrokers.* Bethesda, Md.: Adler & Adler, 1986.

Lindsay, Jack. *Origins of Astrology.* New York: Barnes & Noble, 1971.

Lorie, Peter, and Sidd Murray-Clark. *History of the Future.* New York: Doubleday, 1989.

Low, A. M. *It's Bound to Happen.* London: Burke, 1950.

MacIver, Robert M. *Power Transformed.* New York: Macmillan, 1964.

MacKenzie, Andrew. *Riddle of the Future.* London: Arthur Barker, 1974.

*McCann, Lee. *Nostradamus: The Man Who Saw through Time.* 1941. Reprint, New York: Wings Books, 1991.

McEvers, Joan, ed. *The Astrology of the Macrocosm.* St. Paul, Minn.: Llewellyn Publications, 1990.

McNeill, William H. *Plagues and Peoples.* Garden City, N.Y.: Doubleday, 1976.

Man and Time. New York: Pantheon Books, 1957.

Meerloo, Joost A. *Along the Fourth Dimension.* New York: John Day, 1970.

Merrell-Wolff, Franklin. *The Philosophy of Consciousness without an Object: Reflections on the Nature of Transcendental Consciousness.* New York: Julian Press, 1973.

Moore, Thomas. *The Planets Within.* Great Barrington, Mass.: Lindisfarne Press, 1990.

Murphy, Gardner. *Human Potentials*. New York: Basic Books, 1958.

Naisbitt, John. *Megatrends*. New York: Warner Books, 1982.

Nisbit, Robert. *The Making of Modern Society*. New York: New York University Press, 1986.

Osborn, Arthur W. *The Future Is Now*. New Hyde Park, N.Y.: University Books, 1961.

*Payne, Buryl. *The Body Magnetic*. Santa Cruz: n.p., 1990.

Peat, F. David. *Synchronicity: The Bridge between Matter and Mind*. New York: Bantam Books, 1988.

Pendell, Elmer. *Why Civilizations Self-Destruct*. Cape Canaveral: Howard Allen, 1977.

*Peterson, Scott. *Native American Prophecies*. New York: Paragon House, 1990.

Pickard, Jerome P. *Metropolitanization of the United States*. Washington, D.C.: Urban Land Institute, 1959.

Rivlin, Robert, and Karen Gravelle. *Deciphering the Senses*. New York: Simon & Schuster, 1984.

Russell, Eric. *Astrology and Prediction*. New York: Drake Publishers, 1973.

*Sasportas, Howard. *The Gods of Change: Pain, Crisis, and the Transits of Uranus, Neptune, and Pluto*. New York: Penguin, 1989.

Scheflin, Alan W., and Edward M. Opton, *The Mind Manipulators*. London: Paddington Press, 1978.

Shilts, Randy. *And the Band Played On: Politics, People, and the AIDS Epidemic*. New York: St. Martin's Press, 1987.

Smith, Huston. *Beyond the Post-Modern Mind*. Wheaton, Ill.: Theosophical Publishing House, 1982.

Snow, Chet B. *Mass Dreams of the Future*. New York: McGraw-Hill, 1989.

Stulman, Julius. *Evolving Mankind's Future: The World Institute—A Problem-Solving Methodology*. Philadelphia: J. B. Lippincott, 1967.

Swann, Ingo. *Everybody's Guide to Natural ESP: Unlocking the Extrasensory Power of Your Mind*. Los Angeles: Jeremy P. Tarcher, 1991.

*Taylor, Eldon. *Subliminal Communication*. Las Vegas: Just Another Reality Publishing, 1990.

*———. *Subliminal Learning*. Salt Lake City: Just Another Reality Publishing, 1988.

Testor, Jim. *A History of Western Astrology*. New York: Ballantine Books, 1987.

Thass-Thienemann, Theodore. *The Subconscious Language*. New York: Washington Square Press, 1967.

Timbs, John. *Predictions Realized in Modern Times*. 1880. Reprint, Ann Arbor: Gryphon Books, 1971.

Vandenberg, Philipp. *The Mystery of the Oracles*. New York: Macmillan, 1982.

*Vaughan, Alan. *Patterns of Prophecy*. New York: Hawthorn Books, 1973.

Wheeler, John A. "The Mystery and the Message of the Quantum." Presentation at the *Joint Annual Meeting of the American Physical Society and the American Association of Physics Teachers* (January 1984).

Wieman, Henry Nelson. *The Directive in History*. Boston: Beacon Press, 1949.

Williams, John K. *The Wisdom of Your Subconscious Mind*. Englewood Cliffs, N.J.: Prentice-Hall, 1964.

*Wilson, Robert Anton. *Prometheus Rising*. Phoenix: Falcon Press, 1986.

Winn, Denise. *The Manipulated Mind*. London: Octagon Press, 1983.

Woo, C. H. "Consciousness and Quantum Interference—An Experimental Approach." *Foundations of Physics* 2, nos. 11–12 (1981).

Yates, Frances A. *The Art of Memory*. Chicago: University of Chicago Press, 1966.

INDEX